CASES
IN
MARKETING
MANAGEMENT

EUGENE J. KELLEY, editor
The Pennsylvania State University

PRENTICE-HALL FOUNDATIONS OF MARKETING SERIES

MARKETING: STRATEGY AND FUNCTIONS
EUGENE J. KELLEY   *The Pennsylvania State University*

MARKETING PLANNING AND COMPETITIVE STRATEGY
EUGENE J. KELLEY   *The Pennsylvania State University*

CONSUMER BEHAVIOR
PETER D. BENNETT   *The Pennsylvania State University*
HAROLD H. KASSARJIAN   *University of California*

MARKETING MANAGEMENT AND THE BEHAVIORAL ENVIRONMENT
PERRY BLISS   *State University of New York at Buffalo*

MEN, MOTIVES, AND MARKETS
WROE ALDERSON and MICHAEL H. HALBERT

QUANTITATIVE METHODS IN MARKETING
RONALD E. FRANK and PAUL S. GREEN   *University of Pennsylvania*

PRICING DECISIONS AND MARKETING POLICY
KRISTIAN PALDA   *Queen's University*

PRODUCT POLICY AND STRATEGY
DAVID J. LUCK   *Southern Illinois University*

PROMOTION: A BEHAVIORAL VIEW
HARPER W. BOYD, JR.   *Stanford University*
SIDNEY J. LEVY   *Northwestern University*

SALES MANAGEMENT
JOSEPH W. THOMAS   *Michigan State University*

PRENTICE-HALL FOUNDATIONS OF MARKETING SERIES

PRENTICE-HALL, INC., Englewood Cliffs, New Jersey

SECOND EDITION

CASES
IN
MARKETING
MANAGEMENT

EDWARD C. BURSK

Professor (Emeritus) of Business Administration
Harvard University

STEPHEN A. GREYSER

Professor of Business Administration
Harvard University

Library of Congress Cataloging in Publication Data

BURSK, EDWARD COLLINS
    Cases in marketing management.

    (Prentice-Hall foundations of marketing series)
    Includes index.
    1. Marketing management—Case studies. I. Greyser,
Stephen A., joint author. II. Title.
HF5415.13.B83   1975   658.8'0092'6   75-4825
ISBN   0-13-118893-3

CASES IN MARKETING MANAGEMENT

EDWARD C. BURSK

Harvard University (emeritus)

STEPHEN A. GREYSER

Harvard University

SECOND EDITION

PRENTICE-HALL, INC., Englewood Cliffs, New Jersey

FOUNDATIONS OF MARKETING SERIES

The copyrights on all cases in this book are held by the President and Fellows of
Harvard College with the exception of the following: *Buying an Automobile, Bender
Mattress Company, Schmidt Packing Company, Boling Bros. Department Store, Sym-
phony of the Sierras, Gem Appliance Company, Singh and Sons (A), (B)*, and *(C),
Lightning Aircraft Company, Musselman Department Store, Bolger Company, Thames
Rainwear Company, Ltd., Better Soap Company, Apex Chemical Company, Grandholm Company, Silverdale Drug Company*, and *Rio Railroad*. The cases copyrighted
by Harvard are reprinted by special permission and may not be reproduced in whole
or in part without the written permission of the President and Fellows of Harvard
College. This material is made possible by the cooperation of business firms who
may wish to remain anonymous by having names, quantities, or other identifying
details disguised while maintaining basic relationships. Cases are prepared as the
basis for class discussion rather than as illustrations of the handling of any particular
administrative situation.

Printed in the United States of America

10   9   8   7   6   5   4   3

PRENTICE-HALL INTERNATIONAL, INC., *London*
PRENTICE-HALL OF AUSTRALIA, PTY. LTD., *Sydney*
PRENTICE-HALL OF CANADA, LTD., *Toronto*
PRENTICE-HALL OF INDIA PRIVATE LIMITED, *New Delhi*
PRENTICE-HALL OF JAPAN, INC., *Tokyo*

To KIT and LINDA

Whose support has facilitated our work generally—
and this book specifically

CONTENTS

FOUNDATIONS OF MARKETING SERIES

The Foundations of Marketing is a series of authoritative and concise books prepared to serve the need for teaching materials incorporating the results of recent research and developments in the study and practice of marketing. The structure of the series—its flexibility within unity of purposes—enables the teacher to construct a complete basic marketing course, adjustable to a level of rigor of the teacher's choosing. Certain or all books can be combined to accomplish individual course objectives. Individual books are self-contained, reasonably complete treatments of the fundamental changes taking place in their areas. Students have the benefits of being introduced to the managerial approach to the field and to the socioeconomic process of marketing by authorities actively engaged in study and research in each field.

An overview of the series and of the managerial approach to marketing is provided by

Marketing Planning and Competitive Strategy

Four books treat important aspects of scientific methodology and decision making in marketing:

Consumer Behavior
Marketing Management and the Behavioral Environment
Men, Motives, and Markets
Quantitative Methods in Marketing

Key policy areas of marketing are covered in

Pricing Decisions and Marketing Policy
Product Policy

Promotion: A Behavioral View
Sales Management
Channel Management
Marketing Logistics
Organizational Buying Behavior

Important environmental areas in marketing are emphasized in

International Marketing, 2nd ed.
Marketing and Public Policy
Marketing in the Canadian Environment

All books may profitably use as supplements

Cases in Marketing Management, 2nd ed.
Advanced Cases in Marketing Management
History of Marketing

It is hoped that the series will stimulate independent and intelligent thought about the central issues of marketing analysis and policy and that readers will find the books useful guides to a creative and disciplined approach to meeting complex and changing marketing problems.

EUGENE J. KELLEY, *Editor*

We appreciate the permission of Harvard Business School Deans Stanley F. Teele, George P. Baker, and Lawrence E. Fouraker for the use of case material copyrighted by Harvard. We are grateful to Richard Armknecht and Bonnie Reece for assistance in preparing some of these cases. We are thankful to Elizabeth Knox and Shannon Grady for help in preparing the manuscript.

Edward C. Bursk and Stephen A. Greyser

INTRODUCTION
TO
THE STUDY OF CASES

Like almost all cases, the cases in this book are descriptions of situations in business or other organizations, calling for an appraisal of past action, a decision on future action, or both. These cases are all real—based on problems and events that actually took place—although in some instances, names of people, companies, and geographic locations are disguised.

Students and instructors can readily see that the cases are categorized by major subareas within marketing—consumer behavior, product policy, distribution policy, promotional policy, and marketing planning and strategy. Most of the case problems are rather straightforward in nature. However, some of the cases treat more complex issues, and call on students to consider several aspects of marketing in their analysis and action recommendations.

Moreover, most of the cases—even beyond those which treat marketing research as a primary issue—are built on research information. The student thus should realize that research is an integral part of all marketing decisions. The cases generally provide data that enable the student to undertake solid, rather than merely speculative, analysis of consumer and industrial buyers.

Furthermore virtually every case calls for *both analysis and decision-making*. Logical analysis and a firm grasp of the facts of a situation are crucial. So are judgment, such as is used in sifting through available information to find the *relevant* information, and imagination, such as is needed in developing an action plan that uniquely marshals the company's resources and distinctive capabilities.

Framework for Analysis

Marketing is at best an imprecise art. Although it is almost impossible to predict the results of marketing action, it is likely that most of the important factors entering into a marketing decision can be assessed.

What is needed is a model or framework of analysis that will insure that the process is as orderly and searching as possible. Here is one model of analysis that has been tested again and again in actual practice, as well as in case study.

1. The first step in mapping out the situation is to translate the decision that is to be made into terms of the underlying problem. In marketing, the decision might be, for example, whether to lower the price of a product or not. But the underlying problem would be whether enough more of the product would be bought at the lower price to increase the net return.

2. The next step is to break the underlying problem into a series of component subproblems in the form of more detailed questions. In the case of the marketing decision, the subproblems might be: Will a lower income level be tapped so we will get new users? Will present buyers feel they can afford to use more? Will retailers give it more push?

3. There could be any number of further layers of subquestions or subanalysis. "Will present buyers feel they can afford to use more?" could be further analyzed in terms of the basic motivations people have for this kind of product, the financial resources or credit terms available to buyers, and the competing products that might be more attractive than additional purchases of this one. Note that in every instance the subquestions refer to the causes that bring about the result, represented by the larger question from which they stem.

4. At every point, the cruciality of each question can be weighed and a subdecision made as to whether to seek further information on that question by means of marketing research, and, if so, on what scale and in what form. For example, we might find we need some new research into consumer motivations.

5. Finally, of course, the subanswers are carried back to the questions on the level above them, and subanswers are formulated at that level, to be carried up to the next level, until a final answer to the underlying problem is reached and translated back into the decision.

From a broader perspective, the foregoing can also be structured as follows:

1. Understand the situation, from the viewpoints of the environment, competition, and the company's internal resources.
2. Posit alternative courses of action.
3. Explore the pros and cons of each alternative, including their sensitivity to changes in the environment and in the company situation.
4. Make your decision, recognizing the strengths and weaknesses of your chosen course of action.

Further Suggestions

The above model should not be taken to imply that one's case "homework" stops with a decision alone. Much of the time, matters of implementation are also important—how you would carry out your plan of action, what steps should be taken first, and so on.

For purposes of starting your thinking and getting you to explore as many areas as possible, questions are appended to each case. These are not meant to be limiting; indeed, occasionally some of these particular questions will never get raised in a discussion at all. Remember, you must use your own imagination to find clues to understanding the situation (to be subsequently confirmed or refuted by the test of logic). Many lists of categories, factors, or other kinds of considerations can be secured from various sources as *suggestions* of where to look for cause and effect, but it is the essence of the whole dynamic nature of marketing that people—students or businessmen—continually look for new ways to analyze and understand and plan for action.

Furthermore, you are privileged, and indeed urged, not to disagree with *facts*, but to read between the lines and doubt the *judgments and opinions* of people portrayed or quoted in the cases. Above all, you will gain from the cases to the extent you analyze everything you can.

Keep in mind that the objective is to learn by exploration, discussion, even argument (in as logical a framework as possible). There are no clear-cut solutions, no black-and-white answers. The actions of marketing managers or researchers described in the cases may or may not illustrate good handling of marketing problems or assignments; *that* is for *you* to decide.

Often you will want further information or guidance in how to attack a case. As is the fact in real life, businessmen themselves often do not have such information or guidance either. One of the things a marketer must learn is how to operate as effectively as possible in such imperfect situations. Even when more material might be available subsequently, as a result of research or other sources of help, there are countless times when one must analyze a situation and try to arrive at a tentative decision, just to find out whether it is worthwhile or desirable to go ahead to the point of doing such further searching or preparation.

When considering the need for further information, you should always ask yourself:

1. Is research needed or justified by the nature and magnitude of the particular situation?
2. If so, what specific kind of information do I need; and in what specific ways do I expect to use it?
3. What is the right source of such help; and what must I (putting yourself in the position of the responsible party in the case) do to see that a good job is done (or has been done)?
4. Can I have confidence in the results or in demonstration of the need for still further searching or preparation)?
5. Now, how can I translate this marketing information into marketing action?

CASES
IN
MARKETING
MANAGEMENT

CONSUMER
BEHAVIOR

The success of every marketing action depends ultimately on how consumers react to appeals or stratagems designed to influence them, and on how they then act or fail to act. It is thus necessary to understand consumers' behavior—to gain insights into the way they feel about different kinds of products or services, or different uses of their money—and to determine by what values or criteria they make their buying decisions.

Consumers' motivations have many sources. Some are internally generated: wants that are rooted in physical need for food and shelter, in sex drives, and in more sublimated desires for approval, security, and self-satisfaction. Some impinge on the consumer from outside, as a result of education and social forces generally; as time goes on, and our standard of living rises farther and farther above the level of bare subsistence, these become increasingly important.

But what we are principally concerned with in this section are the kinds of actions that management itself can take—utilizing existing or latent motivations—to lead the consumer to choose the particular product or brand that the manufacturer or distributor is interested in selling. And here there are four kinds of action corresponding to four ways in which the consumer can be appealed to.

1. Product Policy. Offering designs, features, services, or other advantages that are better than competitors' for special segments or for the mass of the market—often only slightly better, often psychologically rather than functionally, but effective if they are attuned to consumers' values.

2. Distribution Policy. Distributing through particular kinds or numbers of outlets for the sake of increased convenience or accessibility of the product, the benefit of the outlets' own standing in consumers' minds, or the extra sales push likely to be received from the outlets.

3. Pricing Policy. Setting basic prices to tap various layers of demand, in accordance with consumers' ability and inclination to allocate their financial resources, including credit, and in relation to competitors' prices for the same or similar products; and then setting discounts, terms, and other variations in form (like odd-cents prices in retailing) to make the basic price more noticeable and more palatable.

4. *Promotional Policy.* Deciding on the amount and content of advertising, display, and personal selling needed to arouse and increase the consumers' interest, acceptance, preference, and intention to buy the particular product or brand, and also to facilitate the distribution or pricing policy.

Just as marketers usually combine or "mix" all these elements together, emphasizing one as their main thrust and making the others auxiliary, so consumers are influenced by a mixture of appeals, with one of them dominant and the others supporting. The mixture can vary both for different marketers and for different buyers, even in the case of similar or identical products.

Notice, also, that the same principles apply to industrial marketers and buyers, except that here there is likely to be somewhat less emphasis on promotion and more emphasis on product, and especially on the services connected with the product (delivery, quality control, technical advice on use, and the like).

BUYING AN AUTOMOBILE

(A man and wife of about 50 years of age come into medium-price automobile salesroom.)

MAN. Saw that sporty hard-top in the window. . . .

SALESMAN. Yes, isn't that a beauty! It really catches people's eyes as they go past.

MAN. Of course, we wouldn't want anything quite that flashy; I'd feel a little foolish. But it does remind me of a car I had once; only then. . . .

WIFE. A little too daring for us. That's more the kind of thing that our seventeen-year-old boy would want. He likes the looks and power and, well. . . .

SALESMAN. I know how you feel. Inappropriate. Now, take a look at this conservative two-door. . . .

WIFE. But I don't like that upholstery. It's so drab.

SALESMAN. Madam, this is the finest nylon-plastic, guaranteed to outwear iron; all the cars are coming with it this year. Why, only yesterday, Mrs. Jones came in and. . . .

MAN. What would my trade-in be on this one—more than on the hard-top, I guess, not to mention the better gas mileage on this one.

SALESMAN. Don't worry, we give you what your old car is worth, no matter what you buy. Actually, this one *would* run you a little less, net. This is a real buy for dependable transportation. . . .

(The salesman goes on talking about the ruggedness and horsepower of the car; economical gas mileage; future trade-in value, and so forth.)

[*If this is all of the picture you had, would you expect the man and wife to buy?*]

MAN.   Of course, with my present car I can still. . . .

SALESMAN.   Let me call the appraiser, and while he's looking at your car —it's a 1971 model, isn't it?

MAN.   No, a 1972.

SALESMAN.   Well, those old ones all look a little alike, I think, particularly when compared with the 1975. See, how it. . . .

WIFE.   John, I think we'd better be getting along. I've got to get dinner started.

MAN.   Haven't you got any of the new economical compacts?

SALESMAN.   Why yes, let me show you. . . .

MAN.   No, don't bother now. We can't really afford a new car this year. We'll be back again later.

(Next week or so, same man and woman are in another *salesroom—this time, foreign cars.)*

MAN.   What do you call that little midget, in the window?

SALESMAN.   That's a Bentaru Bantam, so called because, though it's little, it has a lot of get-up-and-go. . . . Are you interested in a small car, or a foreign car?

WIFE.   Well, not particularly, but it does look a little unusual, doesn't it?

MAN.   And I guess it's economical too.

SALESMAN.   Yes, it is economical on gas, and oil, but I think the most attractive feature is, well, the fact that it looks distinguished, different. . . .

WIFE.   Our seventeen-year-old son is more interested in the sporty kind.

SALESMAN.   My, you have a son that old? I'll bet he does a lot of dating, doesn't he?

MAN.   Too much, much too much, ought to do more studying.

WIFE.   Now, John.

SALESMAN.   I think I know how you both feel, though my problem—and pride—is a fifteen-year-old girl. And I must admit she does like the boys who come for her in a nice-looking car. As a matter of fact, I've learned a lot about cars just from listening to how she feels.

WIFE.   Does she like these little foreign cars?

SALESMAN.   Oh, yes. She says most of the boys have either the conventional, unimaginative cars their families own, or one of those beaten-down and souped-up old wrecks—and it makes her feel grown-up and important to be called for in something like one of these Bentarus.

MAN. You did say it's economical?

SALESMAN. Oh, yes, and not just gas and oil. . . .
(The salesman goes on to talk about maintenance, repairs.)

[*Again, what do you think—will they buy?*]

MAN. But you don't have any model like the convertibles they used to make, on which you can put the top down, do you?

SALESMAN. No, the Bentaru people have found that that adds too much expense to the initial price *and* the maintenance but they give you the same values with this roof panel; and don't forget how easy this is to park, particularly for the ladies.

WIFE. But I don't drive; John, and of course Johnnie, take care of all that.

SALESMAN. But you do like your menfolk to be happy and proud, don't you?

MAN. Let's see what the trade-in is on my car.

SALESMAN. My, you've taken good care of your car, haven't you? I can see you're the kind of person who takes pride in a good car. Now, you understand, don't you, that I can't give you the big allowance you might get toward a big, conventional car—we don't price up our cars artificially just so we can impress you with a big trade-in. . . .

Now, do you think they will buy? Did the couple really want to buy a car? What kind? What happened in the two sales presentations? What good or bad developments took place and at what points? What desirable or undesirable qualities did the two salesmen demonstrate? If you had to pick one personal quality for successful selling in the kind of situation displayed above, what would it be?

ACME CORPORATION (A)

In September of 1973, John Wilson, sales engineer for Ampere Corporation's components marketing division, wondered what action to take in light of his discovery that Ampere had not yet received any releases from the Acme Corporation on a blanket purchase order for room air conditioner thermostats. Acme's purchasing department had earlier issued the blanket purchase order on the thermostats, to be included as components in Acme's 1974 air conditioner line.

Background

Wilson, a veteran Ampere sales engineer, had worked very closely for several years with Acme's engineering group in order to obtain the thermostat business. He ordinarily met once or twice weekly with various members of Acme's engineering group. Ampere (via Wilson) was already supplying Acme with other components, including air conditioner motors on which Ampere was virtually sole supplier. The air conditioner thermostats represented about $40,000 to $50,000 of annual business, which was being supplied virtually in full by Watt Company.

Wilson's efforts to have Ampere approved as a source of supply on the room air conditioner thermostats had begun in the summer of 1971, when he learned that Acme was undertaking a redesign of their air conditioner line for their 1974 models. The planned redesign called for considerable engineering effort on Acme's part. The schedule for the room air conditioner line was that Acme's engineering work would be completed in February 1973. Pilot runs on the new models were to be made in the spring and summer of 1973, with full-scale production planned for the fall.

Engineering Efforts

Wilson was aware of Acme's basic policy to try to have more than one source of supply on its components. Acme's normal procedure was to have equal alternates, and both engineering and purchasing personnel indicated to Wilson that Ampere had a good opportunity for approval as thermostat supplier.

Consequently, Wilson and Ampere's control department spent considerable time resolving basic engineering problems and clearing up details on the thermostat. These efforts with Acme's engineering staff, involving some four to five man-weeks over a twelve- to fifteen-month period, were rewarded in early 1973 when Ampere was approved as an equal source of supply on the unit, along with Watt, prior to the start of pilot runs on the model.

Watt had also worked closely with Acme in developing a thermostat unit for the new model. Watt's control and Ampere's were both priced the same (about $2). However, the former was slightly more expensive (about 10¢ per unit) because it required some added labor to mount and some additional insulation. Although the Ampere control was thus slightly less expensive to use—and Acme's engineers expressed a slight preference for it—both units were approved as equal alternates.

Procedure

Having achieved approval on the thermostat from Acme's engineering department, Wilson's next step was to bring the matter to the purchasing department. This was the second step in the normal three-part procedure at Acme for a supplier seeking a new order. Engineering department specification came first, resulting in approval as a source; a purchasing department order then provided either a blanket authorization or a specified proportion of business on the part; finally, actual orders were released by the material controls department. Further details on how this procedure operated appear in the Appendix.

Pilot Run Experience

In discussions with Acme's purchasing department, Wilson was asked to meet pilot run requirements to commence approximately six weeks later. Under a one-year blanket order, Ampere's control department undertook preparations to meet Acme's production dates. This involved tooling a new cam and cover for the control in order to meet Acme's initial schedules, plus some short-run tooling on the cover to provide units for Acme's pilot runs.

Because Watt needed more time to tool the necessary parts for their control, Ampere was given the initial production orders and the releases for the pilot runs. The control department authorized overtime for the short-run tooling, and placed orders for the permanent tooling.

As is Ampere's usual practice once a purchase commitment is given, the eventual tooling costs of about $3,500 were absorbed by the control department. Acme's tooling order for $750 on the cam of the control was returned, and these costs absorbed, when it appeared that there was another customer for which the same cam would be used.

During the pilot run stage, completed in late June, every one of Acme's production dates was met. By this time, Watt had completed the tooling for its unit and had also received a blanket purchase order from Acme. Purchasing indicated to Wilson that Ampere would get at least half of the thermostat business for the 1974 model year. This production was scheduled to start in October.

September Surprise

Thus, Wilson was considerably surprised to learn in September, at the time of the first releases on the components for full-scale production, that no room air conditioner thermostats were released to Ampere for the first two months of production.

Wilson knew that the control department was very anxious to get its "deserved" share of the Acme thermostat business. In addition to its investment of time and money on this unit, the department was concerned because of a past experience with Acme. In 1970, the department had exerted considerable efforts to extricate Acme from a relays controls supply crisis caused by a strike in the plant of Acme's sole supplier. Despite what was considered by Acme an excellent performance on Ampere's part, once the strike was over Ampere retained no part of the relays business.

However, Wilson also knew that Ampere was currently receiving several hundred thousand dollars' worth of air conditioner motors, capacitors, and cord set business from Acme. These orders were released —as were those for the thermostats—by Fran Austin in Acme's material controls department. Wilson knew that Mrs. Austin, a quiet older woman who was a veteran member of Acme's material controls staff, made many releases on the basis of her own supplier experiences and preferences. Her supervisor gave her considerable latitude in her decisions. Unlike some other material controls clerks, who released, "50-50" on blanket purchase orders to equal alternate suppliers, she followed the practice of making her own allocations on these unspecified orders.

Wilson believed that Mrs. Austin considered Watt an extremely good supplier and was very satisfied with its performance and that of its sales representative. From observation and his own experiences with her, he knew she could overlook minor performance flaws, and that she preferred the status quo. Although Wilson wanted the thermostat releases badly, he was reluctant to take precipitant action with either Acme's purchasing department, Mrs. Austin's supervisor, or Mrs. Austin herself.

What should Wilson do? Why?

Appendix: Acme Purchasing Procedure

Engineering, purchasing, and material controls are the three departments within the Acme organization involved in determining and processing new vendor orders on components. Engineering's role is to concentrate on requirements and specifications. Once it has released a unit for production (e.g., through drawings) on the basis of design and price, and has approved the source(s) of supply, engineering is no longer a factor in the purchasing process. At this juncture, the material controls department prepares a master card on all new parts. It is from this master card that the purchasing department personnel issue purchase orders.

Organizationally, the material controls group acts in an expediting role, works closely with suppliers, and coordinates with the purchasing department in the event of any problems. Purchasing's function is primarily to make the actual decisions on purchase orders—for example, whether to order solely from one approved supplier, how to split the business on a par among alternate approved suppliers, etc. Thus, the purchasing department theoretically dictates the proportion to go to each alternate source.

In ordinary practice, however, for several years the material controls people usually "called the shots" on these proportions, particularly when more than one supplier was specified without an indicated split. The five supervisors working under the head of the material controls department had considerable freedom of authority in their activities, as did the individual material controls clerks working for them. For example, members of the material controls staff varied in their interpretation of blanket purchase orders when releases on them were to be made.

Although they do not have the price information used by purchasing in making decisions, individuals in material controls have considerable experience with vendors and their sales and service representatives.

ACME CORPORATION (B)

In October 1973, John Wilson, sales engineer for Ampere Corporation's components marketing division wondered whether he had taken the best course of action in trying to secure additional releases for Ampere's control department from the Acme Corporation on a blanket purchase order for room air conditioner thermostats. Earlier, in September, he had realized that although Acme's engineering department had approved the Ampere unit, all Acme's pilot production requirements had been met, and the purchase order had been issued, nonetheless no releases had been issued to Ampere on the component for the first two months of production on the air conditioner model.

The source of the problem, in Wilson's eyes, was Mrs. Fran Austin, a veteran member of Acme's material controls department. Although the purchasing department made the decisions on vendors once a part was authorized by engineering, in practice the material controls department often determined the actual allocations when blanket purchase orders were issued to equal alternate suppliers. This was Mrs. Austin's practice, and in this instance what had appeared to be a minimum of 50 percent release for Ampere on the thermostats was in essence being nullified.

Watt Company had long been virtually the sole supplier of Acme's room air conditioner thermostats, business estimated to be worth about $40,000 to $50,000 annually. Wilson believed that Mrs. Austin considered Watt an extremely good supplier and was very satisfied with its performance and that of its sales representative. Similarly, Mrs. Austin considered Ampere an extremely good supplier of room air conditioner motors, an item on which she released several hundred thousand dollars' worth of business a year to Wilson. From observation and his own experiences with Mrs. Austin, Wilson knew she could overlook minor performance flaws, and that she preferred the status quo. He was reluctant to antagonize her.

On the other hand, Wilson strongly believed that the control department's efforts and performance warranted the 50 percent of the thermostat business which Acme's purchasing department had indicated would be the case. He was particularly disturbed—as would be control department executives—because Mrs. Austin's responsibility technically was only to release material on a schedule, rather than to make unilateral allocation decisions.

Wilson's first step was immediately to contact Mrs. Austin personally. He confronted her with the facts of the situation as he understood them, and then asked why Ampere had gotten no releases on the thermostats. Mrs. Austin's reply was that Watt had treated her very well in the past— i.e., they had always met delivery schedules and had not involved her in unnecessary expediting. She did not wish to gamble on Ampere, which she considered unproven on this component. When Wilson explained that Ampere had been set up as an equal alternate by purchasing, Mrs. Austin replied that if purchasing had wanted a 50-50 split, this would have been specified. Further, she asked Wilson whether he would like to give up portions of Ampere's room air conditioner motors business to the alternates set up for that product. By the same token that her experience with Watt thermostats was excellent, so was her experience with Ampere motors.

At this juncture, Wilson's reaction was "How can I argue with that?" He knew that Mrs. Austin had overlooked minor problems on the motors business in the past, such as delayed deliveries. But he still believed Ampere deserved a share of the thermostat business. Thus he contacted the relevant purchasing staff member, who said the matter would be examined.

But several weeks later, further action had yet to be taken.

Appraise Wilson's actions thus far. What should he do now? Why?

ACME CORPORATION (C)

In October 1973, Ampere Corporation's control department had yet to receive any releases from the Acme Corporation for room air conditioner thermostats on which a blanket purchase order had earlier been issued to Ampere as an equal alternate supplier. John Wilson, sales engineer for Ampere's components marketing division, had unsuccessfully attempted to resolve the situation through Mrs. Fran Austin, veteran Acme material controls clerk, who continued to allocate the releases on the thermostats to Watt Company, virtually sole supplier on the thermostats for several years. He had then contacted the relevant Acme purchasing staff member, who promised to look into the matter.

Several weeks later, having heard nothing, a representative of the control department and Wilson visited the purchasing department to try to clarify the matter. In addition to Ampere's investment in tooling on the thermostats, they pointed out to Acme that Ampere's performance had been excellent during Acme's pilot stage, when Watt was still tooling its thermostat unit. Not only did the purchasing staff member agree, but the department's second in command stated that Ampere was being unjustly treated.

The latter then called Mrs. Austin and told her in no uncertain terms that Ampere should be getting 50 percent of the releases on the thermostats. He stated that when she had two blanket orders, she should split the business in half. Only if vendor problems were being experienced should a supplier be shut off, and then only after purchasing is involved and agrees.

Shortly thereafter, releases to Ampere on the thermostats began to come through. It appeared that starting with January releases, Ampere would receive 50 percent of this business. But at the same time, Wilson said that he detected a distinct coolness on Mrs. Austin's part toward him. The thermostat incident was responsible, he believed, and he thought that there would be repercussions because Mrs. Austin was obviously in a position to call any problems with Ampere to the attention of purchasing. "I feel that I have won the battle but lost the war. I wonder whether there is some way I could have handled this situation better, and how I can get back into the good graces of our lady friend in material controls."

Appraise what has taken place. What should Wilson do now?

FARMCRAFTER, INC.

Farmcrafter, Inc., was considering the manufacture and sale of a "do-it-yourself" repair kit for farmers, whereby they could make many kinds of repairs on their farm machinery without having to interrupt their chores to take the machinery to the city.

To test the reaction of the market to this new product, the company mailed five different offers, at five different prices, to 10,000 farmers. The design was so drawn as to produce five mailings of 2,000 each specifying one of the five prices, and divided into five lots of 400 each making one of the five offers. Thus, there were 2,000 of each offer as well as each price.

The offers were: (a) to send further information to those returning the coupon, (b) same as a, except the coupon was to be accompanied by a quarter to cover mailing costs, (c) to send the name of the nearest hardware store carrying the repair kit to those returning the coupon, (d) the same as c, except the name to be sent was that of the nearest farm equipment dealer, and (e) to send a salesman to call.[1]

The results of the mailing, which described the repair kit in glowing terms and illustrated it in color, are shown in Exhibit 1 (percentage of coupons returned).

---

[1] The company, of course, planned to send an appropriate notice to everyone who sent in a coupon, including refund of the quarter, in case it decided not to go ahead with the product.

EXHIBIT 1   Analysis of Returns

Price	Different Offers					
	(a) Informa- tion	(b) Info. for 25¢	(c) Hardware Store	(d) Equipment Dealer	(e) Salesman to Call	Average
$75.00	42%	11%	23%	32%	6%	23%
$65.00	39	14	25	31	9	24
$55.00	43	12	25	34	7	24
$49.75	55	19	35	43	12	33
$45.00	52	20	33	41	13	32
Average	46	15 *	28	36	9	27

* But 2% failed to enclose a quarter.

The reactions to the five prices were also analyzed by size of farms (percentage of coupons returned):

EXHIBIT 2   Returns by Size of Farm

Price	Large	Medium	Small	Average
$75.00	25%	36%	8%	23%
$65.00	27	38	7	24
$55.00	26	34	10	24
$49.75	25	49	24	33
$45.00	27	51	18	32
Average	26	42	13	27

The company had available this information about the number of farms of different sizes:

EXHIBIT 3   Distribution of Farms by Size

Under 100 acres (small)	2,561,185
100 to 500 acres (medium)	1,899,053
Over 500 acres (large)	322,178
Total	4,782,416

What inferences should the company draw about the nature and strength of demand for its proposed repair kit? What do you think of this way of testing reaction to a proposed new product?

BENDER MATTRESS COMPANY

The Bender Mattress Company of Los Angeles, California, manufactured mattresses, box springs, convertible sofas, and some furniture. The greatest portion of its business was in mattresses and box springs, under the brand name Restful. It sold to retail stores in Southern California and the territory up to but not including San Francisco.

The major concern of the company was to increase unit sales. In this industry, according to Bender executives, prices are predetermined by competition, particularly in national companies, and average costs are approximately constant throughout the significant volume range. Thus, increased profits become a function of increased volume, which, in turn, is dependent largely upon the effectiveness of marketing efforts.

Of Restful's annual advertising budget of $400,000, 60 percent was being spent to sponsor the weather forecast on the 11 P.M. newscast on Tuesday, Thursday, and Sunday over Channel 4; 24 percent in cooperative newspaper advertising; and 16 percent on point-of-sale material. This media plan had been in effect for three years.

For Downy, a competing brand, the total amount and breakdown of advertising were estimated to be approximately the same. The Nighttime Company, in contrast, was spending about as much but concentrating it on cooperative advertising in newspapers. Restful and Downy were the only two brands using TV.

Bender commissioned a research agency to test the effectiveness of its advertising program, for a fee of $5,000. Questionnaires were mailed to a sample of 6,000 family units in the Los Angeles metropolitan area selected at random; and 999 usable returns were received. Some of the resulting tabulations follow in Exhibits 1 through 6.

EXHIBIT 1   Brand Decision—All Respondents

Decision on Brand to Purchase Made by:

Husband	9%
Wife	27
Both	46
Do not remember	7
No response	11
Total	100%

EXHIBIT 2   Brand Recognition—All Respondents

Brand Name

Night-time	90% *adv. papers*
Restful	88 *? + V*
Downy	87 *TV.*
Bye-Bye	82
Californian	65
Posture-plus	34
Sleep-Rest	25
Angelic	16
Moonlight	10
Other	12
No response	3

EXHIBIT 3   Shopping Habits—All Respondents

Item

Number of Stores Shopped	
One	33%
More than one	57
Do not remember; no response	10
Total	100%
Furniture Bought with Mattress	
Bedroom set	23%
Springs and bed	16
Springs	28
Purchased mattress only	28
Other and no response	5
Total	100%
Type of Store in Which Mattress Was Purchased	
Department	31%
Furniture	36
Discount	4
Sleep shop	3
Other and no response	26
Total	100%

EXHIBIT 4   Brand Preferences

A. Pre-Purchase Preferences—All Respondents

Restful	7%
Bye-Bye	2
Downy	6
Night-time	10
Californian	2
All other	8
No preference	65
	100%

B. Brand Purchased and Brand Preferred—Respondents with Pre-Purchase Preference

Pre-Purchase Brand Preference

Brand Purchased	Restful	Bye-Bye	Downy	Night-time	Californian	All Others
Restful	77%	-	-	6%	-	-
Bye-Bye	-	82%	-	1	-	-
Downy	2	6	83%	-	-	5%
Night-time	12	6	-	82	-	3
Californian	2	-	2	1	82%	1
All others	2	6	6	6	12	84
Do not remember	5	-	9	4	6	7
Total	100	100	100	100	100	100

C. Recall of Advertising—All Respondents

Recalled Brand Advertised

Source of Advertising	Recalled Mattress Advertising		Restful	Bye-Bye	Downy	Night-time	Californian	All Others	Brand Not Recalled or Not Related to Source	Total
	Yes	No								
Radio	16%	84%	2%	1%	2%	2%	*	*	9%	16%
TV	76	24	26	8	31	4	1	*	6	76
Newspapers	48	52	6	2	4	6	1	3	26	48
Magazines	44	56	5	3	3	9	2	*	22	44
Billboards	15	85	1	1	1	1	1	*	10	15

* Less than 1%.

D. Recent and Non-Recent Purchases by Pre-Purchase Brand Preference—TV Viewers Only

Pre-Purchase Brand Preference	Recent Purchasers		Non-Recent Purchasers	
	Number	Percent	Number	Percent
Restful	23	28	27	19
Bye-Bye	3	4	10	7
Downy	18	21	21	15
Night-time	15	18	43	31
Californian	3	4	12	8
All Others	21	25	28	20
Total	83	100	141	100

EXHIBIT 5   Relative Importance of Factors Affecting Selection of Brand by Brand Purchased—All Respondents

Factors and Relative Importance	Restful	Downy	Night-time	Bye-Bye	Californian	All Others	Do Not Remember and No Response	Total All Brands
Salesman's Suggestion								
Very important	24%	16%	18%	22%	21%	22%	14%	19%
Important	22	23	19	29	28	23	21	22
Not important	24	30	29	18	21	24	21	25
No response	30	31	34	31	30	31	44	34
Total	100%	100%	100%	100%	100%	100%	100%	100%
Advertising								
Very important	19%	24%	13%	6%	10%	8%	8%	12%
Important	27	28	21	20	14	16	13	19
Not important	23	18	28	29	30	36	31	29
No response	31	30	28	45	46	40	48	40
Total	100%	100%	100%	100%	100%	100%	100%	100%
Previous Experience								
Very important	35%	23%	39%	35%	30%	30%	14%	28%
Important	14	21	13	16	9	12	9	13
Not important	18	20	20	16	21	23	27	22
No response	33	36	28	33	40	35	50	37
Total	100%	100%	100%	100%	100%	100%	100%	100%

Factors and Relative Importance	Restful	Downy	Night-time	Bye-Bye	Californian	All Others	Do Not Remember and No Response	Total All Brands
Special Discount								
Very important	17%	16%	13%	29%	30%	18%	13%	17%
Important	20	15	9	11	14	12	16	13
Not important	25	27	32	25	23	30	20	27
No response	38	42	46	35	33	40	51	43
Total	100%	100%	100%	100%	100%	100%	100%	100%
Advertised Sale								
Very important	12%	26%	11%	14%	14%	17%	16%	16%
Important	10	19	9	12	4	9	13	11
Not important	37	30	35	35	39	36	25	33
No response	41	25	45	29	44	38	46	40
Total	100%	100%	100%	100%	100%	100%	100%	100%

17

EXHIBIT 6   Factors Related to Selection of Store Where Purchased
—All Respondents

| | Relative Importance | | | | |
Factors	Very Important	Important	Not Important	No Response	Total
Location of store	14%	16%	33%	37%	100%
Reputation of store	54	19	4	23	100
Generally shop there	20	12	29	39	100
Store advertising	9	15	32	44	100
Special price	31	17	18	34	100
Store salesman	13	13	31	43	100

What can the Bender management learn from the tabulations as to the effect of various factors on the purchase of the brand of mattress? Should it make any changes in its promotional mix?

BRAMTON COMPANY

Mr. W. T. Holderness, director of the Bramton Company's new market research department, was asked to survey the geophysical paper market and recommend whether Bramton—a manufacturer of photographic supplies—should enter it. If so, he was asked also to recommend whether Bramton should sell direct or distribute the paper through dealers.

Geophysical paper is used by petroleum field crews in geologic exploration, to record measurements of seismic shock resulting from charges detonated underground. Bramton scientists had developed an emulsion that they considered similar to emulsions used on competitors' papers, in response to urgent requests from the Bramton branch sales office managers in Dallas and Los Angeles.

Mr. Holderness selected a sample of 11 large companies with 230 field crews—about one-third of the total—for his survey. Results of interviews with purchasing agents of the 11 companies are summarized in Exhibit 1. The interviews also produced the following impressions:

1. Pangar had recently edged out Global as the preferred geophysical paper manufacturer. Interviewees who had shifted to Pangar cited quality as the reason.

EXHIBIT 1   Interview Results

	Number of Companies
Type of Paper Used	
Pangar 100%	9
Pangar 95%, Triumph 5%	1
Pangar 80%, Global 20%	1
Purchasing Practices	
Purchase all requirements centrally from a dealer	5
Purchase locally from dealers	4
Purchase direct from Pangar (i.e., classified by Pangar as a dealer)	2
Inventory Policy	
Minimum inventory—depend on dealer for fast service	7
Maintain inventory of 6 to 10 weeks	4
Equipment	
Manufacture all their own equipment	7
S.I.E. camera	4

2. Consistently high quality paper could not be overemphasized. Interviewees agreed that it must (a) give good contrast at the speeds and light-bulb voltages regularly used by the survey crews; (b) have high wet strength to permit storage in water for several days prior to development in the field; (c) not stain or mottle, because the delicate geophysical traces could easily be obscured; (d) have no splices, because these would interfere with trace analysis; and (e) be versatile enough for the field crews to use in temperatures ranging from below freezing to well over 100° and to develop by mixing their chemicals and fixers in contaminated water or even salt water. Because field crews often lacked qualified photographic personnel, standard instrument settings were used by almost all crews, and variations in paper quality would cause weak or unintelligible traces.

3. Houston and Dallas dominated the geophysical paper market. Although consumers traditionally purchased direct from manufacturers, this trend had recently changed. Local dealers were able to provide prompt deliveries, whereas manufacturers often took up to six weeks; and local dealers were sources of other supplies that the consumers required. Thus

the consumers had become used to purchasing from a dealer. Consumers generally maintained low inventory levels and were accustomed to prompt shipments. In addition to their dealers, both Pangar and Global had factory representatives in touch with the users, offering valuable technical assistance.

4. Price cutting was prevalent in the market. Five different Global dealers were after the account of one exploration firm; one dealer priced so low that the cash discount was his only margin. Pangar had classified some exploration companies as dealers in order to offer price concessions.

Mr. Holderness arranged to have one exploration company field-test Bramton's proposed paper and compare it with Pangar's product. To duplicate the contrast of the Pangar paper at the standard 4.2-volt galvanometer lamp setting, Bramton's paper had to be exposed at a 4.4-volt setting. This was a disadvantage, for increased voltage meant diminished bulb life. The testers found that at 3.8 volts the Bramton contrast was better than the Pangar contrast at the same voltage. But as the voltage increased, Pangar's contrast sharpened more satisfactorily than did Bramton's. Adequate contrast was reached at 4.2 volts with the Pangar paper, but not with Bramton's.

Bramton's paper was judged to have better wet strength, but Pangar's grain texture was better for making pencil notations on the seismic record, an important convenience for the petroleum engineers. The testers' overall opinion was that Bramton was not as good as Pangar but somewhat better than Global.

What recommendations should Mr. Holderness make? Assuming that Bramton cannot match the Pangar finish or contrast at 4.2 volts, even with further improvement by the Bramton scientists, what chance does the Bramton product have on the market? Assuming that the Bramton management does decide to go ahead with this product, how should it plan to appeal to the market? What are the factors that determine demand for this product—price, service, or quality? And how do they compare in importance? Who makes the buying decision?

ABBOTT STEEL CORPORATION

The sales and advertising managers of Abbott Steel Corporation were meeting to discuss the meaning and the implications for promotional policy of the results of a recent research study of purchasing agents. The study concerned reactions to the advertising and personal selling activities of four leading steel firms, and was based on a national sample of purchasing agents who had been prescreened to determine that they were specifiers of steel products.

Abbott, one of the major steel companies in the country, manufactured a wide line of steel products for fabricators and other industrial firms. Abbott's products were sold direct and through a national warehouse distribution system, with the latter accounting for over half of Abbott's sales. In its direct sales effort, like most of its competitors, Abbott had a sizable field force of several hundred sales engineers operating from offices in principal cities. These men called on purchasing agents, and also worked on special applications with development engineers and design people in the plants of customer companies.

In the same way that all the major firms employed extensive sales forces, Abbott also undertook advertising campaigns in vertical and horizontal trade magazines. So in addition to maintaining its sales force Abbott spent over $2-1/2 million in advertising, almost all of it in trade magazines.

Thus it was with considerable interest that Abbott's marketing staff perused the results of a research study conducted by a major trade-publication firm. The study had been conducted with over 2,000 purchasing agents, and focused on their ratings of major steel manufacturers along three specific dimensions: overall preference for the company, preference for the company's salesman, and preference for the company's advertising. The specific questions were:

1. All things considered, based on their overall performance, in what order would you rank these companies?
2. In terms of the performance of the salesmen representing these companies, how would you rank these companies?
3. In terms of the usefulness of the advertising of these companies, how would you rank these companies?

The research was part of a broader study of purchasing-agent preferences, and respondents to the questions about steel companies had been prescreened as to their actual involvement in specifying steel products. The trade magazine considered the study to be a rather accurate reflection of the purchasing-agent population. The Abbott people, although recognizing that there was no way of knowing which purchasing agents bought direct and/or through warehouses, nevertheless thought that the data could provide some vital insights to aid in understanding the impressions made by Abbott's sales force and its advertising. They were also impressed with the rather close correlation between Abbott's own share of market data and the overall company preference ratings in the trade publication's study.

As the sales manager and advertising manager reviewed the key data (summarized in Exhibit 1) they wondered what the results meant, especially in terms of implications for Abbott and for its major competitors. The latter, of course, presumably were also seeing the results of the study.

EXHIBIT 1   Percentage of Purchasing Agents Preferring Company Under Various Conditions *

Brand	Condition 1	Condition 2	Condition 3
Grant	43%**	28%	9%
Abbott	43	38	28
Duluth	58	50	45
Fletcher	19	13	9
Combined "Big 4"	42	34	19

* Conditions:
Condition 1—Purchasing agent prefers *both* the company's advertising and its salesman.
Condition 2—Purchasing agent prefers the company's salesman but not its advertising.
Condition 3—Purchasing agent prefers the company's advertising but not its salesman.
** To be read: When the purchasing agent prefers *both* the company's salesman and its advertising, the probability is .43 that he ranks the company No. 1 overall.
Note: The percentages should not add in either direction.

What are the implications of the research results for Abbott's promotional policy? What does the study suggest regarding the other major manufacturers?

SCHMIDT PACKING COMPANY

Herr Schmidt, president of the Schmidt Packing Company, was considering the information he had gathered on "brown and serve" pork sausages, preparatory to deciding whether the company should produce and market such a product.

The Company

The Schmidt Packing Company was a major regional packer and marketer of pork products. The packing plant was located in Frankfurt, Germany. The markets the company served included all of Hesse, a small part of Württemberg, Baden, and Munich. The company maintained two sales offices, one in Mannheim and the other in Munich. Each sales office was the headquarters for approximately 20 salesmen who sold Schmidt products to grocery outlets. The company had had a net after-tax profit of 1,260,000 DM (Deutschmarks) on sales of 315,000,000 DM during the past year.

The Product

According to the salesmen of the sausage machinery Schmidt used, "brown and serve" sausage had been introduced in the United States with great success by the Fisher Company, an American meat packer, three years before. Essentially, the brown and serve sausage was a sausage that was thoroughly precooked at the packing plant and therefore required only three minutes in the housewife's skillet in order to become hot and brown, in contrast to the thirty minutes or more required to cook the standard sausage and make it ready for the table. Actually, the brown and serve sausage could be eaten safely directly from the package; the frying served only to heat and brown the product, thus making it more appetizing and eye-appealing.

During the cooking process, whether done at the packing plant or in the home, approximately 50 percent of a raw sausage was cooked away. Therefore, in order to present the housewife with precooked sausages in a familiar size, the Fisher Company management had considered it desirable to make them twice as large as normal in the uncooked state and then to cook them down to the standard size. Fisher also priced the product at twice the cost of the same weight of standard sausage.

Required Investment

After some investigation Herr Schmidt had discovered that the process of making brown and serve sausages involved, in addition to new machinery for making the sausages twice as large, a surprising number of cooking, transfer, and temperature change operations, and that components of equipment to make the process efficient on a production-line basis would cost in the neighborhood of 840,000 DM.

Herr Schmidt believed that a six-month introductory program for the areas he wished to cover—involving the hiring of demonstrators along with newspaper and radio advertising—would cost approximately 168,000 DM. The company's financial position was such that the company could not go into the production and distribution of precooked sausages without resorting to a bank loan. On the other hand, its credit was good, and Herr Schmidt did not believe that there would be any difficulty in obtaining a loan on a long-term basis.

Prospects for the Product

Herr Schmidt knew from comparative studies of the buying habits of West German and Austrian housewives that the former were much more inclined to buy prepacked, canned, and frozen foods. He also had the information presented in Exhibit 1.

EXHIBIT 1   Impulse Food Buying: "Why did you buy it?"
(Percent of those who bought on impulse)

	Austria	West Germany	Italy	Nether-lands	Norway
Display reminded housewife	48	39	51	37	25
"Momentary appetite"	25	18	19	20	–
Bargain, low price, sales discount	13	20	7	19	4
Sales staff drew attention	12	8	6	4	5
Reference to sales material	3	16	–	4	1
New product, bought to try	4	3	6	2	5
Scarce product	–	–	1	–	10
Other reasons	–	–	8	9	–

In addition, he had written to a friend who belonged to the American Marketing Association and through this intermediary had obtained from the Fisher Company's director of marketing research the following account of its testing of the product.

After the idea of a precooked sausage was created, the Fisher laboratory perfected its appearance, seasoning, and length of cooking to meet the anticipated consumer requirements. Next, a consumer testing program was initiated. Interviewers recorded consumer problems with package opening, instructions for preparation, degree of brownness, and final taste. Initial reaction to the proposed product was extremely favorable.

Fisher then set out to measure acceptance of the fully cooked sausages by consumers who did not know about the precooking. Half of those tested were asked how well they liked the sausage, and the balance were requested to judge it for seasoning. Two-thirds liked the sausage very much; 30 percent felt it "too highly seasoned," and 64 percent thought it "just right." Several consumer home tests followed, comparing "brown and serve" with the standard fresh product, with degree of freshness as the variable. The precooked variety was again received favorably.

Finally a sales test was set up on a pilot scale in a small Midwestern town. Following three weeks of promotion, name recognition and repeat buying of the brown and serve sausages were found to be very favorable. The penetration of the market and retention of buyers of this brand were checked again six months following the store test by making a house-to-house survey. An expansion to the large area around the original city was made. Sales performance was measured on a store-to-store basis.

With the results favorable at every point, Fisher followed an orderly procedure in advancing the promotion of brown and serve from market to market to the extent that its facilities would permit. Spot checks on consumer reaction followed in several markets.

What can Herr Schmidt glean from Fisher's experience and the data in Exhibit 1? Why should (or should not) demand for brown and serve sausage be different in West Germany from what it is in the United States?

SAMSON BREWING COMPANY

Founded in 1874 by immigrant brewmaster Eli Samson, the Samson Brewing Company achieved early and continued sales success in its three-state marketing area. Five generations of Samsons had inherited and maintained this upward sales trend. Although in recent years Samson had been able to record increases in physical and dollar volume, the company had not been able to hold its traditional share of an expanding regional beer market.

Company executives attributed the sales rise to increases in the number of people in the area reaching beer-drinking age. They charged the decline in market share to an invasion by two supraregional brands, backed by heavy merchandising and promotional budgets within the preceding two years. This encroachment, coupled with increased competition from other purely local brands and continuing promotion by the major national premium beers, led to a realization by Samson management that an "agonizing reappraisal" of its selling climate and marketing activities was necessary for future growth.

The review was not undertaken with any sense of grave necessity for immediate action. Rather, it was to proceed on an exploratory basis, examining several aspects of Samson marketing strategy in an orderly manner. A series of informal meetings for those concerned with each phase of Samson marketing activities was arranged. Paul Samson, the company president, received the following memos reporting the results of these meetings.

FROM THE MEETING OF 9/5

An analysis of Samson sales by geographic subsections within our distribution area failed to uncover any major trouble spots. Traditionally strong pockets of popularity for Samson have maintained sales volume in the face of the increased competition, while areas in which we have never achieved great sales success continue as such.

FROM THE MEETING OF 9/12

A study of Samson's distribution pattern did not reveal any weaknesses that the review conference would label as "major." Samson is carried by most of the major chain and independent supermarkets in the region, and virtually every package store sells Samson. As you know, draft beer business is not a significant portion of our sales, although Samson is on tap in some taverns in our top sales areas. Almost every tavern in the three-state region carries bottled Samson for bar and table sale.

FROM THE MEETING OF 9/29

Our pricing is right in line with the other local beer brands. The appraisal group feels that our retailer margins and prices are competitive. However, we learned that several of our local competitors have made occasional deals with large purchasers, or have instituted special price promotions—both practices we have been reluctant to try.

FROM THE MEETING OF 10/7

Right now, we are spending about $200,000 per year on promotion, mostly on point-of-purchase display and our cooperative deal for tavern and package store signs. Here's the committee's assessment:

1. *Point of Purchase.* The committee thinks that our coverage of package stores and supermarkets is very good in those areas where Samson has always been popular. However, in some other parts of our territory retailers are reluctant to take our signs and banners because of crowding and "not enough back-up promotion."

2. *Lighted Display Signs.* Our cooperative program for package stores and taverns is now four years old. With some variations, we are paying about half the costs of these signs, featuring both the retailer and Samson names. Many major package stores have our signs, and their modernizing effect is popular with the owners. Some committee members do not think that we can go much further with this device, as almost all of the stores we really want have either a Samson sign or their own, and are not interested in changing.

3. *Media Advertising.* Except for minor changes, Samson newspaper ads as well as radio and TV spots are still featuring our traditional themes: Samson is a local beer, brewed by men of long experience. In general, the committee is pleased with the work that the agency has been doing for us, including the point-of-sale material.

There is one more point. The committee thinks we ought to discuss the possibility of expanding our limited advertising spending in response to the increased activity by other beers. Increased advertising might provide something new for Samson. As you can guess a number of previously undiscussed ideas came up—beyond the question of increasing the ad budget. We have scheduled another meeting to discuss whether or not Samson should continue with its traditional advertising themes, regardless of any change in expenditures. This meeting will probably get into our overall approach to marketing Samson.

Subsequently, Alfred Mann, the advertising manager, circulated a shortened version of a study which the company's advertising agency had called "the best research available on consumer attitudes toward beer" (see Appendix). Then another meeting was called to discuss the themes and appeals which Samson should use in its promotion.

Sam Gaines, the sales manager, felt that the company was already addressing its ads to the "middle majority," and that these people were the repeat buyers who constituted Samson's market. According to him:

> The ads we're running now are pretty sensible. They tell people that Samson's been made and sold here for over 80 years . . . that means it *must* be good. Besides, because it's made here, it doesn't cost as much as the big boys' products even though it's certainly just as good. This makes a sensible pitch that has sold, does sell, and will sell our beer. And our package store display signs keep Samson in front of them day and night.
>
> If we do start more advertising—which I guess would certainly help us—I would say that probably just showing plain folks' actual pictures with voices of people who have been drinking Samson for years would really hit this middle majority just right. The agency that did this study certainly confirmed *my* opinions about beer drinking! The only thing the report doesn't do is tell us enough about one real reason people buy a particular beer—price. And that's Samson's real advantage. . . .

Mann emphasized the need to concentrate on basic appeals and motivations and still take advantage of the company's old name and good reputation. As he explained:

> My idea would still appeal to the middle majority but would do it by setting ourselves apart. I want to see us distinguish Samson from all the other local brands, and particularly from some of the new brands that have been invading our territory. We ought to be able to gain respect for Samson as a venerable member of the the regional community.

Paul Samson, Jr., assistant to and son of the president, said that he was intrigued by the parts of the report that did not talk about the "average man," and argued that people would respond to Samson's special story— "the one that no one else around here can tell." He went on to recall how the company had stressed quality ever since Eli Samson founded the brewery in 1874. Then he made this suggestion:

in which area are the new brands succeeding.

Why not show a television tour of our brewery, pointing out
the ingredients of beer, how they are put together, processed, how
Samson is aged, our new and extra sanitary bottling methods, and
so on? That's one sure way in which we can capitalize both on
our long years here and on our product. The report indicates that
people convince themselves that they judge beer by its taste. If
we can *show* them why our beer tastes good, consistently good,
then we can let them convince themselves that their taste tells
them to drink Samson.

Mann said he was afraid that brewing processes would "go right over
the head of the average beer drinker." He argued that Samson should try
to relate itself to the beer drinker in a more personal way, using the
pleasure theme but adding a little style to make the Samson brand more
respected. He said he wanted to create a picture of "an upper-class beer
for the middle-majority drinker."

Arthur Agee, the account man for the local agency that had handled
Samson's advertising for the past two years, welcomed the idea of more
"creativity." He pointed out that as a result of the research study, available to all beer companies, "the middle majority, that great beer-imbibing
mass, has been assailed by hundreds of flannel-shirted, open-necked,
clean-cut, athletic men enjoying their beers with wholesome women or
wives in homey, paneled, do-it-yourself recreation rooms."

Agee argued that the important thing was to get people to taste Samson
beer, and then make up their minds about its quality. So what was needed
was an approach that would attract the attention of people who now had
no opinion about Samson, and thus build "a broader base of people who
would consider Samson the next time they buy or switch brands." His
proposal was a humorous advertising campaign, with much heavier use
of media than in the past.

What kind of advertising strategy should Samson adopt? Does management
know enough now to make a wise decision? What further information would
be helpful? Does the research report give the company any useful clues?

Appendix: Excerpts from Research Report on Consumer Attitudes Toward Beer and Beer Advertising

The study [1] was undertaken to determine the real underlying attitudes and motives which people have toward beer, to determine any
differences in these attitudes by social class levels, and to measure the
impact of typical beer advertising on these different classes. Why do
people drink beer? When? With whom? What advertising can cause them
to switch brands?

[1] Material is based on a study for the *Chicago Tribune* by Social Research,
Inc.

METHOD

The findings in the study were based on over 350 psychological depth interviews with men and women of all social classes. The research question was basically: "*Why* do people do this?" rather than "*How many* do this?"

The two major social class groupings important to the advertiser are the upper-middle and upper classes (15 percent of the population—the quality market), and the middle majority (65 percent of the population—the mass market). The upper-middle and upper classes are made up of the leaders of the community, businessmen, professional men, and their families. These people emphasize values of sophistication, self-reliance, and leadership. Their behavior marks them off from the "common man" by their ability to handle this world to their own social and economic advantage. The middle majority, in contrast, is made up of the large majority of working people—white-collar workers, semiskilled and skilled laborers, and small businessmen. Their jobs mean everything to these people because they have few resources for saving and maintaining themselves in hard times. They emphasize highly conventional behavior. In their world, there is much less leeway for individual variation in social behavior.

With most products, the upper-middles react most positively to advertising that caters to their higher status positions in society—that indicates through sophisticated language, prestige objects, and well-to-do settings that the advertiser feels that those who appreciate the finer things of life will use his product.

The middle majority, on the other hand, often react quite negatively to advertising that appeals to the upper middles. They feel that such advertising is too high-flown, and they prefer advertising that is realistic in terms of settings and people, that sticks to practical details. They react most positively to advertising catering to their needs and interests, giving them information of use, and showing respect for the common man.

By far the largest group of beer drinkers is in the middle majority, and the middle majority consumes the largest amount of beer per capita as well.

HIGHLIGHTS

Up and down the social ladder, we find beer a well-liked drink. People have clear attitudes toward beer and its uses. They know what they want from beer; they get basic social and psychological satisfactions in drinking it.

When do people drink beer?

Beer is a congenial drink. It oils the wheels to make a social gathering enjoyable, relaxing, and refreshing; it breaks down social barriers and lets people be democratic.

When is beer an appropriate social drink?

Beer fits best where equalitarian relaxing is in order. People drink beer in all social classes and for similar reasons. Beer is considered to mark the absence of authority; it is an invitation to informality. Most drinking is done to be socially proper. What is appropriate differs from class to class.

In the upper-middle class (the UMC). People often speak, act, and dress to mark themselves off from the way of life of the middle majority. In drinking habits the mark of UMC status is the mixed drink or the fine wine, not beer. Only when the UMC person is emphasizing his commonality with others does he drink beer to show that he is a good fellow. When he wants to emphasize his membership in a higher status group, as is more often the case, he drinks something else.

In the middle majority (MM). There are fewer occasions when people wish to be formal, to "put on the dog." Most MM people take their "in-between" status for granted and have few needs to appear classier. They consider beer the drink of the common man. They insist that when those above them drink beer, they are bringing themselves down to the "like-me" level. Only on formal occasions (few in middle majority society) do they bring out the high status mixed drinks or wine. Cost also makes beer the drink of the middle majority.

Guides to beer drinking

Middle majority members often express hostility at the suggestion in beer advertising that they should be guided by the upper classes. (Said a 28-year-old clerk: "Those 'man of distinction' ads make me mad. My money will buy just as good liquor as anybody else's.") This feeling manifests itself toward testimonials too. While snob appeal is effective for some prestige items recognized as such, beer is not a prestige item.

What makes beer a good drink?

At the most universal level, the pleasure of beer drinking lies in the throat. Words used to describe beer are more descriptive of how it feels than how it tastes, e.g., "smooth."

Beer is just alcoholic enough to give the drinker a feeling of relaxation and lack of inhibitions. In socializing, this enables him to feel more at home and more willing to be spontaneous. At the same time, there is little likelihood of losing control completely.

A thirst quencher. There is almost complete agreement that beer is a good cooling drink, noticeably more thirst-satisfying than whisky or wine.

How do people feel about brands?

For most people there is "my brand," "the brand that let me down," and "all those others." And people describe their favorite beer(s) with all the good words advertisers have taught them to apply to what a beer should be. With bad words they describe the beer that let them down, e.g., the beer they were drinking "that time the party was no fun." Beer drinkers generally stick to a brand for an extended period; few people will drink *any* kind.

Generally speaking, many people feel that nationally advertised brands are more trustworthy than brands with less advertising or less extensive distribution. Most people are quite willing to accept a less well-known beer once they've tasted it.

What are the common appeals in beer advertising?

Most beer advertisers don't make use of favorable attitudes toward beer. In place of advertising that harnesses these attitudes most successfully, much beer advertising falls into these main categories:

The *prestige endorser theme* is perhaps the most popular theme among beer advertisers. This approach seeks to influence the beer drinker through endorsements by some prominent persons. There are at least three disadvantages:

> People do not believe it; they believe the endorsers are "insincere."
> The situation is usually impersonal; it has few connotations of a friendly relation.
> Many of the figures chosen are not meaningful to the audience.

The *high-class theme* in advertising communicates to the audience by dress, setting, and tone of copy that beer is a "high-class" drink. To the MM (and even the UMC) people this idea is distinctly inappropriate. For them beer is a universal drink, not the formal beverage of the wealthy or prominent. Typical reactions of ordinary beer drinkers indicated disbelief of and resentment toward this theme.

The *scientific proof theme* emphasizes technical phrases, information to prove that one brand of beer is better than others. People do not use technical reasons for their beer preferences. Most beer drinkers judge beer more by the satisfaction they get from it—simply by using it—and have little interest in technical information. Also, this theme is essentially impersonal and does not have the attention-holding power of ads that tie in with the social and personal meanings of beer. The scientific theme has reassurance value but is not a good attention-getter as a major ad appeal.

The *average man theme* is not widely used, but, where it is, it receives a good deal of favorable attention from the audience. Such ads emphasize people who look "average" or slightly better in dress and surrounding and who are doing things that middle majority people commonly do or want to do. People feel that such ads "fit" with beer and the meanings it has for them. The ad is much more likely to arouse interest and a desire to have a beer.

Appeals that elicit response

Appeals *recalling, suggesting,* and *demonstrating pleasure* are those to which people respond most. Beer is bound up with social and personal feelings—what it is used for, what pleasure it can give.

We recommend that advertising:

Should embody and emphasize these appeals:

> Family and friends in informal gatherings.
> Relaxation and refreshment after work or exercise.
> Refreshment of spectators at appropriate sports gatherings.
> Equalitarian festivities such as lodge meetings and Fourth of July.
> Beer with meals.

Should use these kinds of people:

> Hearty, active men of middle majority and upper-middle class in informal clothing.
> "All-American girls" with emphasis on wholesomeness, not sexiness.

Should talk about beer as

> A cool, refreshing drink.
> A friendly, hospitable drink.
> A drink for equals, "for people like you."
> A drink that *feels good.*
> A drink consistent in quality, clean and carefully made.

2

PRODUCT
POLICY

Every marketer must continually make decisions about the products he manufactures or buys for resale. What shall be added to or eliminated from the product line? How shall the products already in the line be modified or improved? Would changing the price make the product more attractive? Such innovative action is not only a means to hold—and expand the purchases of—his existing customers (or to attract new and different segments of the market) but also to keep his own sales force interested and enthusiastic.

Marketing research can provide crucial information about the probable success of a proposed product or product modification. Market testing especially is a powerful technique because it simulates actual buying situations. But no marketing research or test can supply the complete answer. People, themselves, do not always know whether or not they will buy; and if they do know, they won't always reveal it. Much depends on what happens over time—competitors' products or promotional moves, the reaction of distributors, changes in economic conditions, social trends, the cumulative effect of one buyer on another.

Nonetheless, the marketer must make his decisions, knowing that what he is trying is to some extent new and therefore risky, but using whatever information and analysis he can muster, and weighing the potential payoff against the risk.

The risk, of course, can take many forms: complete failure and loss of the total investment in the new product, costs greater than the added revenue, dilution of selling effort on other products, diminution of prestige. But the gain, too, can take many forms: financial success from the product itself, added patronage and traffic, support of other products in the line, enlistment of new and better distributors or salesmen, reinforcement of the corporate or store image in customers' minds.

For the gain to be realized, the product must fit in with buyers' values and their established buying habits or procedures for purchasing; at least, it must not be so inappropriate that buyers' ideas cannot be changed a little.

The product must also offer the buyer some advantage: a saving in money or effort, or a gain in service or satisfaction. How large the advantage must be will depend on how satisfied people are with existing products, and on how important the use or the cost of the product is to them. How they value the product is what counts. Among products that are of the same or similar value to them, they shop eagerly and shrewdly for the best price, yet are willing to pay extra for the product whose value they judge to be better or more closely suited to what they want.

With such provisos—but only with such provisos—the manufacturer has one strong factor in his favor: today's consumer is surprisingly willing to try new products and services and is becoming quite sophisticated in judging value. The industrial purchasing agent (using techniques like value analysis) and the corporate chain buying committee (applying computer analysis of volume, margin, and turnover) are also closer, more discriminating buyers than ever before.

People are also individuals. They regard products differently, and they use them differently. This individualism creates many segments of the market that will respond to special products or special product qualities. It creates increasing opportunities for segmented marketing, as mass production and mass distribution standardize products and the way they are sold.

BOLING BROS. DEPARTMENT STORE

(Harry Higbee, salesman for the Winway Hat Company, is talking to Bill Burnham, buyer for hats in the Boling Bros. Department Store, which caters to the medium-to-high income group.)

SALESMAN.   Mr. Burnham, I appreciate the opportunity to talk to you about carrying our Winway hats. This is the kind of store we'd be proud to have them in.

BUYER.   That's interesting. There was a man in here several weeks ago who was asking if we didn't have a Winway hat in his size. But he took another brand, without much fuss.

SALESMAN.   How many brands do you carry now?

BUYER.   We have the Londoner and the Balmak—both good brands. Our customers like them.

SALESMAN.   They *are* good brands. But why don't you round out your line with the Winway? Our price range is lower, distinctly lower than either of them, too. Then you'd be able to satisfy all your customers, and maybe attract some new ones.

BUYER.   That means increasing inventory about 50 percent, and I doubt if we would get enough extra sales to justify it. I'm sort of cramped for space, too, as you can see.

SALESMAN. We had an independent marketing research agency make a survey for us among men hat buyers. Their brand preferences came out like this—see on this chart—Winway 25 percent, Balmak 20 percent, Londoner only 5 percent—I guess they think *that's* a foreign make—and others, all together, 10 percent.

BUYER. What about the rest—let's see, 25 and 20 and 5 and 10 is 60— the remaining 40 percent?

SALESMAN. They're classified as "don't knows." Couldn't make up their minds, I guess.

BUYER. Well, all I know is those figures don't apply here. The Londoner gets 70 percent of our business, and the Balmak 30 percent. Also, this is the case even though, as I'm sure you know, the Londoner runs a few cents higher than the Balmak.

SALESMAN. That's because you don't carry the Winway. Why, in the Tuscary Department Store—only 50 miles away—the Winway is enjoying 80 percent of the business. You've seen our advertisements in *Esquire*, haven't you?

BUYER. Oh, yes. Nice ads. But our trade is accustomed to the two we have. . . .

SALESMAN. Well, keep us in mind. I'll stop in to see you my next trip through here. And in the meantime, why don't you ask some of your customers what they think of Winway, and see what they say?

Should Burnham take on the Winway hat? What kind of considerations should affect his decision? What kind of analysis should he apply? From the facts revealed in the course of the above conversation, and your own observations of men's hat buying (or nonbuying), what determines the kind of hat the average man buys and, if different, what determines the kind of hat the Boling Bros. customer buys? What do you think of Higbee's salesmanship?

SYMPHONY OF THE SIERRAS [1]

In the late spring of 1970, Douglas Sayer, business manager of the Symphony of the Sierras, was considering whether or not to raise subscription ticket prices for the coming season, and if so, by how much. He was contemplating an increase in orchestra and balcony prices of 50¢ to $1 per ticket both at the box office and for subscription series tickets,

---

[1] "Symphony of the Sierras," in *Cases in Arts Administration*, Thomas C. Raymond, Stephen A. Greyser, and Douglas Schwalbe (Cambridge, Mass.: Arts Administration Research Institute, 1970).

and was also considering introducing special group rates and student discounts. However, setting subscription prices was uppermost in his mind at the moment, because the copy for the first mailing promoting subscriptions had to be prepared for the printer in less than three weeks. It was by no means a foregone conclusion that ticket prices should be raised at all. Sayer thought that the Symphony's financial position made such a move advisable, but he did not want to risk a significant reduction in the Symphony's audience. In view of his uncertainty about the probable effect of a price increase, Sayer was also considering making some sort of a survey in order to get a better idea of the reactions of potential ticket purchasers to any proposed increase. However, the subscription mailing deadline made it imperative to make the decision—at least regarding the price of subscription tickets—very soon. Sayer did not want to miss the printer's deadline, because long experience had shown that the timing of the several preseason subscription mailings was very important in maximizing subscription responses. Moreover, the revenue from these mailings played an important role in the Symphony's off-season cash flow.

Background of the Symphony

The Symphony of the Sierras was located in a major city in one of the Mountain states. Although the Symphony was not a major orchestra (like the Boston, New York, Chicago, Philadelphia, and other very large musical organizations), it was an exclusively professional orchestra with a long tradition in its region. Founded in the early 1920s largely through the efforts and the money of one of the city's wealthiest families, the Symphony was virtually a civic institution. Its concerts, though not sold out, were generally well-attended. (See Exhibit 1.) In 1969–70, the Symphony presented twenty-six concerts, in two series of thirteen programs each, one series on Tuesday evenings and the other on Friday evenings.

The Symphony of the Sierras was not the sole source of orchestral music available to the residents of the city. Within a radius of two and a half hours' driving time was another metropolitan orchestra and also a major orchestra. Moreover, every summer since 1960 a two-week music festival had been held in the mountains near the city. The festival, hosted by the major orchestra in the area, attracted soloists of international reputation and was famed throughout the nation for the calibre of its concerts. Several nearby universities, in addition to having student orchestras, also brought into the area various other musical groups such as chamber ensembles. Finally, one AM and two FM radio stations offered classical music to residents of the city.

In 1960 the present conductor, Eugene Wiegner, had ascended the podium of the Symphony of the Sierras. His tenure had been marked by a strong commitment to presenting rarely performed and contemporary

EXHIBIT 1   Attendance as a Percentage of Capacity

Year	Symphony of the Sierras	Estimate of Basic 11 Major Orchestras
1957–58	73	71
1958–59	74	77
1959–60	72	74
1960–61	75	78
1961–62	74	n.a.**
1962–63	77	n.a.
1963–64	80	82
1964–65	84	82
1965–66	82	79
1966–67	82	78
1967–68	83	n.a.
1968–69	78	n.a.
1969–70	85*	n.a.

* Approximately 78% for Tuesday evenings, 91% for Friday evenings.
** Not available.

works. Although the orchestra's program during the season typically contained many works from the standard classical repertoire, its imaginative programming, coupled with the uniformly high quality of its concerts, had won it national acclaim. Sayer, who had joined the Symphony in his present role in 1964, believed that the Symphony's programming had attracted a faithful and unusually sophisticated audience. He often pointed with pride to the fact that the subscription list included a number of people who lived in towns 25 to 50 miles away.

Background of the Problem

Despite its artistic success and audience approval, the Symphony of the Sierras had in recent years encountered increasing difficulty in covering its costs. In fact, the Symphony had shown annual operating deficits which had grown from $6,000 in 1963–64 to $26,500 in 1969–70. Sayer attributed these mounting operating deficits primarily to steeply rising player costs. Furthermore, the pattern of settlements being negotiated elsewhere with the American Federation of Musicians made it seem quite probable that this adverse trend would continue. To date, the Symphony had not experienced substantial difficulty in covering these deficits. Though the Symphony's box-office revenues had not been covering its costs, the revenue from its annual fund-raising campaign, plus the income from its modest endowment had so far covered the gap.

Since the early 1960s, however, although receipts from both the fund-raising campaign and ticket sales had increased, they had failed to keep pace with costs. The bulk of this financial support came from the Haskills, the family whose forebears had been instrumental in founding the Symphony in the 1920s. Although Sayer recognized that the community generally and the Haskills in particular had shown a strong commitment to supporting the Symphony, he wondered how long the Symphony could continue to rely on their largesse. This was of particular concern to him, because in his view the establishment of the summer music festival so near the city was attracting a growing percentage of the money available for cultural activities in the area.

The Symphony's Pricing Policies

Owing in part to the layout of its concert hall, which seated slightly over 1,000, the Symphony had traditionally offered just two prices for seats, one for all orchestra seats, the other for all balcony seats. Tickets for the Friday evening concerts were uniformly priced 50¢ higher than for the Tuesday concerts. Subscription series tickets for both Tuesday and Friday concerts were uniformly 50¢ less than box-office prices. Ticket prices had last been raised two seasons before, 25¢ per ticket across the board.

More specifically, box-office prices for Tuesday evening tickets were $4 for orchestra seats and $2.75 for balcony seats; tickets for Friday night performances were $4.50 and $3.25, respectively. Equivalent prices for subscription series tickets were $3.50 and $2.25 for Tuesday nights and $4 and $2.75 for Fridays. In effect, subscribers received tickets free to about two of the thirteen concerts per series as an inducement to subscribe.

The Symphony also pursued a policy of retaining a large number of tickets in the lower price range—some 47 percent of total capacity in 1969–70. The intent of this practice was to foster an appreciation of its musical offerings, and to encourage concert attendance by students and others with limited means. During the tenure of Wiegner, this educational role of the Symphony had received particular emphasis, although it had always been important. Another outgrowth of this concern for the student audience was a policy of keeping a certain number of seats for each concert available for sale at the box office, although this number did vary according to the night of the week. Sayer thought it desirable to keep about 35 percent of the total number of tickets per week available for sale at the box office.

A record of subscription series sales for previous seasons appears in Exhibit 2. Although subscription sales had been improving fairly steadily in the past few years, Sayer was interested in increasing them further. The cash-flow exigencies of the Symphony made it essential to collect as

EXHIBIT 2   Subscriptions Sold as a Percentage of All Seats Available

	Tuesday Series		Friday Series	
	Orchestra (%)	Balcony (%)	Orchestra (%)	Balcony (%)
1963–64	42	44	56	70
1964–65	43	48	59	73
1965–66	47	48	60	74
1966–67	45	52	60	76
1967–68	51	55	63	79
1968–69	45	49	59	72
1969–70	53*	58**	65*	81**

* 530 seats = 100%
** 470 seats = 100%

much money as possible before the season started in order to cover preseason and opening expenses. Sayer relied on the sale of subscriptions to cover these and was therefore quite reluctant to risk losing subscriptions.

Other Factors Influencing the Decision

Sayer was confident that the concerts planned for the coming season would attract a record number of subscribers, other things being equal. Experience of previous years had suggested that the Symphony's audience did react at the box office to the programs offered. For example, both he and Wiegner believed that the drop in attendance in the 1968–69 season had reflected the unusually high proportion of experimental music programmed that year. Although they desired to move in future years still further in the direction of the 1968–69 programming, Sayer did not think this was feasible until the Symphony had achieved a sounder financial position. Furthermore, there was some question in his mind as to whether the Haskills would respond favorably to programs similar to those of 1968–69.

As Sayer considered the pricing problem further, he realized that he might undertake some research on the subject with present and/or potential subscribers. He knew he could probably get students from the city's university to help carry out the research. However, he recognized that given the time pressure for the decision on subscription prices, any such research could not be elaborate. He also worried over the reliability of any questions directly addressed to pricing, because respondents might be unwilling to admit that a price increase would make a difference to them. Most important, Sayer wondered whether any new information would be more helpful than working with the data from a survey of the Symphony audience made by a group of consultants during the previous year. Excerpts from their study appear in Exhibit 3. Sayer realized that the sample sizes used in the survey were small, but knew that the study had been carefully done. Thus, he believed the information could still provide some useful insights to aid his thinking on the pricing problem.

EXHIBIT 3   Excerpts from Consultants' Findings on the Symphony of the Sierras' Audience's Composition and Attitudes

A. Demographic Characteristics of Symphony-goers Surveyed

	Symphony/Sierras-goers*	Non-Symphony/Sierras-goers**
Number in Sample (N)	87	60
1. Sex		
Male	35%	47%
Female	65	53
	100%	100%
2. Marital Status		
Single	21%	8%
Married	71	89
Widowed/divorced	7	3
	100%	100%
3. Education		
Completed high school or less	7%	14%
Some college	3	17
College complete	49	53
Graduate work	41	16
	100%	100%
4. Age of Respondent		
18–29	25%	16%
30–39	32	22
40–49	23	32
50 and over	20	30
	100%	100%
5. Family Income		
Under $7,000	20%	4%
$7,000–$10,999	14	19
$11,000 and over	35	60
No answer	31	17
	100%	100%

EXHIBIT 3 (cont.)

	Symphony/Sierras- goers*	Non-Symphony/ Sierras-goers**
6. Distance of Home from Symphony		
5-mile radius	45%	30%
10-mile radius	20	32
25-mile radius	22	36
50-mile radius	13	–
	100%	100%

* People who attended concerts of the Symphony of the Sierras in 1968–1969. *already bias*

** People who attended other symphony concerts but did *not* attend concerts of the Symphony of the Sierras in 1968–1969.

B. Attitudes Toward Ticket Buying of Symphony-goers Surveyed

1. "Would you consider buying a season ticket to the Symphony this year?" (Asked only of current Symphony/Sierras-goers)

	Current Subscribers	Nonsubscribers
Yes	88%	16%
No	6	40
Undecided	6	40
No answer	–	4
	100%	100%
	N = 51	36

2. "Symphony tickets at $4 a ticket are a real bargain."

	Symphony/Sierras Orchestra Seat Subscribers
Agree	49%
Disagree	35
Can't say	16
	100%
	N = 28

3. "Symphony tickets at $3 a ticket are a real bargain."

	Symphony/Sierras Balcony Seat Subscribers
Agree	42%
Disagree	41
Can't say	17
	100%
	N = 23

EXHIBIT 3 (cont.)

4. "Do you remember how much you paid for your Symphony/Sierras ticket?"

Symphony/Sierras
Orchestra Seat Subscribers

Less than $4	45%
$4	14
$4 to $5	14
More than $5	0
No answer	27
	100%

N = 28

Symphony/Sierras
Balcony Seat Subscribers

Less than $3	40%
$3	12
$3 to $4	21
More than $4	5
No answer	22
	100%

N = 23

5. "When you go to the Symphony, which of the following factors do you consider to be most important?"

	Symphony/Sierras-goers			Non-Symphony/Sierras-goers		
	1st Choice	2nd Choice	Total	1st Choice	2nd Choice	Total
Entertainment value	31%	28%	59%	39%	16%	55%
Program itself	42	14	56	25	20	45
Conductor	14	14	28	12	22	42
Orchestra, soloists	10	17	27	22	20	42
Educational value	3	7	10	2	12	14
Other	0	17	17	0	0	0
No answer	0	3	3	0	9	9
	100%	100%		100%	100%	
N =		87			60	

What price schedule should Sayer adopt? Why? Under your plan, how many seats must be sold next year to produce the same revenue as this year? What do you think are the chances of doing better than this year?

GEM APPLIANCE COMPANY

In 1961, Mr. Daniel Goodman, manager of the Gem Appliance Company in Tel Aviv, was considering adding an electric dryer to his product line. Gem already manufactured washing machines, to sell around I£ 400, and the proposed dryer would sell for about I£ 300. A competitor made washers with an air-circulating feature that partially dried the laundry but did not eliminate further drying (priced at around I£ 540). But dryers would be a new product for Israel, as well as for Gem, and Goodman needed a forecast of the possible market.

Aside from some data in the *Statistical Yearbook of the United Nations* (see Exhibit 1), Goodman's only information was a study of the U.S. dryer market made by Curtis Publishing Company's research department in 1948, summarized in the Appendix, plus the U.S. statistics shown in Exhibits 2 and 3. He had also learned that the ratio of electric and gas dryer sales to electric washer sales was uniform throughout the United States.

Should Mr. Goodman go ahead with plans to add the dryer to his line of appliances? What general factors will determine the demand for this kind of appliance? What factors may be peculiar to Israel but not the United States? In particular, just what is the major buying motivation for the dryer in the United States, and will this prevail in Israel, too? Are there important differences between washers and dryers, between dryers and ironers, and so on?

Appendix: Summary of Curtis Research Department Bulletin

The basic requisite for dryer ownership is a home with electric power. As of January 1, 1948, there were 33,050,000 residential electric customers in the United States.

Poor weather conditions often prevent housewives from hanging laundry out-of-doors. According to latest *U.S. Meteorological Year Book* figures, there is cloudy or partly cloudy weather in 180 American cities about 70 percent of the time. This means an average of only 2.07 clear days each week in these cities. In most of the United States, with the exception of the southern half of California and Nevada, most of Arizona, and parts of New Mexico, weather conditions definitely hinder good outdoor drying throughout the year.[1]

---

[1] Note that in Israel, in 1958, Tel Aviv had 26 rainy days and 7 stormy days, while Jerusalem had 24 days of rain or snow and 79 stormy days, according to the *Statistical Abstract of Israel.*

EXHIBIT 1   Economic Statistics for Israel

	1949	1951	1953	1955	1957	1958	1959
Population (In millions)	1.2	1.6	1.7	1.8	2.0	2.0	2.1*
Education (In thousands of pupils)							
Total	141	249	355	381	472	517	551
Higher Education	2	4	6	7	8	10	11
Residential Building (Index)	100	293	138	246	216	259	265
(Number of Dwellings)							
With 2 rooms or less						14,750	15,210
With more than 2 rooms						15,490	17,880
Electric Energy Production (In millions of kwh)		620	914	1,308	1,416	1,766	1,968
National Income (In I£ millions)				1,726	2,399	2,721	3,047
Private Consumption Expenditures (In I£ millions)			1,088	1,603	2,177	2,473	2,785
Manufacturing Employment (In thousands)				81.7	–	99.3	–
Manufacturing Wages and Salaries (In I£ millions)				198.1	269.0	316.2	–
Families with Household Equipment (In thousands)							
With piano							15.4
With gramophone							59.7
With radio							384.3
With electric washing machine					**	43.7	61.6
With gas range or cooking stove						168.0	239.5
With refrigerator—ice box						213.1	216.3
With refrigerator—electric						163.5	204.8

* Average size of family 3.8.

** In 1957, an investigation of 2,911 families revealed that 2.4% had bought an electric washing machine during the past year at an average price of I£ 329. Broken down by size of monthly income, the figures were 0.4% for 872 families with monthly incomes of less than I£ 200, 2.6% for 1,544 families with monthly income of I£ 200–349, and 6.2% for 417 families with monthly income of I£ 350 or more. $1 = 1.8 Israeli pounds, I£, at the time.

EXHIBIT 2 U.S. Homes with Electrical Appliances (Number of appliances in millions)

Wired Homes with:

End of Year	Television Sets		Refrigerators		Freezers		Vacuum Cleaners (Floor)		Electric Washers		Dryers (Electric and Gas)		Air Conditioners	
	Number	Percent	Number	Percent	Number	Percent	Number	Percent	Number	Percent	Number	Percent	Number	Percent
1946	–	–	21.4	69.1	–	–	15.1	48.8	18.8	60.5	–	–	0.1	0.2
1950	10.6	26.4	33.8	86.4	2.8	7.2	22.0	56.5	28.1	71.9	0.6	1.4	0.2	0.6
1955	35.0	76.1	43.3	94.1	7.7	16.8	29.6	64.3	38.7	84.1	4.2	9.2	2.6	5.6
1958	44.0	89.0	48.3	97.7	10.4	21.0	35.0	70.9	44.9	90.9	7.7	15.6	5.8	11.7

Note: Percentages based on total number of homes wired for electricity.

Source: *The Economic Almanac 1960* (National Industrial Conference Board), p. 371.

EXHIBIT 3 Sales of Electrical Appliances in U.S. (Number of appliances in thousands)

Year	Washing Machines		Dryers		Combined Washer-Dryers	Ironers	Dishwashers
	Automatic	Other	Electric	Gas			
1936	1,529		—	—	—	180	—
1940	1,455		—	—	—	176	—
1945	251*		—	—	—	30*	—
1950	1,646	2,626	251	68	—	409	230
1955	3,123	1,268	1,028	369	—	87	295
1958	2,832	938	843	397	170	35	425
1959	2,970	980	923	486	196	40	547
1960	2,616	765	814	444	163	35	555

* Effects of war.

Source: Statistical Abstract of the United States 1960, p. 822; 1961, p. 821.

Contamination of the air from industrial soot and dirt increases the problem of home laundering when clothes are hung outdoors to dry.

The frequent limitations of space for adequately drying clothes is another important element to be considered in estimating the automatic dryer market, particularly in urban areas with heavy population concentrations.

Many women feel that clothes dried in sunlight or by other natural means will turn out better and have a sweeter smell than clothes dried by a mechanical process. This is mainly a problem of consumer education through consistent and intelligent advertising.

The present high level of consumer income is favorable for the dryer market. As costs are reduced and terms of payment adjusted to meet consumer needs, the market should gradually broaden.

Dryer operating costs seem reasonable and are a favorable market factor. West Penn Power Company estimates that the electric dryer uses an average 40 kwh per month, at a rate of 3 cents per kwh. *Electrical Merchandising* puts the cost at $11 per year. Many owners have no definite ideas of their dryer operating cost and do not seem to be concerned about it.

In a recent study of 500 dryer users, 91 percent said they saved considerable time with a dryer; 81 percent said the dryer saved them work.[2] In a typical instance it was found that the housewife walked an average of 0.8 mile for each drying operation before a dryer was installed; this walking was entirely eliminated after the dryer purchase.[3] A number of respondents mentioned elimination of sprinkling before ironing and reduction in the number of items that had to be ironed.

Most of the respondents were quite convinced that clothes come out of the dryer just as fresh as they do when dried in the sun; some even thought it better than outdoor drying because there is no wind to tear or fray the clothes; and clothes seemed to keep their proper shape better in the dryer.

Disadvantages claimed for the automatic clothes dryer include room dampness due to the fact that the dryer removes six pounds of water from each load; lint traps which must be emptied periodically; initial cost (currently $220–$250); and fabric damage due to high operating temperatures. (Some people said that the heat made silk things "harsh," and many feared shrinkage.)

For a number of years the principal market for dryers will be new customer sales. Replacement and second-hand sales will not become an important factor in the market until the appliance achieves a higher saturation status than it now has. There is a good reason to believe that the pattern of market development will closely approximate that of mechanical home laundering in general. Sales of electrical ironers (that is, mangles, not hand irons) may be a clue to what will happen.

In this connection it is important to note that some experts in the appli-

2 *Electrical Merchandising*, May 1, 1948.
3 *Ibid.*, March 1, 1947.

ance field have tied the potential dryer market, exclusively, to ownership and sales of ironers. These people contend that ironer owners are most conscious of the value of mechanical laundry aids and are also better able to afford a dryer.

SINGH AND SONS (A)

Sri K. C. Singh, president of Singh and Sons, private manufacturers of cast iron valves, was considering the matter of how to enter the U.S. market in a meaningful way, taking advantage of the relatively low labor cost rates in India. Singh and Sons was already exporting from India to South Africa, Australia, Canada, and the Scandinavian countries, in what Singh considered reasonable quantities—in each case ranging from 20,000 to 50,000 units per year. On the basis of comparative population figures, he felt that the United States potential for his products could be anywhere between 1 million and 10 million units.

Singh and Sons was part of a large industrial complex, with ample financial and productive resources. There was reason to believe that if foreign exchange was needed it could be secured as long as the company could show that it would be used to build up Indian exports and bring in dollars.

Singh's specialty was an unusually sturdy ball-type valve, particularly popular for use in mining in the countries that constituted its present markets. It was much heavier than conventional ball valves and also cruder in appearance (rough, painted iron rather than stainless steel and/or brass); but by its very mass and strength it compensated in performance for its lack of machined elegance, and could take higher pressures and serve longer in hard use than conventional ball valves. It also offered an added economy in that the rubber seats could be easily reversed and/or interchanged, and because only one side of the four sides of the two seats was subjected to wear and tear at any one time, this feature meant that the valve's life could be extended to four times what it otherwise would have been.

The usual strategy followed by Singh and Sons was to have one wholesale distributor in each country. This was the case in Canada, but the Canadian distributor also had the privilege of selling in the United States. In fact, the Canadian distributor, who carried a full line of mining supplies, was selling about 10,000 valves per year in the United States, almost all of it in the mining districts in the western states. Mr. Singh felt that he could alter the Canadian arrangement to allow for other representation in the United States without seriously damaging his current business with this distributor, but was even willing to risk losing it all if that meant a new sizable volume in the United States.

Singh was realizing a 12 percent margin (after freight and delivery cost) on sales to Canada. The Canadian distributor was realizing a 35 percent margin (also after delivery cost, but before charging in any inventory cost). To take the ½" valve as an example: Singh's delivered cost in Canada was $1.70; the price to the Canadian distributor was $2.05; and the price to final users was $3.15 plus freight (in all cases stated in terms of U.S. currency).

Should Singh and Sons try to enter the U.S. market? What else, if anything, should Singh and Sons try to learn about the U.S. market?

SINGH AND SONS (B)

For the sum of $3,000, Singh and Sons engaged a U.S. agency to study the U.S. market and to furnish information on comparative prices of competing valves.

The U.S. marketing agency reported to Singh that it was difficult to compare prices with other brands of valves because the Singh valves were unconventional. For some uses their extra ruggedness was not needed or wanted; for other uses, their superior performance put them in a quite different category from that of what otherwise would seem to be competing valves. In a very real sense, the Singh valve was halfway between gate valves, which generally were of lower price and performance than most ball valves, and the more sophisticated stainless steel and brass, conventional ball valves; that is, it could out-perform the former, yet could not match the mechanical elegance of the latter.

The U.S. agency reported, however, that on balance it thought that Superior ball valves came closest to being comparable. Superior ball valves were the "second" or lower-price line of the Acme Valve Company, one of the largest ball valve manufacturers in the United States, but it was, in the agency's words, "a very respectable line."

Acme's valves were sold to wholesale distributors through the regular Acme sales force of about forty men. Distributors were allowed a 35 percent discount from list prices. On the basis of Acme's annual report, the marketing agency conjectured that on Superior valves Acme's margin (i.e., difference between manufacturing cost and selling price to wholesalers) was around 30 percent.

The list prices of Superior valves are shown in Exhibit 1, along with what would be Singh and Sons' delivered prices to warehouses located at U.S. seaports if they were to get the same margin as in Canada; the weights of Singh valves by size; and a percentage distribution of the volume of unit sales in the different sizes as experienced by typical U.S. wholesale distributors. Singh's delivered costs in the case of warehouses located at seaports in the United States would be about the same as for the Canadian distributor; however, to serve the whole United States would require shipping into inland warehouses as well, and this would cost an

EXHIBIT 1　Price Comparison and Other Information

Size	Superior List Price *	Singh Delivered Price to Seaport Warehouses in United States **	Weight	Typical Distribution of Sales in United States
½"	$ 7.80	$ 2.53	1.2500 lb.	20%
¾"	8.20	2.63	1.8750 lb.	30%
1"	10.00	2.73	2.5000 lb.	20%
1¼"	13.20	5.52	3.0333 lb.	15%
1½"	14.80	7.90	4.7500 lb.	10%
2"	17.60	11.61	5.7500 lb.	5%
				100%

* Freight allowed (that is, no delivery charge) on orders amounting to 500 lbs or more.

** Includes payment of U.S. tariff of 11½%.

estimated 5¢ per lb. (average for the whole country, including both seaport and inland locations). Note that the cost of larger Singh valves rises disproportionately; this is because of their construction (depending on a heavy mass of iron) and correspondingly high transportation cost.

The marketing research agency also reported that it had shown samples of the valve to about fifty construction engineers and distributors, and that the results had been mixed. About half—for the most part, those of higher caliber—showed interest in the potential of this "new kind of valve," or even enthusiasm. The others—for the most part, those of less imagination and aggressiveness—thought it was "too different to gain acceptance." All interviewees raised questions about quality control and dependability of supply when buying from a foreign source.

In the light of this further data, should Singh and Sons attempt to penetrate the U.S. market? Or do they need still further information?

CARBORUNDUM COMPANY—PRODUCT RESEARCH

Part I

The laboratory of Carborundum's refractories division had recently developed a ceramic fiber of aluminum silicate. As produced, the fiber was a white mass of randomly arranged fine (one-fourth the diameter of silk) fibers ranging up to three inches in length. The research laboratory believed that the new material could find applications as a filtering material, as a thermal insulator, and, in general, as a replacement for asbestos.

The task of evaluating the commercial possibilities of the new fiber, or Fiberfrax® as it was christened, was assigned to the marketing research department. Carborundum had swatches of Fiberfrax® in a limited range of weaves made up by textile firms interested in ceramic fibers. These swatches were used by the marketing research analyst in the course of his calls upon prospective users of Fiberfrax®. The analyst was also equipped with some laboratory data on the physical and chemical properties of Fiberfrax® and the information that its price would "probably be approximately 50 percent higher than that of asbestos." His report follows:

FIBERFRAX® SURVEY

As requested, calls were made on twenty major potential users of Fiberfrax® textiles to determine their reaction to the product. (Included were major electrical, woven belting, electric furnace, and glass companies, as well as armed forces materiel commands.)

The majority of people interviewed expressed the opinion that we were premature with our market research. One large possible user stated, "How can you conduct market research on a product that has not yet been fully developed?" Another, "You are dealing with a practically invisible item."

The interviewees were very interested in our product in its textile form, but could offer no tangible information on the market potential for Fiberfrax® textiles. (See Exhibit 1 for the views of one interviewee.)

EXHIBIT 1   Views on Market Potential

On wire insulation Mr. Johnson estimates the total market for high-temperature asbestos wire insulation to be about 25,000,000 pounds annually. However, Mr. Harrison of Asbestos Associates said that 10,000,000 pounds annually would be made into roving and yarn for wire insulation. The present estimated price of 50 percent over asbestos will be a limiting factor.

They stated that our price was too high and that we could only hope to reach a very small market if we did not attempt to mass-produce our product and get the price down. They indicated that in the development of fiberglas and nylon, Corning and Du Pont first went after the largest markets where they could get the tonnage and actually took losses initially to keep their price down. They also informed me that high-temperature textile installation was becoming more and more important, but unless we could offer other outstanding properties, there were many cheaper products with marginal thermal properties that would do.

From the results of the survey we recommend that the following steps be taken:

1. *The Development of Long Staple Fiber.* Production of a consistent and continuous run of long staple fiber which can be made into roving, yarn, cloth, and thread. It is fundamental to the whole problem that we have the basic products first.

2. *Trial Samples of Yarn, Roving, and Cloth.* When the long staple fiber has shown the necessary consistency so that we can make it in quantity,

---

EXHIBIT 2   Questions from Potential Users

Potential users want answers to the following questions:
1. Tensile strength—before and after heat.
2. Complete "K" factor information.
3. What ability has our product to absorb various liquids and water?
4. More dielectric information.
5. General durability test.
6. Dermatitis—effect on people's skin.
7. Show direct comparison by test of Fiberfrax®, asbestos, and fibrous glass.
8. What is the flexibility of our product compared to glass and cotton?
9. Does the product need a lubricant to be flexible?
10. What is the finest thread and the finest weave material that we can make? What variety of weaves and thread can we make?
11. Can we make a 435, 535, and 635 thread for sewing material together? It is one thing to make the cloth, but what about sewing threads? Have to have very definite strength properties.
12. Have we been able to extrude a filament yarn so as to produce fine tape and cloth of twelve micron?
13. Does Fiberfrax® fluff out and become hard to weave as fibrous glass does?
14. Do we realize that yarn for weaving will not necessarily work on felt-making machines?
15. What temperature will Fiberfrax® stand when wetted down?
16. Does it meet underwriters' approval?
17. Has it been tested by the Army and the Navy?

---

samples should be made up in all the forms of cloth, yarn, roving, and thread in the various thicknesses and weaves. These samples should all be lab-checked for physical and chemical properties. Direct property comparison should also be made with comparable competitive products such as asbestos and fibrous glass. (See Exhibit 2 for the comments and questions received throughout the interviews.)

3. *Pilot Production of Samples in Quantity.* When we are confident that we have developed consistent textile products, we should then produce sizable pilot production runs of this material. The results of our pilot production should be checked in our lab to make certain that they compare favorably with our best original samples. With samples of this production run available, calls should be made on the potential users (safety clothing, insulated wire manufacturers, Air Force, Navy, and so forth). These manufacturers need sizable samples for experimentation and should be given free rein to explore the uses of our various Fiberfrax® textiles. If the results are successful, we can start talking potentials when we are sure of our applications.

4. *Price.* At the same time that we can supply samples of the production run, we should be able to supply prices on all our products. Most companies are looking for two prices:

    a. The present price.
    b. The volume price when we reach mass production

Part II

At about the same time, the refractories division of Carborundum Company asked the marketing research department to study the present and potential markets for Zircon, Zirconia, and Mullite refractories. Of these products, the refractories division made only Mullite. The refractories division indicated that the need for speed was not urgent and so the project was assigned a low priority. Six months later, the report was ready, as follows:

ZIRCON, ZIRCONIA, AND MULLITE REFRACTORIES STUDY

Purpose. Some time ago, the refractories division requested that the marketing research department undertake a study of the present and potential market for Zircon, Zirconia, and Mullite refractories. Specifically, the refractories division indicated that it wished to learn with respect to each of these refractories:

    1. The present and possible applications;
    2. The principal competitive refractory product(s);
    3. The market by type of industry; and
    4. The size (in dollars) of the market.

Methodology. To satisfy these objectives, the necessary information has been gathered through personal interviews and a mail questionnaire. Customers and potential customers—furnace builders, ceramic manufacturers, glass companies, steel producers—were visited by commercial research personnel. Carborundum refractories salesmen were reached by mail questionnaire.

Scope. Interviews were completed with 56 customers or potential customers for either Zircon, Zirconia, or Mullite refractories. Questionnaires were returned by 11 refractories salesmen.

Summary

1. Zircon, Zirconia, and Mullite cannot be considered new products in the super-refractory field. Their competitive counterparts have been available for some time.
2. Of these three products, Mullite appears to have the widest range of applications and possibly the largest potential market. Zirconia, at the moment, has only one principal application. Zircon, on the other hand, appears to have a wide range of applications also, but a rather small potential market.
3. Charles Taylor & Sons Company dominates the Zircon market, while Norton is presently taking the "lion's" share of the Zirconia market. Carborundum is not as yet actively competing in either of these areas.
4. Competition is keenest in the Mullite market. Babcock & Wilcox; Taylor; Remmey; Electro; Shamva Mullite—all are actively participating in this market. Babcock & Wilcox appears to be the leader in this product category.
5. The principal applications for Zircon, Zirconia, and Mullite refractories are to be found in the metallurgical, glass, and ceramic industries. Zircon refractories are used in glass tanks and aluminum melting furnaces. Zirconia refractories in the form of setter tile are presently employed in the firing of barium titanates. Mullite refractories are found in electric steel melting furnaces, glass tanks, and as kiln furniture in the ceramic industry.
6. On the basis of available information, the present market for Zircon is valued at approximately $500,000–$600,000; for Zirconia, $800,000–$1,100,000; and for Mullite refractories, $4,000,000–$4,500,000.
7. In marketing these three refractory products, the refractories division will not be concerned with developing new markets but rather will be confronted with the task of securing a share of the available market.

Product Analysis of Zircon

Product. Zircon refractories are not "new" to the market. Charles Taylor & Sons Company has been manufacturing Zircon refractories since the early '30s; R. C. Remmey & Company has also been marketing a similar refractory for some time; Carborundum has considered the possibility of adding this product to its super-refractory line since 1925. Taylor, in its brochure on Zircon refractories, describes its product as follows:

"Taylor Zircon refractories are made entirely of selected grade of refined zirconium-silicate without the addition of bond clays or similar sources of alumina. Coarse grain sizes are produced by a Taylor process, preparatory to the final blending and mixing of the batch. Uniformly dense structure and high mechanical strength are obtained by a combination of blended grain sizing and special forming methods, and by firing the molded piece to higher temperatures. This process was developed by our engineering staff after extensive research, and it requires the use of equipment not usually available in the ordinary refractories plant."

Although Carborundum has developed and tested several experimental products, none of these has been commercially manufactured or marketed. The test products were essentially a blending of Zircon sand with either ball clay, pure Zirconia, or bentonite powder. An all-Zircon refractory was also developed. Attention is being directed toward the development of a slipcast Zircon refractory brick with greater density and more weight.

Characteristics. Zircon refractories are extremely refractory, possess good spalling [1] resistance, and have excellent insulating properties and hot load strength. Zircon refractories can be subjected to temperatures of 3600°F. They resist the erosive action of iron oxide slag, and molten aluminum, and the corrosive action of molten calcium metaphosphate, sodium phosphate, and sulphur dioxide. Zircon refractories retain heat and are capable of carrying heavy loads at high temperatures.

Applications. The aluminum, glass, and chemical industries present the operating conditions in which Zircon refractories can be utilized.

Zircon refractories have the peculiar property of not being readily "wet" by molten aluminum or dross under normal furnace conditions. Consequently, hearths and side walls which are built of Zircon brick are not penetrated by metal. "Cleaner metal, increased production, longer hearth life, lower refractory cost per ton of metal cast" are realized when Zircon refractories are used.

Zircon refractories are also utilized in the glass industry. Because of their resistance to the corrosive and erosive action of molten glass, particularly of the boro-silicate and opal types, Zircon refractories are found in the paving and superstructure of glass tanks. They are also used as the port-sill, plate blocks, breast walls, and burner blocks. "Longer tank life and less glass contamination" result when Zircon refractories are installed.

In the chemical industry, Zircon refractories have been satisfactorily used in the linings of calcium metaphosphate and sodium phosphate furnaces. They have also been successfully employed in the lining of sulphur

[1] Spalling—chipping, crumbling.

burners and in the curb walls and hearths of enamel frit smelters. Their extreme refractoriness and freedom from volume changes at high temperature make them particularly adaptable for lining the combustion chamber of high temperature stills or generators in refineries.

Market. On the basis of information secured from Carborundum refractories sales and technical personnel, glass manufacturers, and furnace builders, the estimated annual market for Zircon refractories is, roughly. $500,000–$600,000. This estimate appears to be inconsistent with the number of applications suggested for this product. However, one cannot avoid the impression, after talking to people familiar with the product, that Zircon does not enjoy a widespread acceptance. This may be traced to an inadequate knowledge of the potentialities of the product, to an unfavorable price situation, or to an incomplete marketing job on the part of the major manufacturers.

Charles Taylor & Sons Company is the principal manufacturer of Zircon refractories. It offers a complete line of standard and special shapes to the metallurgical, glass, and chemical industries. It secures approximately 50 percent of the total market.

Corning Glass is the only other important manufacturer of this refractory; however, its interests have been restricted to glass applications.

Zirconia

Product. Like Zircon refractories, stabilized Zirconia refractories have also been available for some time. Norton is the principal manufacturer with others—Zirconium Corporation of America, Titanium Alloy Manufacturing Company, Carborundum—attempting to develop an acceptable, commercially competitive product. Carborundum's interest in this refractory antedates the 1930s.

Although the Zirconia refractory which is now on the market is described as stabilized, Carborundum has been experimenting with a partially stabilized product. An unstabilized Zirconia refractory has been completely discarded because of its inherent tendency to increase in size after it is heated and cooled.

The partially stabilized refractory which is now being developed by Carborundum is a mixture of lime and unstabilized grain. The mixture is fired in bulk at Cone 30, after which it is crushed and molded and then refired at the same temperature. To date, experiments have been restricted to a small setter tile shape, 6″ × 6″ × ¼″.

Norton describes its product as an "electrically fused stabilized Zirconia refractory which is produced in two types: (1) dense structure, and (2) insulating structure (50 percent or higher porosity). The dense type can be produced in all the standard brick shapes of the 9″ and 13½″ series, as well as in the form of tubes, plates, discs, and a wide variety of special shapes. Some restrictions are necessary in the variety of shapes that can be made of the insulating type."

Characteristics. Stabilized Zirconia refractories are extremely high-temperature refractories. They may be used where temperatures run as high as 4700°F. These refractories are also chemically inert, resist wetting by molten metals, and have excellent insulating qualities. They are highly sensitive to thermal shock.

Applications. Because stabilized Zirconia is chemically inert and extremely refractory, it has been found to be especially useful in the manufacture of kiln furniture for the firing of barium titanates. Linings of stabilized Zirconia have been installed in gas synthesis furnaces, metal melting furnaces, and ceramic kilns. Electric furnace heating elements have been made of stabilized Zirconia; the possibility of utilizing it in oil black furnaces and in reaction engine parts—jet rocket liners—is being studied.

Of all the applications, the use of stabilized Zirconia for kiln furniture on which barium titanates can be fired is the most important. Titanates which are used in the manufacture of capacitors are a ceramic body and are fired at 2500–2600°F. At this temperature, the titanate becomes very reactive and of the known refractory materials only Zirconia, thoria, and beryllia resist this reaction. The relatively low cost of Zirconia explains its selection as a refractory material over thoria and beryllia.

Gas synthesis processes have been operated in stabilized Zirconia-lined furnaces for long periods of time at temperatures of 4500–4600°F in a neutral to slightly reducing gas atmosphere. The refractories have been exposed to high-velocity gaseous streams and some thermal shock.

Zirconia nozzles have been used in the continuous steel casting process. Molten metal at a temperature of 2200–2800°F passes from the furnace through a Zirconia nozzle into the mold. The metal does not wet or erode the nozzle.

Market. The estimated annual market for stabilized Zirconia refractories is $800,000 to $1,100,000.

The bulk of this estimate is for setter tile, which is used in the firing of barium titanate. Norton, which is the principal supplier of the tile, probably secures 70 percent of this market.

Barium titanate manufacturers are not at all satisfied with the setter tile that is now available. They point out that the productive life of the present tile is entirely too short; that there is too much variation in the productive life between tile shipments; that the present cost is too high in terms of the productive life; and that deliveries are too slow. For these reasons, they are more than anxious to see a second supplier appear in the market.

Of the refractory manufacturers who are attempting to establish themselves in the market, the Zirconium Corporation of America and the

Titanium Alloy Manufacturing Company are the most active. Carborundum is currently experimenting with a product.

Mullite

Product. The Mullite refractory is essentially "an electric furnace synthetic mullite (aluminate silica) comprising some 75 percent of the body, with additions of alumina and silica in the proper proportions to form additional Mullite as the bond." This refractory product was introduced by Carborundum three years ago as a "competitively priced Mullite brick . . . to our standard brick line."

Babcock & Wilcox, Charles Taylor & Sons, Mullite refractories, and R. C. Remmey are all manufacturing a competitive Mullite product. Of these, Babcock & Wilcox appear to have the highest quality product in the intermediate price range.

Babcock & Wilcox describes its product, "Allmul," as a "firebrick with a true Mullite composition . . . which is produced by using an electrically fused grog in connection with an unusually high final burning temperature." Unlike Carborundum, which is attempting to restrict its production of Mullite to bricks and brick shapes, Babcock & Wilcox's product is available in both standard and special shapes and sizes.

Characteristics. Carborundum Mullite is a high-temperature refractory —3000°F—with good volume stability, high resistance to thermal shock, good hot-load strength, and high slag (iron oxide) resistance.

Applications. The principal applications for Carborundum Mullite and similar Mullites are to be found in the metallurgical, glass, ceramic, and chemical industries.

Roofs of electric steel melting furnaces, side walls of zinc smelting furnaces, and side walls of lead reverberatory furnaces represent potential installation for Mullite. Linings of steel ladles and hot metal mixers—welding furnaces and billet heaters—are other areas in which the refractory might be used. Linings of nonferrous melting furnaces, particularly Ajax Wyatt furnaces, have been successfully constructed of Mullite refractories.

In the glass industry, Mullite refractories are being used in the superstructure and checkerbrick of glass tanks.

Because of their resistance to thermal shock, excellent load-carrying ability, and chemical stability, Mullite refractories are being used as kiln furniture, setter tile, and girders by the ceramics industry. Piers of the combustion chambers of enameling furnaces have also been constructed of Mullite refractories.

Oil black reactors in the petroleum industry and HCN reactors in the chemical industry appear to offer other applications for these refractories.

Market. The estimated annual market for Mullite refractories is

$4,000,000 to $4,500,000. The bulk of this market appears to be in the metallurgical and glass industries.

R. C. Remmey, Charles Taylor & Sons, Mullite Refractories, Carborundum, and Babcock & Wilcox are the principal manufacturers of Mullite refractories. As a result of a price and product quality advantage, Babcock & Wilcox is securing a major share of this market.

Because of manufacturing considerations, Carborundum's participation in this market is largely limited to standard brick shapes and sizes. However, the other major producers are now supplying this refractory material in special shapes and sizes as well.

Are these two studies indicative of a sound approach to new product planning? Compare the two in the light of their own particular situations (including timing); on this basis which is the better, or more appropriate? Should Carborundum go ahead with Fiberfrax® development? Should it explore further the Zircon, Zirconia, or Mullite markets for reasons of either (a) some opportunity in the form of a need or want or (b) some ability of Carborundum to do a better job than competitors?

LIGHTNING AIRCRAFT COMPANY

In 1959, the Lightning Aircraft Company, which manufactured single-engine planes, bought for purposes of sport and business use, was considering expanding its line to capture a larger share of the latter market. More and more corporations were buying planes to transport their top executives on business trips, and the Lightning management was attracted both by the number of possible buyers and by the size of the unit sale (because business planes tended to be larger than the existing Lightning models).

Lists of present corporate owners of planes were found and questionnaires were mailed to a stratified sample, as follows:

EXHIBIT 1   Mailings and Responses

	Companies Owning Planes	Mailings	Responses
a. Single-engine	12,760	640	183
b. Light twin	2,083	1,689	530
c. Heavy twin	450	450	173
	15,293	2,779	886

EXHIBIT 2   Speed, Capacity, and Price Matrix

Cruising Speed (in miles per hour)

Number of Passenger Seats	150	200	250	300	350	400	450	500
3	$ 12,000	$ 25,000	$ 65,000	$100,000	$ 150,000	$ 200,000	$ 230,000	$ 260,000
4	$ 16,000	$ 50,000	$ 75,000	$120,000	$ 175,000	$ 225,000	$ 260,000	$ 300,000
5	$ 40,000	$ 75,000	$120,000	$175,000	$ 220,000	$ 300,000	$ 400,000	$ 500,000
6	$ 80,000	$100,000	$165,000	$210,000	$ 280,000	$ 375,000	$ 500,000	$ 700,000
8	$110,000	$160,000	$200,000	$260,000	$ 400,000	$ 500,000	$ 800,000	$1,000,000
12	$180,000	$220,000	$300,000	$400,000	$ 600,000	$ 800,000	$1,100,000	$1,200,000
20+	$250,000	$350,000	$500,000	$700,000	$ 800,000	$1,000,000	$1,500,000	$1,800,000
30+	$360,000	$450,000	$600,000	$800,000	$1,000,000	$1,600,000	$2,300,000	$3,000,000

Cross-checking of respondents against the original lists and follow-up of nonrespondents seemed to indicate that returns were representative geographically, by size of company, and so forth. About two-thirds of the returns came from company presidents, to whom the questionnaires had originally been addressed, except in the case of heavy twin-engine owners (mostly large companies), where about half of the returns were filled out by the aviation department or chief pilot.

Because management considered three variables important—speed, capacity, and price—the principal question provided a matrix with 64 possible combinations of the three factors (see Exhibit 2), and respondents were asked to enter in the appropriate box or boxes the number of planes of that type they expected to purchase over the next three years. The 64 combinations were then divided into six classifications as follows:

  I. Single-engine planes
     3–4 passengers
     150 to 200 miles per hour
     $12,000 to $25,000; average $20,000
 II. Light twin-engine planes
     3–5 passengers
     150 to 250 miles per hour
     $40,000 to $75,000; average $65,000
III. Heavy twin-engine planes
     5–6 passengers
     150 to 250 miles per hour
     $75,000 to $165,000; average $125,000
 IV. Turboprops
     6–8 passengers
     300 to 400 miles per hour
     $210,000 to $500,000; average $350,000
  V. Turbojets
     8–12 passengers
     400 to 500 miles per hour
     $800,000 to $1,200,000; average $1,000,000
 VI. All others (mostly existing military or commercial airline planes converted to private use)

Further, returns were analyzed according to present ownership of planes: (a) single-engine; (b) light twin-engine; and (c) heavy twin-engine. Turboprop and turbojet planes were not being offered to the corporate market at this time. The results were as follows:

EXHIBIT 3   Purchase Expectations

	I	II	III	IV	V	VI	All
a. Single-engine	61	30	10	–	–	–	101
b. Light twin	52	80	158	17	3	46	356
c. Heavy twin	2	2	19	14	16	30	83
Total	115	112	187	31	19	76	540

Analysis of present owners by brand showed no meaningful relationships. That is, a present Lightning owner was no more or no less likely to buy a Class II plane than owners of other, competing Class I planes.

It would cost Lightning about three-quarters of a million dollars to develop and tool for a Class II or Class III model, and at least several million dollars for a Class IV or V model. The company figured that manufacturing, selling, and administrative costs would be approximately 90 percent of selling price, and that it would need to recover development costs in three years. The company was currently enjoying a market share of 9 percent in the single-engine field, but management realized it would take two years to get to the market with twin-engines and then five or six years before it could make as much headway in the twin-engine field as in the single-engine field. The turboprop and -jet market was even further away because it would require considerable changeover in the company's operations, but management still felt it should try to gauge future potentials fully.

An additional mailing to a random sample of 757, with 203 returns, uncovered 17 purchase indications on the part of present nonowners of planes, over half of them qualified by "maybe." Of the 17, the majority (11) favored Class I planes. The names of this mailing were taken from a list of 70,000 firms believed to be large enough to afford a company plane and find it useful. The numbers of planes delivered for other than military or commercial airline use had been 6,413 in 1958, with twins accounting for 894 of these.[1] As of January 1, 1958, the business aircraft fleet was reported to be composed as follows: [2]

EXHIBIT 4　Business Aircraft Fleet

Single-engine	24,470
Twin-engine	3,842
Miscellaneous	171
	28,483

Can the results of the survey be projected to the total market? Will the results hold over time? What class of plane—II, III, IV, or V—is likely to be most profitable for Lightning's expansion move?

HAWKINS KNITWEAR, INC.

The management of Hawkins Knitwear, Inc., was considering several alternative proposals for changing the packaging and pricing of its Style 2B7 "Fashion Dot" women's cotton underpants. Hawkins sold the

[1] *Aviation Week,* March 9, 1959.
[2] *Ibid.,* March 9, 1958.

2B7 to retail accounts for $4.85 a dozen, to retail at 69¢ each. The retailer's markup was, therefore, 41.4 percent. The 2B7 was sold in both pastel colors and white, but white was the best seller. The pants were individually packaged in heat-sealed, polyethelene envelopes.

Market Position

Hawkins Knitwear, Inc., was a leading producer of men's and women's quality knit cotton underwear. The company's women's line was promoted under the Fashion Dot name.

According to a study which had been prepared for the company by its advertising agency, Hawkins' share of the total women's cotton underpants market was 8.8 percent. This figure was not greatly different from the market share percentages computed for the preceding ten years, and was derived by comparing the industry figures (available only as expressed in dozens of garments) for "manufacturers' shipments of women's cotton/wool circular knit panties and bloomers" with Hawkins' shipments of dozens of women's underpants. (The advertising agency researcher had telephoned the Bureau of the Census and ascertained that cotton garments accounted for approximately 95 percent of the merchandise included in the "cotton/wool" classification.) While accepting the 8.8 percent share of market figure, Hawkins' executives were convinced that the company had a far higher share of the "quality" market, and that Fashion Dot was, in fact, one of the two leading names in the quality women's cotton underwear market.

Total company sales were running at an annual rate of slightly over $10 million. Of this total, 40 percent was in women's styles and 60 percent in men's styles. The company's lines were distributed nationally by a sales force of twenty people—including three district sales managers who reported to the vice-president of sales. The Hawkins sales force sold Hawkins' products exclusively, and each salesman was compensated on the basis of salary, commissions, and bonus.

Distribution

The company sold direct to department and specialty stores; it did not distribute through discount stores, variety stores, mail-order stores, or supermarkets, and it did not use jobbers or other middlemen. The company sold under resale price maintenance laws in the states where such laws were in force, and encouraged price maintenance throughout the country by preticketing its merchandise.

Hawkins had over 5,000 accounts. Recently, Hawkins' marketing research manager, who reported to the vice-president of sales, had sent Census Bureau definitions of various types of retail outlets to each of the company's salesmen. Each salesman had also received an IBM card for each of his accounts and had been asked to indicate the census category to which each account belonged. After their return to the Hawkins headquarters, the IBM cards had been punched and tabulated. The results (together with U.S. census figures on the number of each type of outlet) were as shown in Exhibit 1.

EXHIBIT 1 Hawkins Account Types and Volume

	Number of Hawkins Accounts	Number of Outlets in U.S.	Percentage of Hawkins Dollar Volume Moving Through Type of Outlet
Department stores	747	3,157	40.3
Junior department stores	520	14,971	5.7
Family clothing stores	744	13,551	16.4
Men's & boys' clothing stores	853	9,969	5.6
Men's & boys' furnishings stores	546	8,147	4.6
Women's specialty stores	1,870	26,559	27.4

The 2B7 Packaging Question

In sales volume, the 2B7 Fashion Dot pants were a leading Hawkins style, in terms of both sales and profits. For the last fiscal year the figures had been as shown in Exhibit 2.

EXHIBIT 2 Sales and Contribution of 2B7 Line

	Sales		Contribution to General Overhead and Profit
	Dozens	Dollars	
White	72,702	$352,600	$28,300
Color	27,975	135,700	8,900

For some time there had been a trend toward multiple packaging of underwear items, and the company had, in recent years, a number of requests that it multipack Style 2B7. These requests, transmitted by the

Hawkins salesmen, had seemed particularly numerous and insistent during the company's spring sales meeting. The salesmen also reported that while Fashion Dot's major branded competitor still single-packed its comparable pants, most department store private brands were in double- or triple-packs. In addition, while the branded competitor sold its pants at the same wholesale price as the 2B7 to retail at the same price, the private brands were typically retailed at 5 to 15 percent less, yet allowed the retailer 2 to 3 percent additional markup. A major department store typically carried either Fashion Dot or one of its branded competitors plus a private brand. Specialty stores typically carried either Fashion Dot or one of its branded competitors.

Upon his return from the sales meeting to Hawkins' headquarters, the general merchandise manager began to look into the question of multiple packaging for Style 2B7. In addition to the retailer requests, there were such factors as additional sales which might be generated through multiple packaging as well as savings in packaging costs to be considered.[1] The general merchandise manager was responsible for styling, pricing, markup, and packaging decisions, but he generally consulted with the sales vice-president on pricing and markups, and with both the sales vice-president and the advertising department on packaging.

The general merchandise manager and the vice-president of sales discussed Style 2B7. Together they decided that the style should be double-packed, but that more information was needed on retailer reaction to several possible pricing and markup alternatives. The vice-president of sales asked the marketing research manager to get reactions to three alternative ways of handling the pricing and markup on the double-packed 2B7. The marketing research manager drafted, for the sales vice-president's review and signature, the letter that appears as Exhibit 3. This letter explains the three alternatives. Time was now considered important and the marketing research manager decided that the reactions of the company's thirty top department store Fashion Dot accounts and a small sampling of its more knowledgeable specialty store Fashion Dot accounts would develop sufficient information to provide some guidance for the general merchandise manager and the vice-president of sales. He therefore sent the letter contained in Exhibit 3 to those salesmen handling the thirty top department store accounts. He also asked each of six additional salesmen whose reporting had been good in the past and whose judgment he particularly trusted to contact and survey the two specialty store managers in their territories who, in the salesmen's opinions, were the best merchandisers.

---

[1] It was estimated that double-packing would save 10¢ per dozen in costs.

EXHIBIT 3   Letter on Alternatives

HAWKINS KNITWEAR, INC.

As you know, we currently single-pack our 2B7 Fashion Dot pant, in both white and colors.

We are about to change to double-pack for white *only* and plan to change the wholesale pricing of this style at the same time. We are asking that you contact the buyers in the accounts listed on the sheets accompanying this letter in order to find out which alternative they prefer, both in terms of their own operations and of their feelings about customer reaction. Please indicate which alternative each account prefers and the reasons given by the buyers.

It goes without saying that while we want their advice, we can't be bound by it.

The alternatives follow:

		Wholesale	Retail	Markup
Alternative A	White	$4.70/dozen	2/$1.35	41.9%
	Colors	4.85/dozen	.69	41.4
Alternative B	White	$4.75/dozen	2/$1.38	42.6%
	Colors	4.75/dozen	.69	42.6
Alternative C	White	$4.75/dozen	2/$1.40	43.4%
	Colors	4.75/dozen	.70	43.4

Buyers' comments as to the *reasons* for their choice will be particularly interesting.

We need this information just as soon as possible.

Please give us a separate evaluation for each account.

Vice-President—Sales

Need for Decision

Selected responses to the questions are reproduced in Exhibit 4. The marketing research manager's tabulation of all the responses received

EXHIBIT 4   Selected Reactions to Questionnaire

Madisons. "The overall reaction goes with Alternative A. The buyer concerned with our Style 2B7 believes that giving a better price to the consumer is the best approach, and the additional .5% markup would be welcomed also. This is the thinking even though we would bring our price closer to their own private label which has been 2/$1.19—although there are rumors that that price will go up."

Monroes. "Out of the 3 alternatives, Monroes' buyer indicated preference for Alternative B. Her reasons for choosing this alternative were that the retail price would be the same on white and colors; she wouldn't have to reticket existing stock; and her markup would be improved."

Adams. "The buyer in Adams' would prefer our Alternative C Plan, 2 for $1.40. Because of the particular way we bill this store (due to a credit situation) they do not get their usual 40% markup on our Style 2B7. The buyer feels that we will not hurt our sales by increasing the price, and that the customer will go along with it, because of our preticketing. Adams sells its own brand at 3 for $1.75—for a 40% markup."

Jeffersons. "Discussed the matter with Miss Henry today and was subjected to a very stormy interview. She has absolutely no interest in multiple packaged underwear at this time and is adamant against it—as well as against any price (such as 2/$1.35) which doesn't make the price of an individual garment come out to the even penny. She threatens to look for another resource if we carry out this move."

Specialty store. "The reaction is decidedly in favor of Alternative A. Specifically, the split in cost price between color and white is much easier to take than a true split in price or, rather, a higher price on colors. Since colors have always been 69¢, it remains the same, and that is okay; the white is reduced in price, so that is acceptable. There was some feeling that $1.38 (Alternative B) would be a "weird" price. I should mention that all of my specialty stores do poorly with colors and that the reaction to dual pack—either pro or con—is negligible. Additional markup, however slight, is always welcome."

---

is reproduced in Exhibit 5. The market research manager believed that the results of the retailer survey did not point to any clear-cut conclusion and that he could not base a recommendation on these results alone. He therefore suggested a further alternative, with both single- and double-packing as illustrated in Exhibit 6.

EXHIBIT 5   Responses to 2B7 Pricing Questionnaire

DEPARTMENT STORES

	Preference	Comments
Bon Marché	No change	If forced, only A acceptable.
Heatherington	B	
Hertz	B	
Campbell	No change	If forced, only B acceptable.
Hopedale	No change	If forced, only B acceptable.
Gulliver	No change	Nothing else acceptable.
Jeffersons	No change	Nothing else acceptable (violent).
Hemberger	No change	If forced, prefer B.
Kelly	A	
Madisons	A	
Levines	A	
Adams	C	
Davidsons	C	
Gurdines	A	With $1.39 (not $1.35) and, possibly, double-packed colors as well as white.
Albrights	C	But B is O.K.
Sampson	C	
MacReady	C	
Cornwallis	C	
Monroes	B	Object to having to reticket existing stock.
Foxwell	B	
Jacksons	C	With $1.39, not $1.40.
Wainright	C	
Goldberg	B	
Atkinson	C	
Sachs	C	But B is O.K.
Belkson	A	
Kendrick	B	
Marx	B	
Janrack	B	
Fuller	A	

SPECIALTY STORES

Preference	Number of Stores
A	9
A or B	1
No change	2

EXHIBIT 6   New Alternative

	Wholesale	Suggested Retail	Markup
White single	$4.85/dozen	$ .69	41.4%
Color single	4.85/dozen	.69	41.4
White double-pack	4.75/dozen	2/ 1.38	42.6

He backed this up by saying, "I don't think it would cost us anything—really, in incremental costs—to offer the two packages in white, and we would actually save by not reticketing our present inventory; further this gives the stores an option to do what they want with a high-volume item."

However, the general merchandise manager disagreed strongly; he stated that, just because it was a major volume style, the company would "need to build another warehouse" in order to handle the two packages. The general merchandise manager was also becoming increasingly concerned with time pressures. He pointed out that a decision to double-pack the 2B7 had already been made, that the salesmen were aware of it, and that many store buyers were now also aware of it. He believed that, under these circumstances, it would be wise to move quickly to implement the multipack decision.

What action should the company take in regard to packing and pricing the 2B7 pants, taking into consideration sales, costs, and profits?

3

DISTRIBUTION POLICY

The problems of securing effective selling action are compounded when the manufacturer does not sell directly to the ultimate buyers or users of his product but deals through wholesalers, retailers, or other intermediaries.

It is helpful to think of products flowing from their manufacturing source, down through various channels of trade (made up of different combinations of different kinds and numbers of intermediaries), to their multiple destinations in the hands of individual buyers. Marketing decisions in this area are crucial. The number of intermediate distributors and final outlets and their degree of interest will determine how well they handle the product—carry it in inventory, give it sales push, and service the buyers. Also, the kind of dealers, wholesale and retail alike, will have a strong bearing on how the product will be regarded by buyers down through the channels of trade to the market; and this, of course, will affect the speed and strength of the distribution process.

Sometimes, of course, the manufacturer will bypass wholesalers and sell directly to retailers, industrial buyers, or even consumers. This usually means, not that he has eliminated the wholesale function, but rather that he has taken it on himself because he feels he can do it more effectively or economically. And, of course, no one (except agents or distributors who handle nothing but his product) will have the same degree of interest in pushing his product or will have salesmen with the same specialized knowledge for that particular product. On the other hand, wholesalers can usually offer the manufacturer a wide range of customers whom they can afford to call on and serve frequently, because they have a chance to sell not only his product but many other products as well.

If the manufacturer does use (1) brokers or agents (who do not stock or take title to the merchandise but receive a commission from the manufacturer for arranging the sale, and who usually represent a number of noncompeting lines), or (2) various forms of wholesale distributors, or (3) various forms of retail stores or dealers, or all three, there are a number of things he can do to get more drive in their selling efforts in behalf of his products on down the line. For example, he can provide assistance in the form of displays and merchandising aids; send out his own "missionary" salesmen to call on important prospects with the broker's, wholesaler's, or retailer's salesmen; arrange contests or incentive plans for those who handle or sell his product; and so on. He can offer his product on an exclusive basis to selected brokers, wholesalers, or retailers, sacrificing some coverage of the market for the sake of the extra push that those who represent him exclusively will exert for his product because they are assured of all the business in their territories. And he can provide larger margins than are usually made available, in the hope that this will stimulate more enthusiasm in behalf of his product.

Some products need less push, either because they are already established on the market or because they answer some existing need; some, for the opposite reasons, need more push. Also, there will be differences in the degree to which the product should be carried extensively by a large number of wholesalers or retailers, as against a smaller number of selected outlets. If its sales depend on its being available or getting mentioned and displayed at the moment it is needed, then the emphasis will be on more outlets. If it is the kind of product people will make a little effort to get when they want it, and/or if it actually gains prestige from being handled by a few particular kinds of outlets, then the opposite will be the case.

MUSSELMAN DEPARTMENT STORE

(In the Musselman Department Store—located in Milltown and catering to the low- to middle-income group—David Dirkson, salesman for the Zenith Drug Company, a wholesale drug firm, is calling on Beatrice Bishop, the buyer for the Cosmetics and Drug Sundries Department.)

SALESMAN. Miss Bishop, I represent the Zenith Drug Company. We're expanding our services to offer a wholesale prescription service, which I'm sure your customers would find attractive.

BUYER. A wholesale prescription service? I've never heard of that.

SALESMAN. It *is* novel, isn't it?—and that's why it should mean some new, plus business for you.

BUYER. But what is it? How does it work?

SALESMAN. When your customers are here in the store, shopping for other items, no doubt right here in your department, they leave their prescriptions with you, and we pick them up at 5:00 P.M., fill them overnight, and have the medicine all neatly put up in bottles and labeled—

with the store's name, Musselman Department Store Prescription Service
—back at 9:00 A.M. the next morning, ready for delivery.

BUYER.   But where is the advantage?

SALESMAN.   Your customers save 25 percent of the retail price, 25 percent
off what they'd pay in a drugstore. There is a lot of talk these days about
the high price of drugs; 25 percent—that's a lot of money on some of the
new miracle drugs that cost $10 or $15 a prescription.

BUYER.   That does sound interesting. Tell me more about your firm.

SALESMAN.   Oh, we've been in business in Exeter County for over 75
years, and now we're operating here in Monroe County—have been for
several months now. As a matter of fact, we've chosen Monroe County
as the scene for this new prescription service.

BUYER.   Why?

SALESMAN.   Well, partly because we don't have as many retail drugstore
accounts here; they might not welcome this particular kind of competition.
We think Monroe is a good county. And Milltown, particularly, is a real
shopping center.

BUYER.   What kind of markup would we get?

SALESMAN.   If you want to give your customers the full 25 percent
saving, you'd still get the traditional department store figure of 40 percent of the selling price; or you could fatten your share by giving them
a saving of only 15 or 20 percent.

BUYER.   Do you think it would fit in with cosmetics, vitamins, bathing
caps and so on? We don't carry any medicines now, you know.

SALESMAN.   Of course it would. And it might be the entering wedge for
a full-scale drug business. The regular drugstores carry enough department store merchandise, Lord knows!

What is the problem underlying the decision Miss Bishop must make? What
are the questions she must ask herself—and answer? Should she take on the
new service? Why would Musselman gain competitively by this move? Why
would Zenith Drug gain? How good a salesman is Dirkson?

GRANGER FURNITURE COMPANY

In January 1973, Donald Brown, president of Granger Furniture Company, was reviewing the previous year's results with his advertising
agency in preparation for a group meeting later in the week. One of the
major topics of discussion at that meeting was to be Granger's distribution policy and what changes, if any, should be made during 1973
to maintain and improve Granger's position with retailers and consumers.

In particular, Mr. Brown was concerned about the dealer situations in Hillsburg and Greenton, two of the company's top twenty-five markets.

History and Background

The Granger Furniture Company of Granger, Tennessee, manufactures case goods and upholstered furniture in correlated groups, suites, and occasional pieces. Each furniture group is a complete assortment of living room, dining room, and bedroom pieces (75 to 100 different pieces exclusive of color and finish options). These groups cover the major styles now in vogue with consumers and are shown in Exhibit 1.

EXHIBIT 1   Furniture Styles and Granger Groups

Style	Granger Group
Mediterranean	Esperanto
Italian	Triune
	Di Moda
French	French in the Country Manner
English	
18th century	Wallace Nutting
17th century	Guildhall
Eclectic (all periods)	Rapport Collection
Contemporary	
Transitional	Collage
Oriental influence	Plaudit
Scandinavian modern	Index

Until the 1930s, Granger manufactured for and catered to the mass market in the lower price ranges. At that time, management decided to change its approach and try to win a dominant position in the middle- and upper-quality markets, which are the style markets. (For a profile of Granger's present customers, see Exhibit 2.)

In conjunction with this new orientation, a decision was made to build a brand name for Granger products. This decision was based on management's belief that as more consumers move from area to area, a nationally advertised brand name would influence their purchases as much as the reputation of the retailer. The how and why of furniture purchasing, as analyzed in a consultant's report, is summarized in Exhibit 3.

EXHIBIT 2   Customer Profile for Granger Furniture

Studies performed for Granger by both the Hearst Corporation and by *Better Homes & Gardens* established the following profile of the typical Granger customer:

1. "Some college" or more education characterized 65% of the women and 77% of the men. Company executives believed that this higher level of education was definitely related to an appreciation of the styling of Granger furniture.
2. Granger owners are in the upper to high income brackets; i.e., 60% have incomes of $10,000 and over.
3. Of the people surveyed, 61% were in the young- to middle-married years of 25 to 44. Some 40% had been married less than ten years, and an additional 31% had been married ten to twenty years.
4. For nearly two-thirds of the respondents, it was a first-time purchase.
5. Slightly more than 45% of the purchasers were looking for Granger when they went to buy furniture. Of these people, 40% looked in one store only, 23% in two stores, 15% in three stores, and 22% in more than three stores.

Until 1952, distribution of Granger's products was handled by commission sales agents whose responsibility was to obtain maximum volume in their territories in whatever ways they thought best. Patterns of distribution varied widely. In some cities, one department store and one furniture store were "authorized." In others, wide distribution to many dealers was the pattern. Exclusives on certain "correlated furniture groups" were given to key dealers occasionally. Wholesalers were included in the distribution in still other territories.

EXHIBIT 3   Excerpts from a Consultant's Report on Consumer Behavior

---

A. Why Furniture Is Purchased

A significant group of the furniture-consuming public is composed of newlyweds, who buy an estimated 25 percent of the furniture sold. On many occasions, this group purchases only those items which are not donated by their parents. Such donations create a replacement need in the home of each mother.

Mobility is another major cause of furniture purchases. The move usually comes as the result of a better job, a larger family, or increased family income. It frequently involves larger quarters requiring furniture over and above that being used.

A third predominant market segment is that group of stationary families who continue to replace and upgrade furniture of earlier years when motivated by such things as socioeconomic advances, home enlargements, children reaching their teens, children leaving home, or a new child.

B. How Furniture Is Purchased

Because furniture represents to most women both a sign of their husbands' status and a reflection of their own personality, its purchase is taken quite seriously. Women are afraid they will pick a style which does not show "good taste." Add to this the long life of the product and a high cost factor, and it is easy to see why American women approach the purchase of furniture with great apprehension. It is a high-risk item, and most people shop around before making a final decision.

Studies indicate that it is the wife who first decides to purchase new furniture. However, in nearly half the cases, the husband helps to shop and approves the style, quality, and price. About one-third of all purchasers complete this process in less than three months, while nearly one-half take longer than six months to plan and purchase furniture.

In 1952, the company decided to abolish sales agencies in favor of a company-controlled and -managed sales force; establishment of this sales force ran counter to industry practice. Granger also began to initiate a national policy of selective distribution. Because of the earlier relationships set up by the commission sales agents, this policy was slow to reach completion nationally.

Industry Distribution Pattern

The principal outlets through which furniture products were sold to consumers were the 36,000 retail furniture stores in America. These stores were typically low sales volume outlets, with only 1 to 2 percent having sales in excess of $1 million annually. As described in an industry analysis:

> Additional outlets range from giant retail merchandisers, such as Sears Roebuck & Co. and the larger department stores to smaller volume department stores and various kinds of specialty stores, including floor covering and decorator shops. The independent interior decorator selling from wholesale showrooms represents still another means of selling home furnishings to the customer.[1]

By the early 1970s, exposure of manufacturers' product lines by retailers in the furniture industry was far from the static situation that existed in most home goods lines such as appliances, television and stereo, rugs and carpets. The furniture dealer would vary the size and importance of his display from each manufacturer from season to season, depending to a great degree on his evaluation of new goods. He would

---

[1] "Home Furnishing Trends to 1975," prepared by Stanford Research Institute for an All Industry Conference, 1965.

continue to carry and show best-selling patterns, but in his desire to keep his store "updated" he placed emphasis on the merchandise he considered to have the best sales potential. Thus a major objective of furniture firms' marketing was to obtain greater area for displaying and selling furniture—i.e., retail "real estate."

Brand-name recognition of furniture by the consumer was generally an important objective of the distribution policies of various manufacturers. As with almost any consumer product, the better known the name, the easier to convince a retailer to handle the line. Inevitably, though, the larger retailers insisted on some kind of protection, in the form of exclusive rights to certain merchandise, when asked to support some national program. Their concern stemmed from three reasons: (1) fear of losing their reputations for style distinctiveness, (2) fear that smaller dealers on the fringes of their trading areas would use them as "showrooms" for merchandise they (the smaller dealers) could not keep in inventory, and (3) fear of being undersold.

In being urged or forced through fair trading in some states to sell goods at a manufacturer's nationally advertised suggested retail price, many retailers considered that their markup and profit potential, as well as their ability to "merchandise" the prices, were being restricted.[2] Further, they objected to having their stores used as price umbrellas subject to discount selling by other retailers. These retailer feelings were exemplified in the extreme by one of the nation's largest furniture dealers who as a matter of policy would not identify a manufacturer by name in any newspaper advertising, would change the manufacturer's nationally advertised name of a correlated group, and would even obliterate the manufacturer's brand name from the goods. It was within this general industry framework that Granger's distribution policies had been developed.

Granger's Basic Distribution Policy

In 1972, Granger goods were sold through 2,963 outlets retailing directly to the consumer. Three-quarters of these outlets were furniture stores, the rest were department stores. Granger no longer sold to wholesalers and to showrooms where goods were available to consumers through third parties (mainly interior decorators). The displays in Granger outlets varied from very small showings to complete "Granger galleries."

These nearly 3,000 dealers were "authorized." Authorization to become a dealer was determined by Granger management following a recommendation by the Granger sales representative (salesman) for that area. Dealer qualifications relative to credit, location, size and type of store,

---

[2] It should be noted that fair trading was not a general industry practice. Only Granger fair-traded its merchandise, and this was done in just a few states.

merchandising and advertising practices, warehouse and service facilities, community image, and growth potential were reviewed and evaluated by management personnel before a dealer was permitted to carry the line. Granger management expressed a preference for stores with an established reputation for quality merchandise.

Becoming a Granger dealer meant that a representative segment of the entire Granger line was made available to the store. The company reserved the right, however, to deny access to the dealer to any portion of the line it wished. Similarly, the dealer was under no compulsion to buy stock and display any portion of the line he did not find acceptable or desirable. A typical store carried only part of the Granger line along with several other furniture lines. In many small trading areas, there was only one dealer authorized to carry any given group of Granger furniture. In larger cities and for the best-selling furniture lines, however, groups were "shared" and would be shown by several key dealers in the same trading area. Granger's entire line ordinarily would be represented by the stores collectively in most trading areas. As an example, Exhibit 4 shows the 1972 distribution pattern in Megacity.

After the relationship had been established, the dealer was provided with all merchandising and selling aids pertaining to those patterns which he carried. Such materials included newspaper mats, counter cards, point-of-purchase displays, consumer booklets, salesmen's handbooks, proofs of national advertisements, suggested floor displays, and material for retail sales training. Mr. Brown believed that dealers valued and used Granger material because requests for consumer literature, much of which was paid for by the dealers, had increased 27 percent during the 1968 to 1972 period. Also, although Granger provided no cooperative advertising money,[3] retailer advertising linage for Granger merchandise had increased 22 percent during those five years, and now totaled several millions of advertising lines annually.[4]

Retailers were visited regularly by a company sales representative. As part of their jobs, these men could recommend that a retailer be dropped. Such action might be taken when a retailer's volume declined markedly, when a store decided to take on more low-quality lines, or when a retailer became substantially less aggressive in his promotion of Granger merchandise than was considered desirable by Granger. Typically, some 75 retailers were dropped annually, and an additional 25 resigned the Granger line. In most cases, the salesman also recommended a new account as a replacement.

Despite a decrease in Granger's number of retail accounts from 3,440 to 2,963 between 1967 and 1972, Granger sales increased 40 percent. Additional sales and distribution statistics can be found in Exhibits 5 and 6. These exhibits show the increasing concentration of Granger's

---

[3] Many manufacturers, particularly in radio, TV, appliances, floor covering, and textile products, reimbursed their dealers for a portion of the latter's local advertising (placed at local rates) on behalf of the former's products.

[4] A typical full-size newspaper page contains 2,400 lines.

EXHIBIT 4 Retail Distribution of Granger Groups in Megacity, 1972

Retailer	Wallace Nutting	Esperanto	DiModa	Triune	Guildhall	Rapport	Plaudit	Collage	Index	French in the Country Manner
Store A	X	X	X	X	X	X	X	X	X	X
Store B	X	X	X	X	X			X		X
Store C	X	X	X	X	X	X	X	X		X
Store D	X		X		X	X				
Store E	X	X		X		X			X	
Store F				X						X
Store G	X									
Store H		X					X			
Store I									X	

EXHIBIT 5   Concentration of Granger's Volume in Largest Trading Areas

Top Trading	Volume as % of Total			
Areas	1968	1969	1970	1971
5	28.1	27.2	27.4	29.0
10	37.1	38.1	39.0	40.4
15	43.5	45.1	45.7	45.7
20	48.1	49.9	50.4	50.9
25	51.4	53.7	54.2	54.6
Remainder of Continental U.S.	48.6	46.3	45.8	45.3

Granger's Top 25 Markets 1971 (alphabetically):

Atlanta	Los Angeles
Baltimore	Milwaukee
Boston	Minneapolis–St. Paul
Chicago	New Orleans
Cincinnati	New York
Cleveland	Omaha
Dallas	Philadelphia
Denver	Pittsburgh
Detroit	St. Louis
Hartford–New Britain	San Francisco
Houston	Seattle
Indianapolis	Washington
Kansas City	

EXHIBIT 6   Distribution of Granger Furniture Sales (Percentages)

	Furniture Stores					Department Stores				
	1967	1968	1969	1970	1971	1967	1968	1969	1970	1971
Top 100 accounts	57.4	63.5	68.0	66.5	56.1	42.6	36.5	32.0	33.5	33.9
Remainder of regular accounts	87.3	87.6	88.0	88.0	89.5	12.7	12.4	12.0	12.0	10.5
All accounts	76.9	78.6	80.0	80.0	79.6	23.1	21.4	20.0	20.0	20.4

1967 column to be read: 76.9% of Granger's total 1967 sales were through furniture stores; 57.4% of the sales represented by the top 100 accounts were through furniture stores; 87.3% of the sales represented by all other accounts were through furniture stores.

sales in larger cities, in bigger volume outlets, and in furniture stores. A further important factor in Granger's overall distribution picture was the amount of volume contributed by the top 100 accounts, as shown in Exhibit 7.

EXHIBIT 7   Volume of Top 100 Accounts

Year	Percent of Sales
1967	34.8
1968	37.3
1969	40.0
1970	39.9
1971	42.0

Key Accounts

Mr. Brown and other company executives believed that such greater volume concentration reflected Granger's Key Account Program, which had been instituted in 1968.

This selling approach was based on the concept of obtaining larger volume through a few actively developed accounts rather than through wider distribution. In this program, Granger attempted to develop one prominent store—furniture or department—in each trading area into a "prime" dealer, but not an exclusive dealer. Each dealer then set up a "Granger Gallery," a segregated area in the furniture department where all Granger goods carried were displayed in an attractive, homogeneous area. In return for the large amount of floor space devoted to Granger goods, Granger gave the dealer certain benefits. These included the normal selling aids plus retail sales training, retail forums (at Granger, in a nearby city, or at the particular store), preferred handling in expediting orders and other correspondence, and an opportunity to consult with company officials on the planning and introduction of new goods. Such benefits were available to any retailer who would give a like amount of space and effort.

As of late 1972, there were about sixty Key Account Programs in effect. Each of these accounted for annual sales of $100,000 or more. Granger Galleries of varying dimensions or methods of display were in place in about 150 stores, among them some of the nation's largest dealers. Exhibit 8 shows sales volumes for nine of these Key Accounts in recent years.

EXHIBIT 8   Sales in Key Account Programs

Store	1967	1968	1969	1970	1971
A	$185,192	$395,526*	$446,935	$581,826	$747,498
B	113,191	86,288	354,695*	541,160	678,495
C	155,031	268,562	428,653*	440,769	574,498
D	207,753	174,712	283,550	386,433*	419,490
E	47,873	86,590	164,351*	309,510	264,042
F	80,986	91,437	178,733*	233,393	254,835
G	98,693	94,785	123,817	195,590*	219,663
H	70,386	159,078*	218,122	226,355	208,821
I	37,071	79,934	150,471*	173,358	202,187

* Indicates the year in which the program
began to operate.

The Megacity Situation

Because of the authority which former sales agents had wielded over dealer authorization, Granger's present distribution in various cities ranged from wide through selective to exclusive. From time to time, management had an opportunity to alter these patterns, to bring them closer to the company's goal of selectivity, by discontinuing exclusive arrangements on one hand, or wide distribution on the other. One example of such a change was in the Megacity area.

Starting in 1967, Granger had begun to terminate a number of fringe and marginal accounts in this trading area and to concentrate on the more prominent department and furniture stores. At this same time, relationships with several of the aforemential "third party" showrooms were terminated. Exhibit 9 shows operating statistics for 1967, and for 1972 after the distribution changes had been completed.

EXHIBIT 9   Megacity Operating Statistics

Year	Number of Accounts	Volume Ratios	Company Volume Ratios	Percentage of Company Volume
1967	42	100	100	4.9
1972	27	150	120	6.2

The Problem Cities

Mr. Brown was concerned about several important trading areas which he believed were not keeping pace with area potential and company growth. In these cities, the same basic approach to distribution (as that followed in Megacity) was presumably in effect, but in some, sales volume had declined or had not followed company growth. Hillsburg and Greenton were good examples. Exhibit 10 gives a comparison of total company sales and sales in these cities.

EXHIBIT 10   Company and Trading Area Sales Ratios

Year	Granger Total	Greenton	Hillsburg
1967	100	100	100
1972	120	70	81

Because of these disappointing results, Mr. Brown had asked for all the statistics and facts available on these two cities so that he and the advertising agency could analyze more closely the patterns of distribution. From this study, Mr. Brown hoped they could develop some ideas which would help sales management make the selective distribution strategy more effective.

Between 1967 and 1972, only two accounts had been dropped from the active list in Greenton. The remaining outlets, two department stores and fourteen furniture stores, were served by one sales representative. Mr. Brown recalled that the former salesman for this area had retired and had been replaced in 1970.

In 1972, Granger shipped approximately $180,000 worth of furniture to the stores in the Greenton trading area. However, over half of this volume had gone to just two stores. (See Exhibit 11 for the percentage breakdown

EXHIBIT 11   Granger Shipments to Greenton in 1972

Retailer	Percent of Total Shipments
Department store A	10.0
Department store B	27.7
Furniture store A	27.7
Furniture store B	10.6
Furniture store C	4.5
Furniture store D	7.6
Others	11.9

EXHIBIT 12 Distribution of Granger Groups in Greenton, 1972

Greenton Retailer	Wallace Nutting	Esperanto	DiModa	Triune	Guildhall	Rapport	Plaudit	Collage	Index	French in the Country Manner
Department store A						X	X			
Department store B	X	X		X						
Furniture store A	X	X		X		X		X	X	X
Furniture store B			X	X	X					
Furniture store C					X			X		
Furniture store D			X		X		X			

of 1972 shipments to various Greenton retailers.) These two high-volume outlets had enjoyed "first refusal" privileges and occasional exclusive arrangements for a number of years. Exhibit 12 shows the resulting distribution of Granger groups.

The Advertising Checking Bureau [5] figures in the Greenton file indicated that Granger linage in Greenton was approximately 50,000 for 1972. When Mr. Brown compared this with another trading area of nearly equal size, he discovered that this other city had sales 50 percent greater than Greenton, and its newspaper had carried 65,500 lines of Granger retail advertising.

Although Hillsburg was a more populous trading area than Greenton, Granger sales were lower there than in Greenton, totaling only some $130,000 in 1972. Salesman turnover in this territory was considerably higher than in Greenton. New sales representatives had been appointed in 1970, 1971, and 1972. During the 1967 to 1972 period, the number of stores carrying Granger had declined from fifteen to thirteen, but fewer than half of them were considerd by the sales manager to be "active" accounts. The 1972 shipments to Hillsburg are broken down in Exhibit 13, and the Granger groups carried by these stores are shown in Exhibit 14.

EXHIBIT 13   Granger Shipments to Hillsburg in 1972

Retailer	Percent of Total Shipments
Department store A	5.2
Department store B	5.3
Furniture store A	45.0
Furniture store B	18.0
Furniture store C	22.2
Others	4.3

The smaller outlets in Hillsburg generally used in-store promotions (window and floor displays), although the current sales representative had not been impressed by their quality or size. These retailers gave folders describing Granger merchandise to customers who came into their stores, but other advertising efforts were virtually nonexistent. There was no record of ACB figures for Hillsburg.

Without a full-fledged, in-the-field study, Mr. Brown was naturally reluctant to draw firm conclusions and to propose specific actions for Greenton and Hillsburg. However, he asked the sales manager to draw up some specific prospective policy directions as the basis for a field investi-

[5] Advertising Checking Bureau (ACB) figures indicate the amount of newspaper advertising space devoted to a manufacturer's brand name by retailers.

EXHIBIT 14 Distribution of Granger Groups in Hillsburg, 1972

Hillsburg Retailer	Wallace Nutting	Esperanto	DiModa	Triune	Guildhall	Rapport	Plaudit	Collage	Index	French in the Country Manner
Department store A								X		X
Department store B					X					
Furniture store A	X	X	X							
Furniture store B		X		X						
Furniture store C		X		X	X	X				X

85

gation. Such an investigation might lead to consideration of changes in Granger distribution policies in these two cities. Mr. Brown hoped that from this investigation might come guidelines for placement of new goods (i.e., lines of furniture) as well as plans for a general review of Granger's distribution of existing goods. He also hoped that the policy proposals would take into account the nature of the pressures likely to come from both important and fringe accounts.

What specific changes, if any, do you recommend for Greenton and Hillsburg? What changes, if any, should be made in Granger's distribution program? Why? How does consumer furniture buying behavior affect your decision? As Granger, what do you expect your retailers to do for you? As a Granger retailer, what do you expect Granger to do for you?

CARBORUNDUM/CANNON

The district manager in charge of the Carborundum Company's Memphis area complained to his vice-president at headquarters that Carborundum was not getting the service it should from the Cannon Company, which was its major distributor in that area.

The vice-president asked the marketing research department to analyze the Memphis situation with a view toward determining whether Carborundum should: (1) maintain the status quo; (2) retain Cannon but add another distributor in the Memphis area; (3) replace Cannon with another distributor. In the case of either alternative (2) or (3), which of the available distributors would be best for Carborundum?

Carborundum, like its major competitors, sold directly to large users. However, large users also bought from distributors when they needed items in a hurry, or the items were ones they used infrequently, and therefore did not buy in quantity. The Carborundum salesman called on both these large users and the Carborundum distributors.

The district manager submitted to the marketing research department a list of important Memphis area accounts then buying both Carborundum and competitors' products.

A marketing research department analyst was dispatched to Memphis. He spent two weeks interviewing in the area, returned to headquarters, and after summarizing the distributor situation as presented in Exhibit 1, wrote the following report.

A Study of the Memphis Industrial Abrasive Market

Purpose. The objectives of this study were to: (1) determine the relative effectiveness of the principal industrial mill supply houses; (2)

evaluate the service aspect of the Carborundum distributor; (3) secure an estimate of the size of the abrasive market; (4) ascertain Carborundum's participation in this market.

Scope. Personal interviews were completed with forty abrasive users in Memphis, Tennessee; Dyersburg, Tennessee; Blytheville, Arkansas; and Jonesboro, Arkansas. Calls were also made on the more important Memphis industrial supply houses.

Summary

Cannon, Brady & Goldsmith, and Mason Supply are the three largest and oldest mill supply houses in the Memphis area. All three can be classified as general hardware and industrial mill supply houses; each represents in excess of 200 manufacturers. However, the smaller specialty houses that are springing up are vigorously challenging these "Big Three" in the industrial supply field.

As a result of certain weaknesses in its operation and its inability or unwillingness to recognize them as such, Cannon's stature in the industrial mill supply area is diminishing. Of the three top houses, its market position is undoubtedly the most vulnerable to the attacks of the smaller industrial supply specialty houses.

The principal problem which faces the older supply houses is that of adjusting their operation and attitude to the industrialization which is occurring in the area. Cannon, like Brady & Goldsmith and Mason Supply, is cognizant of the change that is necessary to meet this situation. Unlike its two chief competitors, however, Cannon, perhaps because of its size, has not been able to translate this recognition into effective action.

The growing Memphis industrial market is becoming highly competitive. As evidence of this, several suppliers are resorting to price-cutting tactics.

The industrial abrasive potential for the Memphis area is slightly in excess of a half-million dollars. Carborundum is securing only about one-fifth (19 percent) of the total abrasive business in the Memphis market.[1]

Market Analysis

DISTRIBUTOR COVERAGE

Mill Supply Market. Because of the large number of popular lines which they carry, Brady & Goldsmith, Cannon, and Mason Supply are the prin-

---

[1] This was less than its share of the national market. Potential is based on salesmen's adjusted estimates; share of market represents actual sales as a percentage of potential.

cipal mill supply houses. Reed & Redmond, whose operation is patterned after that of the "Big Three," is the regular mill supply source for a small but growing number of the industrial manufacturers in the area. Jones Supply, Hartwell, and Walwood Supply, who are essentially distributors of small tools and allied lines, are the more aggressive limited-line distributors. (See Exhibit 1.)

EXHIBIT 1   Distributor Coverage in Memphis, Dyersburg, Blytheville, and Jonesboro (Percent of abrasive users who consider distributor a regular or occasional source of supply)

	For General Mill Supplies		For Abrasives in Particular	
	Regular	Occasional	Regular	Occasional
Cannon	70	8	43	7
Mason Supply	68	7	18	2
Brady & Goldsmith	63	5	65	3
Reed & Redmond	20	20	5	10
Jones Supply	18	22	–	–
Hartwell	15	10	–	–
Walwood Supply	10	5	–	–

Abrasive Market. There are only three important abrasive suppliers in the Memphis market: Brady & Goldsmith, Cannon, and Mason Supply. Although Reed & Redmond also is active in this market, its strength is not nearly as great as that of any one of the "Big Three." (See Exhibit 1.) Jones Supply sells a negligible amount of coated.

Although 43 percent of the abrasive users stated that Cannon was their regular abrasive source, Cannon's position in this market is largely attributable to the efforts of the Carborundum representative located there. Cannon is the regular source of supply for many customers *only* because it carries Carborundum and *not* because of any abrasive service which it renders.

ABRASIVE POTENTIAL

Bonded. The estimated bonded abrasive potential for Memphis is $438,000. Slightly more than half of this potential figure is to be found in six accounts. Carborundum's share is 18 percent. Roughly $35,000 of the bonded abrasive business in this area is not available to Carborundum because of reciprocity arrangements between two manufacturers and Brady & Goldsmith.

Coated. The estimated coated abrasive potential for Memphis is $123,000. More than one-third of this estimate is concentrated among six accounts. Carborundum's share is 16 percent. The two largest coated abrasive users in this territory account for 25 percent of the available coated business.

Abrasive Grain. The estimated grain potential for this market is $17,000. Almost half of this estimate is found in two accounts. Carborundum's share is 73 percent.

Distributor Analysis

CANNON (CARBORUNDUM)

Warehouse and Office Operation. Cannon's main warehouse and outlet are located in downtown Memphis. It is only a few blocks from one of its principal competitors, Brady & Goldsmith.

Our distributor occupies two large bulidings, each with four floors. Industrial mill supplies are warehoused in one building while automotive supplies and electrical appliances are located in the other. Although these buildings are quite old, their outward appearance is not unattractive. Large windows contain displays of their more important lines. Two railroad sidings and ample loading platform space are important features of these buildings.

The internal operation can be classified as "old-fashioned" in appearance. Although the warehouse is orderly, it does not appear to be efficiently arranged. The office is organized on a functional basis, but here, too, there is an evident lack of planning and clear-cut departmentalization. The absence of a receptionist is evidence enough of a "dated" operation.

Sales Organization. In addition to its main warehouse in Memphis, Cannon maintains a chain of twenty-five stores throughout the territory which it serves. These branch operations are principally outlets for automotive supplies and equipment.

Cannon has an outside sales force of seventy-five men. These salesmen solicit business in Arkansas, Tennessee, and the northern sections of Mississippi and Alabama. Of its outside sales force, only nine are classified as industrial mill supply representatives. The industrial mill supply salesmen are assigned on a geographical basis, and each man has approximately seventy-five accounts.

Because none of these men has had formal or informal abrasive training, none can be classified as an abrasive specialist.

Cannon's inside sales force consists of six desk men and seven counter men. Two desk men handle all abrasive inquiries. One of them, who attended an abrasive training course at Carborundum 15 years ago, is classified by Cannon as an abrasive specialist.

All salesmen are on straight salary. Each salesman is furnished with a company car. The average age of a Cannon salesman is roughly 55 years, and the average length of service is approximately 35 years. At least one salesman is 80 years old.

Stock. Cannon is the Memphis distributor for over 400 different manufacturers. As such, this house stocks industrial mill supplies, general hardware items, automotive supplies, and electrical appliances.

Although total inventory figures were not available, Carborundum stock is a very small part of the total inventory. The total Carborundum investment of this distributor is $15,000–$20,000. Of this, less than $1,000 is in Carborundum coated inventory. Strictly on a physical basis, the 3-M stock in the automotive department appeared to be considerably larger than the Carborundum coated inventory in the industrial mill supply branch. Abrasive stock turnover is estimated to be 2.5 times per year.

Service. Cannon is an old house. As a matter of fact, it has been in business for eighty-five years and has been the Carborundum distributor for forty years. If size is any criterion for success, then Cannon must be considered successful.

Despite its apparent success, many of the customers in the Memphis area voiced strong criticism about the service they are receiving from this distributor. Indifferent telephone service, infrequent sales calls, inadequately trained salesmen, no order follow-up, unsatisfactory counter service, and inefficient order expediting are service areas which customers cite as being particularly irritating and frustrating.

To phone Cannon for information or to place an order can be both trying and time-consuming: "Phone service is terrible. Explained to Cannon salesman that we would not call for merchandise or information again. Seems as though you can never get the department or person you want. You've got to wait for a considerable time before any action is taken on your call."

Salesmen in the outlying area do not call frequently on the trade: "Carborundum gets 75 percent of the business only because of the service which your salesman extends to us. Cannon salesman, although located here in town, calls on us infrequently. In fact, your salesman, even though he lives in Memphis, comes in more often than your distributor's salesman." Cannon representatives have little or no knowledge about any of the products or lines which they "peddle": "Cannon salesmen do not know a damn thing about anything they sell, abrasives included. I'd be ashamed to let a Cannon salesman talk to our engineers or to the men in the shop. Hell, I know as much about their products as they do, and you know that isn't too damn much! You can't blame the salesmen, though. They just have too many lines. Nothing but a bunch of order-takers."

Order follow-up, or the lack of it, is a sore point with quite a few customers: "Cannon's poor order follow-up was responsible for our request to Carborundum to handle our business on a direct basis. Acknowledgments, delivery dates, order status were never provided by Cannon."

Even though there are seven men available to handle over-the-counter business, Cannon's counter service, in the opinion of many customers, is far from satisfactory: "The counter service stinks, and we will not send a truck to Cannon unless it is absolutely necessary. I don't know why it takes so long, but we just can't afford to have a man sitting around Cannon waiting for merchandise."

Order expediting is another weakness in Cannon's operation: "Takes too damn long to get an item when Cannon has to go to the manufacturer. Cannon would rather airmail an order to a manufacturer than send a wire or phone long distance."

Service from Cannon to its customers can very definitely be improved. There is no indication, however, that it will be.

Cannon-Carborundum Relations. The service from Carborundum is not all that Cannon would like it to be. Up-to-date stock information and a better working relationship with our salesman are two things which this distributor thinks will make for a more effective relationship with The Carborundum Company. Cannon's abrasive specialist pointed out that frequently an item which is reported to be in stock in Chicago is not there when he orders it. He does not feel that this is too serious a problem, but if something could be done to correct it—that is, more frequent revisions of stock sheets—he would have more confidence in the delivery dates which he quotes to customers on shipments out of Chicago.

In Cannon's estimation, the working relationship between our representative and its sales people is not what it should be to produce maximum results. Both Cannon's industrial sales manager and abrasive specialist frankly admitted that they dislike and resent some of the things our salesman is doing. In particular, they are annoyed with the "haphazard" way that he quotes delivery dates to customers. They also feel that he is doing Cannon an extreme disservice when he explains to customers that Cannon is responsible for delivery delays which are actually caused by The Carborundum Company. They also cited the fact that certain of their own salesmen refuse to accompany our representative on customer calls.

If our relationship with this distributor is to be a mutually profitable one, these points of friction will have to be removed.

General. Cannon is not an aggressive, up-to-date organization. It does not have the proper management attitude, the appropriate sales tools, or the trained personnel to cope with the competitive industrial market which is developing in Memphis. Nevertheless, Cannon will probably maintain its position as the largest hardware and mill supply house in Memphis for some time to come. Undoubtedly, it will continue its present method of operation indefinitely and in doing so, to quote a competitive distributor, "secure more business by accident than any one or all of the smaller houses in Memphis can develop by design."

Warehouse and Office Operation. Brady & Goldsmith's main warehouse and office are located in downtown Memphis. It is just a few blocks from Cannon.

This distributor occupies only one building, four stories high. This building, like other buildings in the area, is quite old but not unattractive. As at Cannon, large windows contain displays of its more important lines.

The office appears to be departmentalized and well-organized. It has an air of efficiency about it which Cannon's did not have. The warehouse, as seen only from over the counter, appeared to be arranged in an orderly and efficient manner.

Sales Organization. The Brady & Goldsmith outside sales force consists of thirty men who cover a territory that encompasses a 600-mile radius of Memphis. Of the outside sales force, eight are located in Memphis and the surrounding area. Sales territories are assigned on a geographical basis. The number of accounts per salesman varies from ten accounts for older men to 200 accounts for newer men.

The average age of the sales people is roughly forty years, while the average length of service is approximately fifteen years. All salesmen are compensated on a salary-plus-commission basis.

All eight men of the Memphis sales force have attended Norton's Abrasive School. The sales manager and the assistant sales manager have also attended the school. According to the assistant sales manager, none of the eight Memphis men, however, can be thought of as an abrasive specialist. Brady & Goldsmith's inside sales force consists of nine desk men and three counter men. One of the desk men has also attended the Norton school. The sales force is supported by one Norton salesman and three Behr-Manning salesmen. The Norton man and two of the Behr-Manning men are new to the territory as of the first of the year. The previous Norton representative had been assigned to this distributor for four years.

Brady & Goldsmith maintains branch operations in New Orleans and Houston. Each of these is described as being half the size of the Memphis organization.

Stock. Brady & Goldsmith is a general hardware and industrial mill supply house. As such, it represents over 200 manufacturers. This house maintains a total inventory of approxmiately $1,000,000. No estimate as to the size of the industrial mill supply inventory or the industrial abrasive inventory is available.

General. Brady & Goldsmith is moving to a new location the first of next year. The purpose of this move is to leave the congested downtown area. The new location will also permit the house to consolidate its stock which is now warehoused at several different locations in the city. This distributor considers Cannon to be its principal competitor only because of Cannon's size. Reed & Redmond in its estimation is the most aggressive house in the area. Although the distributor alluded to the current practice of price cutting by the smaller distributors, it refused to identify the house or houses doing so.

Although many customers indicated that service from Brady & Goldsmith was better than than from Cannon, few could explain in what way it was better. Several customers intimated that Brady & Goldsmith had undergone a change, but they were at a loss to explain the change. Even the Brady & Goldsmith assistant sales manager, when asked if any organizational or policy change had occurred recently, replied, "Not to the best of my knowledge."

MASON SUPPLY (SIMONDS AND 3-M)

Warehouse and Office Operation. Mason is located on the fringe of the downtown wholesale district. It is only a short distance from Cannon and Brady & Goldsmith. This distributor occupies a two-story corner building. The building is not new but appears to be of more recent structure than that of either Cannon or Brady & Goldsmith. Large display windows are on two sides of the building. The building is divided into three sections: paint store, steel warehouse, and industrial mill supply warehouse. A small alley in the rear of the building provides access to an ample loading platform.

The counter, which is just inside the main entrance, is well manned. The "Will Call" section is prominently marked. The office and warehouse appear to be well organized.

Sales Organization. Mason has an outside sales force of twelve men who cover all of Tennessee, eastern Arkansas, northern Mississippi, and northern Alabama. Of these men, seven operate exclusively in the Memphis area. Sales territories are assigned on an account basis. Each salesman has from seventy-five to one hundred accounts. This distributor does not have a branch operation at the present time.

The inside sales force is composed of eight desk men and eight counter men. One inside man is classified as an abrasive specialist. The counter trade is particularly heavy, even though there are no customer parking facilities. The president of the company is especially pleased with his "Will Call" arrangements.

The sales organization is supported by a Simonds representative and a 3-M representative. The latter is permanently assigned to the area, while the former travels out of New Orleans and visits Mason once a month.

Stock. Mason, like Cannon and Brady & Goldsmith, is a general hardware and industrial mill supply house. It, too, represents over 200 manufacturers.

This distributor estimates its bonded abrasive stock to be between $10,000 and $15,000. The coated abrasive inventory is considerably smaller. Stock turnover is estimated to be 5 to 6 times a year. Abrasive sales volume last year was in the vicinity of $60,000.

General. The president of Mason explained that he is planning to add a salesman in the very near future. He also pointed out that he is seriously contemplating setting up a branch operation. These things, he feels, are necessary to remain competitive in a growing market.

He considers Cannon to be his principal competitor. In his opinion, Cannon is not the aggressive house it was ten years ago. He believes our distributor is giving more and more attention to the development of automotive business and less and less attention to the acquisition of industrial mill supply business. He bases this last observation on the fact that Cannon's executive officers are strong automotive men.

The chief executive of Mason further stated that the small, limited-line specialty houses are extremely aggressive. This is particularly true, he added, of Reed & Redmond, Walwood, and Hartwell. He remarked, "There has been a considerable increase in distributing houses in the last decade and the 'Big Three' have got to keep moving if they don't want to lose out."

REED & REDMOND (BAY STATE & 3-M)

Warehouse and Office Operation. Reed & Redmond's main warehouse and office are located in the industrial section of Memphis. It is quite a distance from the downtown Memphis area, which is the location of the "Big Three."

The building which houses Reed & Redmond is about two years old. It has only one story, but it has between 25,000 and 30,000 square feet of space. The lot on which the building is erected is large enough to permit expansion.

The interior of the building is very attractive, and the office is extremely well organized. Of all of the distributors in Memphis, Reed & Redmond, without question, has the most impressive internal operation.

Sales Organization. Reed & Redmond covers a territory within a radius of 400 miles of Memphis.

The outside sales force is made up of twelve men, none of whom is an abrasive specialist. Territories are assigned to these men by type of account. They are paid on a straight salary basis.

This distributor has fifteen inside desk men and eight warehouse and counter men. One of the desk men recently returned from the advanced abrasive training course at the Bay State plant, and he is classified as an abrasive specialist. Of the fifteen desk men, ten are former Cannon personnel. The sales manager is also an ex-Cannon employee.

The distributor sales force is supported by both Bay State and 3-M specialists. The Bay State salesman is located in Louisiana, and he visits Reed & Redmond for a ten-day period every month. The 3-M representative is located in Memphis.

Stock. Reed & Redmond is a "junior" edition of the "Big Three"; and it, too, can be classified as a general hardware and industrial mill supply house.

An estimate as to the size of this distributor's abrasive stock was not available, nor were estimates of its annual abrasive volume. The sales manager's only comment was that he was quite satisfied with the Bay State line and would not now consider a change.

General. Reed & Redmond opened its doors twenty years ago. It was first located in the wholesale district. It moved last year to its present location.

The sales manager explained that on several different occasions his company attempted to secure the Carborundum line. The latest of these attempts was just two years ago. He implied that the reason Carborundum refused to appoint this house as distributor was because of its "small size."

The organization is growing rapidly. It began with only four individuals; today it has over 200 people on its payroll. The sales manager pointed out that the operation has already outgrown the building in which it is now located—this in only two years.

HARTWELL (J. K. SMIT)

Warehouse and Office Operation. Hartwell is the only distributor located on the south side of Memphis. Its warehouse and office are situated in a small retail commercial area. This distributor is quite a distance from the downtown area, which is the location of the "Big Three."

The building that the distributor occupies is small. It is a one-story structure with approximately 3,000 square feet of space. A small cellar is also available for storage. Loading platform facilities are somewhat limited.

The office, which occupies about one-fourth of the building, has a very businesslike appearance. Directly behind the office is the stock room. Although small, it is, nevertheless, neat, and well organized.

Sales Organization. Hartwell has three salesmen who solicit business in the eastern part of Tenessee. Mr. Sam Hartwell and Mr. Jack Hartwell, partners in the organization, cover territories in the northern and southern parts of the state. The third salesman, a former Cannon employee, calls on accounts in Memphis and the surrounding areas.

This supply house has one inside man who is the stock and shipping clerk. Two clerks complete the internal organization. This distributor discourages counter service and, consequently, has no full-time counter man.

Stock. Hartwell is a distributor of small tools. It is the representative for J. K. Smit's diamond wheels. Mr. Sam Hartwell estimates that his company maintains an inventory valued at between $25,000 and $30,000. He indicated that the stock turns over every six weeks. Last year's volume was approximately $200,000.

General. Mr. Sam Hartwell and Mr. Jack Hartwell started operating four years ago. Mr. Sam Hartwell is an experienced tool and die man. Mr. Jack Hartwell is a graduate engineer. Although the company is organized as a partnership, stock in the company is available to the employees. Under the present agreement between the two partners, control of the company cannot pass to relatives. As a matter of interest, the company has a firm policy against hiring relatives.

Mr. Sam Hartwell explained that their organization is a limited-line specialty house and they wish to keep it that way. He pointed out that they are "interested in securing lines on which service is the big selling point." He stated very emphatically that they are "not interested in acquiring many lines for the sake of business; nor are we interested in lines which can be classified as 'buy' or 'order' items." He also indicated, "We are interested in associating ourselves with manufacturers who will support us in our sales effort."

Mr. Sam Hartwell would not hazard a guess as to the size of the abrasive market in Memphis, but he certainly provided sufficient evidence of his being aware of it. He estimates that there are twenty-five "significant" abrasive users in this area. He supplemented this with the information that there are, roughly, twenty-five centerless grinders in this territory. He added that all of these people are customers of theirs.

Mr. Sam Hartwell is of the opinion that Carborundum is not getting the solicitation which it should. His personal observation is that Cannon salesmen do not discuss abrasives when they call on their customers. He feels that if Cannon representatives were just to ask, "Any grinding wheels today?" Carborundum's business would increase appreciably.

Mr. Sam Hartwell stated that they would be complimented if Carborundum should consider them as a possible distributor. "We realize the problems in selling abrasives, but that would not stop us from entertaining the possibility of taking on the line. In fact, although we wouldn't particularly like it, we would even be the second distributor in this area for you."

This distributor, although it has not made too large a mark in the market to date, has a reputation among its customers for being aggressive. Both Hartwells have a lot of confidence in themselves and in their organization, and they have the ability to substantiate this confidence. Above all, they are thoroughly imbued with the policy of "service for the customer."

JONES SUPPLY (CARBORUNDUM COATED)

Warehouse and Office Operation. Jones Supply is located in the industrial section of Memphis. Like Reed & Redmond and Hartwell, it is quite a distance from the downtown area where the "Big Three" maintain their operations. The building this distributor occupies is small. It is a one-story structure with roughly 3,000 square feet of space. The building is not too old or unattractive. A large window in the front of the building contains displays of the lines which it carries. There is ample space along the side of the building for customer parking. The office is small but efficiently arranged. The warehouse, which is to the rear of the office, is orderly. Counter space is very small.

Sales Organization. Jones Supply has two full-time salesmen and one part-time salesman. The two full-time salesmen, one of whom is the president, cover Memphis and the nearby areas. Each of these salesmen has approximately 150 accounts upon which to call. Neither of these men can be considered an abrasive specialist.

The inside sales organization consists of the office manager, who is also the company treasurer; the part-time salesman, who is also the counter man and shipping clerk; and two clerks. The office manager, a former Mason Supply employee, has been in the industrial supply field for some time.

Stock. Jones Supply, which is a limited-line specialty house, handles principally small cutting tools. It also stocks a line of small machinery. Although it was recently appointed a Carborundum coated jobber, it does not have a stock of coated abrasives. Stock inventory is valued at $75,000–$80,000.

General. Jones Supply has been in business for fifteen years, and it has been at its present location for ten years. It was established and operated for some time by a Mr. Jones. Several years ago, the Hamilton Company, because of an outstanding debt owed them by Mr. Jones, took over the operation. To look after their interest, the Hamilton Company appointed Mr. Klunk, who is now president, as manager.

Jones Supply has a reputation among its customers for being an extremely service-minded organization. "They'll go all out to get anything that we need. I just called them for an off-size screw which they don't stock. We don't need too many of them, but Klunk will give this request the same treatment he would give an order a hundred times larger."

Mr. Klunk is eager to secure the complete Carborundum line—he is now a Carborundum coated jobber. He stated that he would accept our line on a dual distributor basis, if necessary. If he is successful in securing our line, he plans to invest initially between $4,000 and $5,000 in abrasives.

EXHIBIT 2 Memphis Industrial Abrasive Market (Evaluation of principal distributors)

Product Lines	Cannon	Brady & Goldsmith	Mason Supply	Reed & Redmond	Hartwell	Jones Supply
Bonded	Carborundum	Norton	Simonds	Bay State	J. K. Smit	None
Coated	Carborundum & 3M	Behr-Manning	3M	3M	None	Carborundum
Total abrasive inventory (est.)	$15,000–$20,000*	Unknown	$10,000–$15,000	Unknown	Unknown	None
Perishable tools	Extensive	Extensive	Extensive	Large	Limited	Limited
Machine tools	Extensive	Extensive	Extensive	Large	Limited	Limited
General supplies	Extensive	Extensive	Extensive	Large	Limited	Limited
Total mill supply inventory (est.)	$500,000–$1,000,000**	Approx. $1,000,000	$300,000–$500,000**	$300,000–$500,000**	$25,000–$30,000	$75,000–$80,000
Management						
Aggressiveness	Below average	Average	Average	Above average	Above average	Above average
Experience	Below average	Above average	Above average	Above average	Above average	Average
Attitude	Below average	Above average	Above average	Above average	Above average	Above average
Plans	Unknown	Moving to less congested area of city.	Considering a branch operation and addition of salesman.	Unknown	Intend to remain a limited-line specialty house, but add a few new lines.	Intend to remain a limited-line specialty house.

Sales Organization	Cannon	Brady & Goldsmith	Mason Supply	Reed & Redmond	Hartwell	Jones Supply
Total no. of salesmen	75	30	12	12	3	3 (1 part-time)
Total no. of ind. mill supply salesmen	9	Unknown^a	Unknown^a	Unknown^a	3	3 (1 part-time)
Outside abrasive specialist	None	None	None	None	None	None
Inside salesmen	13 (7 counter men)	12 (3 counter men)	16 (8 counter men)	23 (8 warehouse men)	1***	1†
Inside abrasive specialist	1	None	1	1	None	None
Facilities and Location						
Office	Fair	Good	Good	Excellent	Good	Good
Warehouse	Fair	Good	Good	Excellent	Good	Good
Location	Good	Good	Good	Excellent	Good	Good
Parking	Fair	Poor	Fair	Excellent	Fair	Good

* Carborundum only.

** As reported in the *Directory of Industrial Distributors.*

*** Arrange to have one of the outside salesmen present in office most of the time.

† Part-time salesman who operates both as inside and outside sales person.

^{a} All salesmen sel industrial mill supplies to a degree.

Because of the small sales staff, Mr. Klunk admits that his organization will not be able to do a thorough job among the smaller abrasive accounts. However, he implied that this might be more than offset by the business he may secure as a result of his contacts at large firms.

WALWOOD SUPPLY

Walwood Supply is located in the heart of the downtown wholesale district. It is a distributor for sheet metal and tinning supplies. This house has ten salesmen who call on hardware stores, lumber yards, and builder supplies.

Because of its salesmen's indifference to abrasive products, this distributor discontinued handling our line two years ago. This house is not now carrying an abrasive line, and it indicated it did not desire to do so.

Summary and Evaluation

Pertinent data on the Memphis industrial abrasive market and distributors are summarized in Exhibit 2 (on pages 98-99).

Conclusions

1. Cannon is one of the largest and oldest mill supply houses in Memphis.
2. Cannon's success is almost completely attributable to the variety and number of lines which it carries.
3. Cannon, at present, is one of the most ineffective distributors in the industrial mill supply field in Memphis. The absence of an aggressive management attitude, appropriate sales tools, trained personnel, and adequate customer service is responsible for this situation.
4. Many of the criticisms which are made of Cannon can also be be made of Brady & Goldsmith and Mason Supply. However, while Cannon's major competitors have recognized the need for change and are adapting their operations accordingly, the Carborundum distributor is not doing so.
5. Smaller limited-line specialty houses will become more and more important in this market. Manufacturers are awakening to the realization that the service which the small houses render is too often not available from the larger houses.
6. Customer service will become increasingly important as the Memphis industrial mill supply market continues to become more competitive.
7. Carborundum's position in this market is largely the result of the efforts of the Carborundum representative. In an expanding abrasive market, this is not enough.

Recommendations

1. Because of the long-term association between Carborundum and Cannon, the two names in the Memphis market have more or less become synonymous. This is of obvious value to The Carborundum Company. Consequently, our company should make a definite effort in assisting this distributor to become a major factor in the industrial abrasive market. This may very well be impossible, but the attempt by The Carborundum Company should be an honest one.
2. In the event that our assistance proves unfruitful or unavailing, The Carborundum Company should not hesitate to appoint another distributor.
3. Of the distributors which were visited and which expressed an interest in handling our line, Hartwell appears to have the greatest potential for furthering Carborundum's interests in this territory.

Do you have confidence in the analyst's appraisal of the situation? Do you agree with his recommendations? What action should Carborundum take? Apart from the question of the individual distributors' relative quality, what should Carborundum's basic strategy be as to (a) whether to have one or more than one distributor in a market like Memphis; and (b) what kind of distributor or distributors to have—large or small, with wide coverage of accounts or specializing on a smaller number of accounts, with large inventory and service or an aggressive seller, and so on?

SCHWARTZBRAU BREWING COMPANY

Mr. C. F. McCord, the marketing vice-president of the Schwartzbrau Brewing Company, was considering what moves he should make regarding the organization of his sales force in the light of market trends. The company had tried changes in its sales organization on an experimental basis. Mr. McCord now had available the results of a study by a management consulting firm.

In the past year, the Schwartzbrau Brewing Company had sales approximating $22 million and an after-tax profit of approximately $200 thousand. The company had intensive distribution in the metropolitan Chicago area and within a radius of forty miles of Chicago.

Mr. McCord stated that it was common knowledge in the brewing industry that sales of packaged beer and consumption in the home had increased markedly. On the other hand, the percentage of beer consumed in public places had declined. Concurrent with this decline, there had occurred a change in the character of the outlets at which beer was consumed on the premises. The old-time "brass-rail saloon" was giving way to the "pouring spot" or lounge. This newer type of tavern was much more likely to sell bottled beer for consumption on the premises in addition to, or rather than, draft beer.

The gross margin on draft beer was about twice as high as that on bottled beer. Schwartzbrau's dollar sales were currently about evenly divided between draft and bottled beer but draft sales were expected to decline. For Schwartzbrau, delivery costs were three times higher than "selling" costs, which did not include advertising and public relations.

Sales Force

For some years, Schwartzbrau salesmen had been organized into two separate sales forces—one selling only bottled beer (mostly to grocery and package stores) and one selling only draft beer (to taverns). In almost all cases accounts were called upon once a week. These two sales forces were trained to do two different jobs.

The "bottled" salesmen's main functions were to get good shelf space for Schwartzbrau, put up point-of-sale promotional material, check the status of the retail stock, and do merchandising in the store. They averaged seventy calls a day.

The "draft" salesmen, on the other hand, were expected to set up promotional signs and to spend some time cementing personal relations with the proprietor, as well as spending some money on free rounds and buttressing the loyalty of that portion of the saloon's clientele which happened to be present at the time. The draft salesmen averaged six calls a day.

There were within the Schwartzbrau territory 8,000 outlets selling packaged beer only and 11,000 selling at least some draft. Not all of these carried the Schwartzbrau brand.

Schwartzbrau had forty-five bottled and forty draft salesmen. With the increasing trend toward the sale of bottled beer by taverns, the salesmen of bottled beer had been calling on taverns that had at least partially swung over to bottled beer. Thus, many taverns were called upon by a Schwartzbrau bottled salesman as well as a Schwartzbrau draft salesman.

This situation created a number of problems. The bottled beer salesman calling on a tavern sometimes found himself misunderstood because he had no expense account with which to buy beer for the patrons. Conversely, the effort of the draft beer salesman was only partially as effective as it might have been considering the total consumption of beer in the tavern. Furthermore, the draft salesmen found their sales going down through no fault of their own. From the company's point of view, the expense of distributing a barrel of draft increased because it took just as many salesmen spending just as much time to call on stores which sold only part of their beer in draft form as it had taken to call on all-draft outlets.

Mr. McCord believed that serious consideration should be given to realigning the duties of salesmen so that the present bottled salesmen would become "off-premises" salesmen and would sell bottled beer to grocery and package stores only, while the present draft salesmen would become on-premises salesmen and sell both draft and bottled beer to taverns. As an objection to such a change, however, Mr. McCord felt that the draft salesmen, who had better salaries, better expense accounts, and generally greater seniority, might feel they were "losing caste" if they were assigned some of the duties now handled by bottled salesmen. In addition, he felt there would be a real problem in teaching the draft salesmen the new selling techniques which they would need to sell bottled beer.

The draft salesment were paid approximately $200 a week plus car allowance, and the bottled salesmen were paid $20 a week less. Company figures indicated that out-of-pocket cost for a salesman was approximately $20,000 a year, plus $10,000 for the allocation of sales management and other overhead.

Special Study

One of Mr. McCord's first moves had been to call in a leading management consulting firm. The consulting firm sent its men out with a sample of salesmen in order to get some feel for what the jobs involved. The management consultants also went over every bottled account with the salesmen—surveying them for (1) type of store by volume, (2) merchandising job that could be done, (3) whether the store would let the salesmen do much merchandising, (4) Schwartzbrau sales from that store, (5) total beer sales from that store (estimated by the salesmen).

After a preliminary look at the outlets the management consultants were very hopeful that a plan of calls could be worked out whereby some accounts would be called upon once a week, some once every two weeks, and some once a month, with a resulting saving in the manpower required to do Schwartzbrau's selling job. They stated that this plan had worked effectively for a number of other clients, particularly in the drug trade.

After the survey, the management consultants reported that more time should be spent in merchandising (doing such things as building special case displays) in the stores where it was possible in terms of available space and where the store managements would allow it. So much added time would be needed for this merchandising that the company would need more salesmen than before even if some stops could be eliminated through fewer calls on less important accounts.

After more investigation, the management consultants also stated that, contrary to their hopes, Schwartzbrau salesmen would have to call on almost all accounts once a week, or else the company would lose more sales through fewer calls than it would gain by increased merchandising. The consultants did not believe it would be wise to leave an account uncovered for longer than a week because the opportunities of competing salesmen to call and tie up the retailers with inventories of their brands (in terms of both space and money) would thus be multiplied. In addition, the retailers would lose their image of the Schwartzbrau salesman as a "regular" salesman and this would soon impair Schwartzbrau's share of market.

The consultants concluded that the company—considering the desirability of using displays more intensively and the inadvisability of calling on any account less frequently than once a week—would need fifteen more salesmen to do its selling job.

The management consultants' survey of Schwartzbrau's outlets had shown that in only 20 percent was there sufficient space to make it physically possible to do a merchandising job via display building. Location of these display prospects was spotty, and this fact prompted the consultants to believe that the job could best be done by a separate force of merchandisers—otherwise the job of salesmen of the bottled or off-premises type would vary widely, making control extremely difficult. Therefore, the consultants recommended, as an alternative to adding fifteen salesmen, that a specialized force of about twenty merchandising men be used to do the display-building job. The salesmen were to pre-schedule displays with store managers, and the merchandising men were to follow up.

Mr. McCord estimated that each merchandiser would cost $15,000 a year out-of-pocket when car allowance was considered in addition to salary. He was aware of the usefulness of displays from the company's past experience and knew that they would move some additional volume, and he liked them as a method of getting into the storeroom in order to check stock and possibly sell more beer. He believed, however, that displays could achieve their greatest usefulness only when tied into a local current event or some seasonal theme. He recalled one instance in which displays featuring a winning Chicago baseball team, in conjunction with Schwartzbrau beer, had for a brief period boosted sales 300 percent in those stores using the display.

What is the company's basic problem—organization, promotion, personnel, or what? As a local or regional brand, how should it try to compete with strongly advertised national brands? Does it have or can it make a market for itself? Evaluate the two sides of the business—draft and bottled—for the present and for the long pull. Draw up the outline of a plan of action.

SINGH AND SONS (C)

Sri K.C. Singh, president of Singh and Sons, an Indian manufacturer of valves, wanted to secure more information about distribution systems for valves in the United States.[1] He thus commissioned a study by an American marketing agency.

Distribution Report

The marketing agency reported that the largest potential market for Singh valves appeared to be in the construction industry, for use in heating and air conditioning of large plants and office buildings, where both price and performance were important to the building contractor.

Building contractors usually bought this kind of product from wholesale distributors of plumbing and heating supplies, who maintained inventories, provided delivery, and extended credit. Their margins ranged from 25 to 40 percent for different products—usually toward the high end of that range for products like valves (35 to 40 percent). There were some 10,000 such wholesalers in the United States, with 30 percent of these accounting for 70 percent of the total market.

In turn, wholesale distributors usually bought either from manufacturer's representatives ("reps") or from the manufacturer's sales force. Manufacturers using reps often provided "missionary" assistance in the market; that is, they would send a man of their own to call on architects and engineers to acquaint them with the product and to persuade them to specify it in their plans. A rep typically received commissions of from 5 to 15 percent, depending on the size of the sales volume he might get and on the ease of making sales. Thus, for a fast-selling product requiring little sales effort, he might receive 5 percent, while for a slow-moving product which required a large amount of aggressive selling skill and technical know-how he might receive 15 percent. New and unfamiliar types of products calling for a large amount of introductory effort tended to draw higher commissions, especially in their initial stages in the market. In general, values like the Superior line (a U.S. valve similar to Singh's valve) provided commissions of 8 to 10 percent.

Most manufacturers found it desirable to maintain ten or more regional warehouses in order to supply their wholesale distributors with prompt and dependable service. However, a new trend in industrial market distribution was developing in the United States—the emergence of "warehousing reps." They invested their own money in sizable inventories instead of merely drawing a commission on sales shipped from the manufacturer's warehouse or warehouses directly to the wholesale distributors, took title to the goods, and resold and delivered to the typical wholesale distributors. A distribution system using such reps allowed the manufacturer to dispense with regional warehouses. These reps were given an "entrepreneurial" discount of 20 to 50 percent. In effect they acted as super-wholesale distributors covering a whole region of the country—each with a market comparable in size to the whole national market in other, smaller countries. From fifteen to twenty such warehousing or "entrepreneurial" reps could cover most of the United States.

[1] See the cases Singh and Sons (A) and (B) earlier.

Alternative Actions

Singh realized that he must proceed with caution, because his valves were unconventional, were manufactured outside the United States, and of course the "Singh" brand name would be new to the U.S. market. Singh and Sons had received inquiries from a prominent U.S. manufacturer of plumbing and heating supplies with a well-established salesforce of fifty men selling direct to typical wholesale distributors. This manufacturer did not have a valve line of his own, and apparently felt he could increase his volume of business without incurring additional sales costs of any consequence. He "promised" to build up annual sales of several hundred thousand units of Singh valves if Singh would mark them with his brand name rather than the Singh name. Singh felt that the most he could get in the way of price would be 10 to 15 percent over his delivered cost. However, he would be relieved of promotional and warehousing costs and the risks associated with conducting his own marketing operation.

The alternative, of course, was to organize his own marketing company. The U.S. marketing agency volunteered to assist him, and even offered to invest some of its own money in such a company. Thereafter, the agency would supervise and manage the company for 2½ percent of sales revenue. The initial capital required would be about $60,000, although more might be needed later. Estimated expense budgets are shown in Exhibit 1. Included in the expenses was the $36,000-per-year salary of a man experienced in the construction industry and well known among wholesale distributors, architects, and engineers, who would spend full time doing missionary work in the field, as shown in Exhibit 2. This proposal envisaged the recruitment of fifteen to twenty warehousing reps, which involved persuading that many of the most successful of the typical reps to shift over to the warehousing basis and to invest up to $25,000 each in inventories. A number of such reps, when questioned by the U.S. marketing agency, said they would be interested in this kind of proposition.

Another possibility was for Singh and Sons to set up regional warehouses of their own. Warehousing costs would probably amount to about 1¢ per pound. Freight costs, from port to regional warehouse, if inland, and from regional warehouse to wholesalers would average about 6¢ per pound. In the case of warehousing reps, however, the freight costs would be about 5¢ per pound; and there would be no warehousing costs. (For weights and distribution of sales by size see Exhibit 1 in Singh and Sons (B).)

Of course, it would also be possible to follow a more gradual approach—taking one region of the country at a time. Thus, one rep could cover the New England area, three could cover the Northeast. If the decision were to start this way, only one regional warehouse would be

EXHIBIT 1   Estimated Budgets

	Recommended Budget		Minimum Budget	
	Month	Year	Month	Year
General and Administrative				
Office rent	$ 150	$ 1,800	–	–
Telephone & telegraph	150	1,800	$ 150	$ 1,800
Stationery, postage, supplies	100	1,200	50	600
Secretary	500	6,000		
	$ 900	$10,800	$ 200	$ 2,400
Travel				
Air (40 trips @ $150)	$ 500	$ 6,000	$ 500	$ 6,000
Auto rental & expense	200	2,400	200	2,400
Lodging (80 nights @ $20)	133	1,600	133	1,600
Food (120 days @ $8)	80	960	80	960
	$ 913	$10,960	$ 913	$10,960
Entertainment				
Lunches (60 @ $10)	$ 50	$ 600	$ 50	$ 600
Dinners (60 @ $20)	100	1,200	100	1,200
Miscellaneous	187	2,240	187	2,240
	$ 337	$ 4,040	$ 337	$ 4,040
Executive Costs				
Vice-president	$3,000	$36,000	$3,000	$36,000
Secretary-bookkeeper	600	7,200	200	2,400
Fringes, insurance, taxes	300	3,600	200	2,400
Insurance on key executive	150	1,800	–	–
	$4,050	$48,600	$3,400	$40,800
Advertising				
Space	$1,000	$12,000	$ 750	$ 9,000
Catalogs & literature	300	3,600	200	2,400
Direct mail	300	3,600	150	1,800
Sales promotion	300	3,600	150	1,800
Sales samples	100	1,200	75	900
Miscellaneous	83	1,000	75	900
Total	$2,083	$25,000	$1,400	$16,800
		$99,400		$75,000

Notes for Exhibit 1 are found on p. 108.

EXHIBIT 1 (cont.)

Notes:

1. Minimum budget—first year only.

2. Office and/or full-time secretary-bookkeeper would not be necessary for first year.

3. Because personal selling is the key to the operation, travel and entertainment should not be reduced from suggested levels. Based on a six-day week, above budgets allow for three days travel, one day paperwork, one day on advertising, and remaining time where required.

4. Life insurance would be payable to company.

5. Travel estimates are based on Exhibit 2.

EXHIBIT 2   Travel Estimates

	January–March	April–June	July–September	October–December
India	3		3	
Chicago	6	4	4	4
Cleveland		2	4	
Pittsburgh	4	2		
St. Louis		2	2	2
Kansas City	3	3		
Dallas	3	3	3	
Houston	3	3	3	
San Francisco		3	3	3
Los Angeles		3	3	3
Boston	4	1	1	
New York Metro	3	3	3	3
Philadelphia	2		2	2
Washington-Baltimore			2	4
Atlanta	3		3	
Total per quarter	34	29	36	21

required initially. Using four full black-and-white pages (one every three months) in the Northeast edition of *Construction News Record*, for instance, would cost $4,000.[2]

However, one of the reps interviewed thought this approach would be a mistake; he said that it would be difficult to get good representatives

[2] The New England region included the states of Maine, New Hampshire, Vermont, Rhode Island, Massachusetts, and Connecticut, and represented approximately 5 percent of the U.S. market. The Northeast region included the same states plus New York, Pennsylvania, New Jersey, and Delaware, and represented approximately 20 percent of the U.S. market.

unless it were known that Singh was operating on a national basis, and that a foreign manufacturer needed the "image" of a national company doing a national business in order to develop credibility as a dependable supplier. He also pointed out that there would be a reinforcing effect from having a number of reps; the more active reps all knew each other, and met and talked on the phone with each other frequently. Thus, if one or more were having good success with a product, the others would hear about it and be stimulated to push the product themselves.

What strategy should Singh and Sons adopt?

BOLGER COMPANY

As part of the Bolger Company's annual program of appraising progress and planning for the future, the company was undertaking an analysis of its market—and marketing—situation. Topics of concern were:

1. Is our position in the market vulnerable?
2. How can we keep abreast of market trends?
3. What kind of changes, if any, should we make now, or contemplate making soon, in our sales organization?

The Bolger Company, headquartered in Irving, Ohio, was a major producer of automatic pressure and liquid level controls. Company sales had reached $76.8 million, with profits of $7.3 million in the latest fiscal year. Over the preceding decade, the company had enjoyed an 8.5 percent compounded growth rate in sales. Over the same period, net profits grew at an 11.8 percent compounded rate, and net income as a percentage of sales ranged between 6.8 percent and 10.5 percent.

Bolger's Market

Bolger's products were used in process control. (See the Appendix for a description of process control systems.)

The total market considered to be part of Bolger's operating environment included equipment performing each of the five essential functions described in the Appendix, plus equipment performing such tasks as transforming controller output signals to valve action (actuators) and graphically recording the operations for future reference and analysis. Exhibit 1 illustrates the product classes and examples of equipment in each class.

EXHIBIT 1   Products in Bolger's Operating Environment

Product Class	Examples
Sensors	Thermocouples; magnetic flowmeters; orifice plates; flow and pressure transducers; instruments to analyze chemical composition and physical properties; weighing devices; thickness gauges.
Control valves and actuators	Flow regulating valves; dampers; solenoid valves; pneumatic, hydraulic, and electric valve actuators.
Controllers	Mechanical and electrical devices such as on-off and proportional controllers that produce output regulating signals in response to input information signals.
Recorders and indicators	Graphic chart recorders; miniature recorders and indicators (but not switchboard meters); digital indicators.
Control computers and data acquisition equipment	All components of a computer system, including central processor; bulk memory; A/D and D/S converters; multiplexers; peripheral equipment such as printers, tape readers, or tape punches.
Accessories	Maintenance supplies; annunciators; alarms; panel boards.

Bolger's product line included the following products, which accounted ror shares of Bolger's total sales as shown:

Diaphragm control valves	43%
Gas regulators	18
Liquid level and pressure controllers	10
Butterfly valves	10
Repair parts	9
All other	10

The majority of the company's sales were concentrated on pneumatic and hydraulic equipment to accomplish final control (final control elements, or valves, and actuators). Specialization in this area of the total market had enabled Bolger to concentrate its engineering talent, obtain a 40 to 60 percent market share in all of its major lines, grow profitably well above the industry average, and compete successfully with much larger companies—for instance, the controls division of Worthington Corporation, Honeywell, and IT&T.

Exhibit 2 breaks down the process control equipment market by industry, along with annual growth rates for each. Exhibit 3 shows Bolger's customer distribution. No single customer accounted for as much as 4 percent of total sales.

EXHIBIT 2 Instrumentation Market
(in millions of dollars)

Industry			Annual Growth
Chemical	$181.5	33%	8.9%
Power generation	49.5	9	6.3
Steel	44.0	8	9.8
Pulp and paper	38.5	7	9.3
Food and beverage	38.3	7	9.3
Petroleum	33.2	6	7.0
Water and sewage treatment	33.0	6	15.1
Gas and petroleum production and distribution	27.5	5	8.2
All other	104.5	19	6.6
Total	$550.0	100%	8.7%

EXHIBIT 3 Bolger Customers

Industry	Percentage of Business
Petroleum, petrochemical, chemical	36
Gas utility and pipeline	16
Steam-generated electric power	8
Liquefied petroleum gas	9
Pulp and paper	11
Metal production	4
All other	16
Total	100

INDUSTRY SPECIALIZATION

Companies in the process instrument industry had typically developed around a specific product, control function, or industry. Leeds & Northrup, for example, concentrated much of its effort on metals and power generation. Foxboro emphasized flow measurement for chemicals and petroleum. Taylor gave particular attention to instrument applications of food companies. Both Honeywell and Leeds & Northrup stressed graphic recording and temperature measurement devices. Fisher Governor concentrated on pneumatic control. As a result, control equipment was supplied by over 1,000 manufacturers, competing all the way from a single product to a total "system." Of the many competing manufacturers, however, a relatively small number shared most of the market; six companies had 40 percent, and some twenty firms had 75 percent.

The major reason for the various specializations had been the different technologies involved, both from a product standpoint and a customer standpoint, in the different product classes and industries. For example, the mechanical engineering capabilities needed to design a control valve were very different from the technology needed to manufacture and market a process-control computer.

Because of the multitude of competing firms, overlapping of product lines among companies, and the fact that many were either divisions of large companies or closely held without published reports, information available about the industry was minimal. It was thus difficult to compare the successes of competitors in obtaining sales and profits or to evaluate competitive strategies. Consequently, Bolger was operating in a vacuum regarding detailed knowledge of competitors, market research, and product trends.

Industry Trends

Bolger executives were highly optimistic about the growth prospects for the industry. They also saw tremendous opportunities for the company to increase its own sales as the market expanded. On the other hand, they realized that new firms and new technologies could be expected to enter the market, and that product innovation would become more rapid and competition tougher. In particular, there were two trends developing that the company would have to take into account: (1) direct digital control, and (2) systems selling by competitors.

DDC AND ELECTRONICS SYSTEMS SELLING

The direct digital control (DDC) concept simply involves replacement of as many individual instrument blocks (see Exhibit 5 in the Appendix) as possible with an equivalent function performed by a digital process-control computer. This has significant impact directly on equipment manufacturers centered around the error detecting and controller functions, but only indirect impact on others, as it is not feasible to replace the sensor, valve, or valve actuator wth a computer-based function.

Bolger executives believed that the advances in process-control capabilities through DDC were certain to be great, and that the computer would be the fastest-growing product class, doubling in size within five years. Along with the increased use of computers would come more electronic controls. Previously, most process instruments had been pneumatic.

Electronics, however, were faster, more precise, and more compatible with digital computers. About 30 percent of process controls were now electronic, and the percentage was expected to rise to 60 percent within five years. According to Bolger's vice-president of marketing, who had been studying the market:

> These developments have already had an impact on the industry. Companies have had to develop or acquire (at no small cost) electronic and digital computer know-how. Furthermore, with digital computers and electronic equipment becoming important parts of the total process system, some companies with capabilities in those fields—notably GE and IBM—have been trying to "back into" the process control business.
>
> Some process-control companies—particularly the larger and more diversified companies—recognized the importance of these trends, and built up their competence at an early stage. Although the investment has had a temporary impact on profit margins, it is now paying off. The industry's largest factors, Foxboro and Honeywell, certainly have little to fear, for both have impressive digital and electronic capabilities. Most of the smaller factors in the process-control industry, however, have not yet acquired the necessary digital and electronic know-how. To succeed, they must catch up.
>
> These technological trends have affected the industry's competitive structure, but not to the degree once feared. A few years ago many believed the computer would be such an important part of the total system that it would be the "tail that wagged the dog"; we feared that computer companies would soon dominate the process-control industry. This hasn't happened. The computer companies have neither had good process-control marketing organizations nor have they had the necessary knowledge of the process themselves. In total, companies such as GE and IBM certainly will not force out today's leaders.
>
> DDC and electronics have affected the control valve and actuator classification in only a minor way thus far, compared to other equipment. This will not continue. The use of DDC and automatic sequencing will certainly increase valve sales, but will also force a need for improved valves and actuators outside the familiar technologies. The pneumatic actuator, whose resistance to obsolescence has been the most significant characteristic of valve technology, will be replaced in many cases because DDC will require valve components with greater speed and accuracy than are now available. This will present great opportunities for the companies that can:
>
> 1. Combine valve design capabilities with electronic knowledge to eliminate costly digital/analog transducers
> 2. Increase the valve performance to meet DDC capabilities
> 3. Offer a broad line of both pneumatic and computer actuated valves

Risks of obsolescence will be great for those who can't accomplish the above.

In these areas, therefore, Bolger will be confronted with the need for electronic capabilities greater than those we currently possess and a probable degree of change in consumer requirements that we haven't faced previously.

As for designing, specifying, selecting, and installing a collection of instruments to integrate into a control loop or loops, that is becoming more difficult. Inadequacies in any single instrument result in inefficiencies and costs for the system as a whole, which can far outweigh equipment savings.

To take advantage of the increasing need for complete process understanding and a systems approach, some companies, notably Foxboro and Honeywell, have begun attempting to sell their complete systems capabilities. The degree of success they are having and may have in the future is subject to considerable debate among experts. Those in technical (engineering and design) positions express great optimism over the future of "package selling" and great apprehension about the effects it might have on companies like Bolger. Their beliefs are based mostly on technical literature and contact with other engineers. On the other hand, sales personnel and general managers are less optimistic about the future of systems selling by the manufacturers themselves, though all agree that systems engineering services, from within the companies or from external systems engineering firms, are bound to grow rapidly because of the need to help the customer with the increasingly difficult problem of analyzing his process and requirements.

So far, the idea has been pushed only by manufacturers, with little pull from the customers. There are several reasons for the lack of customer enthusiasm:

1. No one manufacturer has the best of all equipment, and many customers require the best components for the system.

2. Company systems engineering groups are being established by most big companies to study their processes and control equipment needs. These groups can do an adequate job of selecting the best equipment for their purposes and, at the same time, safeguard their company's process secrets. This is very important in many industries.

3. Companies with technical expertise would rather bid separately and get the best prices available on each instrument.

4. Outside systems-engineering firms can and do make up for lack of trained personnel. Companies would rather have them engineer a job as a qualified and impartial third party than have an equipment supplier do the job.

5. Technical knowledge of all instruments in a system is extremely difficult for a sales force to learn. Separate sales groups would almost certainly be required.

For these reasons, it appears that currently the package system has appeal mostly to small companies, with limited capabilities of their own, and in a very few industries, notably paper. Bolger is not being greatly hurt and should not be affected in the near future. However, these trends are sure to continue, and they must be watched carefully.

Bolger Customers

Bolger products were sold to eight classes of buyers:

Original equipment companies (OEMs)
Instrument manufacturers
Contract engineers
Contractors (buy and build)
Jobbers and distributors
Stocking agents
End-users
Licensee arrangements (foreign)

Three general types, however, encompassed almost all of the market environment: (1) end-users, (2) engineering contractors, and (3) OEMs and instrument companies.

END-USERS

Sales to the end-user made up the majority (approximately 60 percent) of Bolger sales and were even more important in creating consumer pull for the Bolger brand name. To these people, service was the most important factor, because failure of a single valve could shut down a multimillion dollar plant and cost thousands of dollars. It was in this segment of the market that the Bolger sales organization, with its high-quality engineering, maintenance, and quick delivery was making its biggest impact and allowing the company to obtain a premium price for its products.

The great majority of purchasing decisions were made by instrument engineers, who were relatively sophisticated buyers. Nevertheless, the ability of Bolger representatives to engineer the installation and provide other technical assistance was of vital significance in the final purchase decision. The following remarks by a valve customer illustrate the dilemma faced by purchasers and points out the importance of a high quality sales force:

Valve catalogs by more than a score of manufacturers in the U.S. alone would fill a sizable library. When you add up all the combinations of features of valve design, sizes, types, shapes, connections, materials, etc., the total would reach at least 100,000 or more.

No longer is it easy and simple to select a valve for a given application. To keep costs within reason, it is necessary to study the flow control problem in great detail. Then, after all the factors that affect a valve problem have been pinpointed, it is necessary to sift and screen all the makes, types, features, designs, and ratings available. . . . There are many flow control situations where a variety of valve types will work.

Besides equipment bought directly for new investment or replacement by end-users, much of the equipment installed via OEMs, instrument companies, and engineering contractors was bought subject to specifications by the end-user that Bolger valves be included in the package.

ENGINEERING CONTRACTORS

Sales to engineering contractors made up approximately another 20 percent of Bolger sales. Prices were slightly lower in these bidding situations, but this was compensated for somewhat by the larger volume on most jobs and the lesser engineering that had to be performed. Contractors were also highly interested in service, delivery, and quality, particularly on fixed-cost projects, and, as mentioned before, were highly sensitive to specifications by their customers for Bolger valves.

It was expected that as process control became more complicated with the development of DDC and other sophisticated technology, engineering contracting firms would become a more prominent factor in Bolger's sales. With only two or three firms normally accepted to bid for a contract, gaining acceptance was, and would continue to be, a key factor. Currently, Bolger was one of the few suppliers acceptable to almost all contractors, and was able to obtain 45 to 55 percent of all the projects on which it bid, even though its bid was often higher than others'. The key to maintaining this acceptance was the ability to obtain end-user pull through high-quality service and products.

OEM AND INSTRUMENT COMPANIES [2]

These two categories combined constituted approximately 20 percent of Bolger's sales. Bolger's OEM philosophy is described in the following company memorandum:

> The problems involved with handling OEMs normally center around discount and commission. The OEM discount is the discount beyond consumer net enjoyed by an OEM customer and is intended to provide the OEM a reasonable profit on Bolger products as well as to cover the costs of engineering and marketing the Bolger product line. In order to enjoy this additional discount, the OEM must in some way be able to provide the consumer with some special service that cannot be provided by Bolger or our selling agents.

[2] Instrument companies were not considered OEM customers by Bolger.

OEM business is attractive because our agents do not normally have an opportunity to quote this product to the eventual consumer, and the OEM provides an otherwise not obtainable market. OEM business keeps up our volume base and because of its repetitive nature is attractive to both Bolger and our agents.

The sales to instrument companies constituted special problems, because they often resold the equipment in systems in competition with Bolger representatives all over the country. Service was of little direct importance; price and quality were the main consideration. However, the force of end-user desire for Bolger valves did play a useful role; instrument companies often found it necessary to incorporate Bolger valves into their systems in order to obtain package sales.

Bolger Marketing

The basic objective of all Bolger strategy was profitable growth, with profitability being emphasized in marketing as well as in other strategies. The company continually endeavored to place itself in market segments where its skill would allow it to command premium prices above the competition.

PRODUCT LINE

As previously stated, Bolger specialized its efforts around the final control element, expanding into liquid level and pressure controllers and transmitting instruments.

Although there had not been any revolutionary change in Bolger's product line in the last fifteen to twenty years, over half of the present products had either been developed or received major engineering revisions within the last five years. The company had shown unusual ability in taking a basically standardized product and designing product variations to solve special processing problems. Thus, the company had taken the leadership in promoting expanded applications for butterfly valves and pioneering the use of ball valves in the pulp and paper industries. This major strength depended on the technical excellence both of the company's engineering staff and of the field sales representatives.

CUSTOMER SERVICE

Service to customers was not limited to technical assistance. The company had recently instituted an assembled stock program (ASP), which was expected to result in the building for stock of 700 basic assemblies. Eventually 50 percent of the company's total sales volume might be delivered in two to four weeks, compared to current ten- to fourteen-week delivery schedules.

In addition to delivery, special customer education classes were held continually at the Irving headquarters to keep Bolger in touch with the market and to inform customers of new developments.

MARKETING ORGANIZATION

The current marketing organization at Bolger is shown schematically in Exhibit 4.

EXHIBIT 4 Bolger Marketing Organization

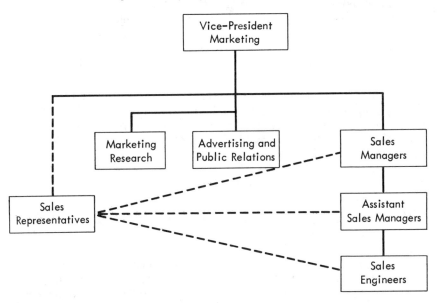

Bolger was unique in that it marketed in the U.S., Canada, and Mexico *exclusively* through its own company-trained manufacturer's representatives. There were currently forty-five manufacturers' representatives employing approximately 260 technically trained sales and service people. Each firm was an independent company, although in every case a major amount of their sales effort was devoted to the Bolger account (in some of the larger offices as high as 90 percent of their total business).

The typical sales representative had forty to fifty customers and called on them once or twice a month. There was little or no specialization by industry except to the extent that a particular industry was concentrated in a given locality.

The sales representatives working for agents were evaluated continuously, and agency contracts were subject to renewal annually. Evaluation was done on an informal basis by the vice-president of marketing and the sales managers, who visited the agencies frequently, where they went over records and talked with the sales representatives and other personnel. There was no reporting system for sales representatives or agents, but through the questions and suggestions of the vice-president of marketing and the sales managers, Bolger, in effect, exercised control of basic field office policies, personnel, and pricing.

The typical agent's sales representative had undergone lengthy and intensive training as a sales engineer at Bolger headquarters, often for several years, before going to work for the agents. (Although not all agents' sales representatives had come from headquarters, most of the newer ones did come to the agents from this source.)

Agents were supported by thirty home office sales engineers. The complex nature of Bolger products required that these men be engineering graduates. Even so, it took three to five years, on the average, for a new engineering graduate to acquire sufficient background to be transferred to field selling. Though these men could progress into managerial positions in the home office (and some of them did), in actuality these positions were few in number, and most men planned to become sales representatives in the various agencies.

The high technical quality of sales representation at the agency level was a reflection of the commissions the company paid for the selling, engineering, and servicing functions performed by the agencies. Commissions to the agents varied between 15 and 20 percent of net selling price. As a result, field sales jobs could be made financially quite attractive—more attractive, indeed, than most management positions—so that these field jobs were sought by most sales engineers. Company management believed that even with such high commissions, the true cost of sales (selling, engineering, and servicing) was no greater than that of many competitors. Most of Bolger's competitors, particularly its larger ones, employed a direct sales force. These sales forces were understood by Bolger to be compensated on a salary plus bonus arrangement.

Management attributed much of its present marketing success to the high quality of the sales representatives and the services they performed for customers, plus the speed of delivery from agents' warehouses (the various agents carried the best inventories in the field).

Progress Appraisal

In the course of Bolger's annual progress appraisal, the newly hired marketing research director, a recent MBA, said that he thought some kind of system should be developed to analyze territory potentials, establish sales quotas (by volume, customer, and/or product line), and evaluate the company's agents against such a sales plan. He felt that it might even be possible to compensate the agents (manufacturer's representatives) according to their performance so measured, rather than as at present as a percentage of sales; and then they might put stronger effort behind Bolger products.

The executive vice-president, on the other hand, said that he felt it might be advisable to move toward abandoning the agents entirely.

He pointed out, for example, that one of the company's agents—a typical one, for whom the Bolger line accounted for some 80 percent of his business—was showing an annual net profit of almost $100,000, and that the various salesmen working for this agent were earning up to $22,000 per year. He calculated that such a move initially might increase marketing costs by 10 percent or more, but felt that in the end it could increase sales to far more than enough to cover the additional costs. He thought that direct contact with the market might also be beneficial, particularly in connection with new product possibilities.

To both these proposals, the reaction of the vice-president of marketing was cold. In his words:

> Why tamper with what we know is a successful way of doing things in order to get some doubtful benefits? Maybe we are strong just because we do it this way. Perhaps our agents support us because they know we are 100 percent in our use of agents— rather than selling some or all customers directly as most of our major competitors do—and because we allow them the status of independent businessmen. Do we want to lose that loyalty? Besides we owe something to our agents for helping us to build up our business. Maybe there is some other way to compensate for any deficiencies in our agents' operation. Or, perhaps even more important, we should seek further improvement through attention to our product lines and product policy.

What changes, if any, should Bolger make now, or plan to make subsequently, in its sales organization or procedures? How well will it be equipped to meet market conditions in the future?

Appendix: Process Control Industry

Since World War II, automatic controls have largely replaced manual control methods for continuous manufacturing processes and are now beginning to replace manual control in batch processing. There are five basic reasons why practically every industry uses at least some process control instruments:

1. In spite of high investment costs of instruments, it is more economical to amortize control instruments than to employ large numbers of men to monitor and control processes manually.
2. They result in products of higher and more consistent quality.
3. They speed the processes.
4. They reduce waste.
5. They make possible much safer operations.

In sum, process control instruments provide more efficient operations.

TYPES OF SYSTEMS

There are two primary classes of control systems: (1) open-loop control systems, and (2) closed-loop control systems. Closed-loop control systems are the more important of these two classes, but it is essential to understand the principles of each class because both have important applications.

A typical block diagram is shown in Exhibit 5. It contains all of the five

EXHIBIT 5   Components of Typical Closed-Loop Control System

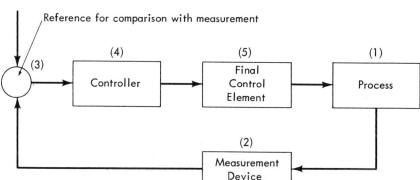

essential elements of a closed-loop control system, which include: (1) the process, (2) measuring element, (3) error detecting mechanism, (4) controller, and (5) final control element.

The easiest example to use for explaining the interrelationships in such a system is the heating of a building. In this case the process is the circulation of a heating medium (steam) through the pipes. When the measuring element (thermometer in the room) registers a temperature below that set as the reference, the controller (thermostat) detects the difference and initiates action on the valve (final control element) to open and let more hot steam flow through the pipes. The valve remains open until the temperature in the room equals the reference temperature, at which time the controller emits a signal to close the valve. Similar systems control chemical reactions, refinery operations, steel making, liquid levels, pressure, and many other processes.

A closed-loop system such as this enables the process to be controlled by an operator who sets the reference, or set point, and lets the system continually adjust itself to comply with the set requirements.

An open-loop system differs from a closed-loop system in that a human operator reads the measurement and adjusts the control element.

THAMES RAINWEAR COMPANY, LTD.

In January 1970, the management of Thames Rainwear was considering the question of whether it should launch a full-scale program to invade the U.S. market.

Thames Rainwear, located in Belfast, Northern Ireland, was one of a number of divisions comprising the Bateson Group, a large integrated textile company. Other divisions were located in Scotland, England, India, and South Africa, manufacturing yarn, fabrics, and a wide range of apparel. Thames' sole product was rainwear, and the company accounted for a major portion of the U.K. market for that product.

Thames was also an active exporter to Western Europe, but had never done more than token business in the United States. Thames sold both men's and women's rainwear to large-scale chains, department stores, and wholesalers in its home market (U.K.) and Western Europe. However, it sold only men's rainwear, and only through a few specialty stores like Brooks Brothers, in the United States. The U.S. product featured a considerably higher-than-average quality of fabric and workmanship and sold at a somewhat higher-than-average price, compared with the most popular raincoats in U.S. department stores. Thames' sales in the United States had never amounted to more than $100,000 per year.

In terms of expanding its role in the U.S., Thames was contemplating the possibility that it might be able to win 10 percent or more of the U.S. market if it made an all-out attempt to penetrate the same price segment in which London Fog was dominant—$30 to $50 retail. However, Thames' executives were frankly apprehensive of London Fog's strength, and awed by the size of the U.S. market.

With the resources of the Bateson Group behind it, Thames could match the promotional outlays of any U.S. manufacturer except London Fog. Also, it could deliver garments of quality superior to London Fog's at $60 per dozen less (manufacturer's price) than London Fog.

Thames commissioned Multinational Business Associates (MBA), to study the U.S. market, for a fee of $10,000. MBA, using published sources and the results of a questionnaire mailed to a national sample of over 10,000 consumers, reported the data summarized in Exhibits 1 through 20. In addition, MBA interviewed department store and specialty store buyers, and made these comments:

> Most large department stores in the United States are usually part of national chains, each store, however, having its own distinct name and usually maintaining its own local "image." For example, Allied Stores Corporation, with headquarters in New York City, has annual sales of over a billion dollars and 45,000 employees, with stores in New York City, Boston, Miami, Dallas, Seattle, and 115 other cities.

(Text continues on p. 132.)

EXHIBIT 1   U.S. Rainwear Shipments, 1958–1975
(Millions of dollars at factory prices *)

	Total	Men's & Boys'	Women's & Misses'	Children
1958	$102	$ 60	$ 38	$ 3
*				
1963	171	79	82	10
1964	177	71	93	13
1965	188	84	91	13
*				
1968	200	90	94	16
		—estimates—		
1970	217	100	100	17
1971	225	104	104	17
1972	233	108	108	17
1973	240	111	111	18
1974	248	115	115	18
1975	256	119	119	18

* The typical wholesale markup is 15%; the typical retail markup, 40%. Most large manufacturers, like London Fog, sell directly to all large retail outlets.

Source of 1958–1968 figures: U.S. Department of Commerce.

EXHIBIT 2   Retail Sales of Apparel, Population, and Income by Region
(as percent of total United States)

	Apparel Sales	Population	Disposable Income
New England	7%	6%	6%
Middle Atlantic	22	18	20
South Atlantic	14	15	14
East North Central	19	20	21
West North Central	7	8	8
East South Central	5	6	5
West South Central	9	10	8
Mountain	4	4	4
Pacific	13	13	14

Notes for Exhibit 2 are found on p. 124.

EXHIBIT 2 (cont.)

> Note: Total U.S. annual sales of general merchandise stores, including department stores, are approximately $70 billion; department stores, $45 billion; specialty apparel stores, $20 billion. Total population is 200 million; total disposable income, $780 billion.
>
> Source: Adapted from *Sales Management,* Survey of Buying Power; U.S. Bureau of Labor Statistics.

EXHIBIT 3 20 Metropolitan Areas in 6 Rainfall Categories, 1955–1967 averages

Annual Amount of Rainfall (inches)	*Area*
0–10	Phoenix, Arizona
11–20	Los Angeles, California
	San Francisco, California
	Denver, Colorado
21–30	Minn.–St. Paul, Minnesota
	Detroit, Michigan
31–40	Chicago, Illinois
	Pittsburgh, Pennsylvania
	Cleveland, Ohio
	St. Louis, Missouri
	Kansas City, Missouri
	Seattle, Washington
41–50	New York, New York
	Philadelphia, Pennsylvania
	Boston, Massachusetts
	Washington, D.C.
	Houston, Texas
	Atlanta, Georgia
51–60	Miami, Florida
	New Orleans, Louisiana

Source: U.S. Department of Commerce.

EXHIBIT 4   Rainwear Distribution by Type of Outlet

	Men		Women	
	Last Purchase	Next Purchase	Last Purchase	Next Purchase
Department store	47%	55%	59%	72%
Specialty store	30	30	19	15
Chain clothing store	8	8	7	7
Discount store	6	4	7	3
Other	9	3	9	4

Source: MBA Consumer Survey.

EXHIBIT 5   Rainwear Prices, 1958–1968
(average dollars per dozen, wholesale) *

	Men's & Boys'	Women's & Misses'
1958	$ 69	$53
1965	124	83
1968	141	80

* This average is calculated using *all* price ranges, including the low-priced plastic coats.

Source: U.S. Department of Commerce.

EXHIBIT 6   Retail Rainwear Prices Paid by Consumers

	Men		Women	
	Last Purchase	Next Purchase	Last Purchase	Next Purchase
Under $10	8%	3%	9%	2%
$10–19.99	17	8	28	13
$20–39.99	40	37	38	44
$40–69.99	31	46	22	38
$70 and over	4	7	2	3
	100%	100%	100%	100%

Source: MBA Consumer Survey.

EXHIBIT 7   Style Preferences for Next Purchase
             Percent of Total Reporting

Preferred Style	Men	Women
With belt	19	42
Without belt	81	58
Slash-through pockets	81	72
Regular patch pockets	19	28
Tailored	34	53
Loose	66	47

Source: MBA Consumer Survey.

EXHIBIT 8   Brand Identification
             Percentage of Raincoats Owned which Respondents
             Identify by Brand (see important note at bottom of table)

	Most Recent Purchase		2nd Oldest Coat		3rd Oldest Coat	
	Men	Women	Men	Women	Men	Women
Alligator	8	0	6	1	1	0
Gleneagles	5	0	1	0	0	0
Cable	0	1	0	0	0	0
Baracuta	2	1	1	0	0	0
Rainfair	3	0	2	0	0	0
London Fog	22	15	7	6	1	5
Aquascutum	1	1	0	1	1	0
Other Brands * (mainly private brands)	34	76	24	35	4	7
Unidentified by Brand	25	6	59	41	93	87
TOTAL	100	100	100	100	100	100

* Other brands row consists of numerous private brands and dealer brands with no specific one being predominant.

Note: In terms of absolute figures only the *most recent purchase* scores are meaningful, because the form of the question asked did not insure faithful reporting on the *second oldest* and *third oldest*. In relative terms, however, it is significant that London Fog's gain over the three years is so much greater than that of any other brand.

Source: MBA Consumer Survey.

EXHIBIT 9 Brand Preferences
(percent of those responding)

	Alligator	London Fog	Other Brands	Don't Care
Total Respondents *	10	44	8	26
By age:				
Under 20	5	58	13	16
20–35	5	50	8	24
36–55	15	42	6	26
55+	12	36	8	32
By income:				
High	13	43	9	23
Medium	11	46	5	27
Low	8	41	3	37
Students	1	53	16	20
By education:				
High school	12	44	4	28
College	9	47	9	24
Grad. school	10	41	9	27
By sex:				
Male	12	45	6	25
Female	4	43	10	30

* Some 12% did not answer the question.

Note: Answers to a question on what the respondent wanted if his/her name was drawn for a free raincoat are almost identical with the above.

Source: MBA Consumer Survey.

EXHIBIT 10   Ranking of Brands *

	Actual Price	Appraised Price **	Appraised Quality **
Aquascutum	1	4	5
Gleneagles	2	3	3
Alligator	3	2	2
London Fog ***	4	1	1
Baracuta	5	6	4
Rainfair	6	5	6
Cable	7	7	7

* #1 for the highest price, #2 for the next highest price, and so on.

** Appraised: that is, as ranked by consumers on returned questionnaires.

*** 19% of the men and 21% of the women who owned a London Fog thought it was made in England (actually manufactured in the United States).

Source: MBA Consumer Survey.

EXHIBIT 11   Men's and Boys' Rainwear Imports to the United States—
1967

	Value ($ thousands)	$ per doz.
Japan	$1,870	$ 58.54
Israel	805	68.78
Italy	800	176.90
United Kingdom	738	233.99
Spain	720	149.60
Canada	592	197.05
Hong Kong	578	55.73
Jamaica	415	61.21
Other	1,500	82.04
Total	$8,018	

Source: U.S. Department of Commerce, U.S. Imports of Merchandise for Consumption, FT 125-135 series.

EXHIBIT 12   Raincoat Prices, by Income Levels *

Price Paid	High		Medium		Low	
Under $10	8%		9%		12%	
$10–19.99	15		23		28	
20–39.99	42	} 72	39	} 65	36	} 60
40–69.99	30		26		24	
70 and over	5		2		1	

* Questionnaires were coded to indicate the income level of the areas to which they were sent.

Source: MBA Consumer Survey.

EXHIBIT 13   Raincoat Prices, by Age Groups

Price Paid	Under 20 years		20–35		36–55		Over 55 years	
Under $10	5%		5%		10%		12%	
$10–19.99	34		21		20		17	
20–39.99	37	} 61	40	} 70	38	} 66	41	} 67
40–69.99	24		30		28		26	
70 and over	0		3		4		4	

Source: MBA Consumer Survey.

EXHIBIT 14   Raincoat Prices, by Education Levels

Price Paid	High School		College		Graduate School	
Under $10	14%		7%		6%	
$10–19.99	26		18		17	
20–39.99	41	} 59	37	} 70	44	} 75
40–69.99	18		33		31	
70 and over	1		6		2	

Source: MBA Consumer Survey.

EXHIBIT 15   Outlets, by Income Levels

Where Bought	High	Medium	Low
Department store	51%	54%	50%
Specialty store	32	21	21
Discount store	5	6	11
Chain clothing store	6	7	6
Other	6	12	11

Source: MBA Consumer Survey.

EXHIBIT 16   Outlets, by Age Groups

Where Bought	Under 20 years	20–35	36–55	Over 55 years
Department store	50%	45%	53%	56%
Specialty store	18	29	26	26
Discount store	16	6	7	4
Chain clothing store	13	10	6	5
Other	3	10	8	9

Source: MBA Consumer Survey.

EXHIBIT 17   Outlets, by Education Levels

Where Bought	High School	College	Graduate School
Department store	54%	49%	49%
Specialty store	20	29	31
Discount store	11	4	5
Chain clothing store	6	8	8
Other	10	9	7

Source: MBA Consumer Survey.

EXHIBIT 18   Multiple Ownership of Raincoats by Rainfall Areas

Areas in Rainfall Inches	Total Respondents	Total Reporting at Least One Coat	Those with Second Coat	Those with Third Coat
0–10	39	34*	4*	1*
11–20	136	84	44	4
21–30	122	60	49	7
31–40	301	149	109	35
41–50	331	183	110	27
51–60	56	37*	13*	3*
Total	985	547	329	77

* The number of respondents in these categories is too small to be significant.

Source: MBA Consumer Survey.

EXHIBIT 19   Timing of Last Purchase of Raincoat by Rainfall Areas

Rainfall Areas in Inches	Less than One Year Ago	1–2 Years Ago	Over 2 Years Ago	Total
0–10*	8*	7*	24*	39*
11–20	38	48	50	136
21–30	46	38	38	122
31–40	128	91	82	301
41–50	137	8	113	258
51–60*	19*	13*	24*	56*
Total	376	205	331	912

* The number of respondents in these categories is too small to be significant.

Source: MBA Consumer Survey.

EXHIBIT 20   Profile of London Fog Customers

Percent of London Fog Customers who:

Bought last coat from:	Men	Women
Department store	48%	85%
Specialty store	40	15
Paid for last coat:		
$20–$39.99	34%	41%
40– 69.99	58	56
70 and over	4	0
Are willing to pay for next raincoat:		
$20–$39.99	25%	36%
40– 69.99	62	59
70 and over	10	5
Are in age group:		
20–35 years	45%	31%*
36–55 years	36	51
Have education through:		
High school	20%	31%
College	53	51
Graduate school	27	18

* There is some indication from buyer interviews and scattered consumer questionnaires that, in the younger women's market, London Fog is being eroded by Misty Harbor.

Source: MBA Consumer Survey.

Department stores, including the national chains, are well staffed with professional buyers. They do much of their buying of rainwear in New York City, where manufacturers, at stated periods, hold "shows" to display their merchandise and take orders. Frequently the "orders" are for manufacture and delivery of styles and types that the buyers request on the basis of their knowledge of what will sell best locally at their various stores.

These buyers can be a big help to any manufacturer entering the market for the first time—or a big obstacle. So it is significant that our buyer survey indicates some definite dissatisfaction with the currently dominant brand, London Fog, and some apparent readiness to welcome a strong newcomer, particularly if the newcomer should be disposed to market and merchandise in line with their (the buyers') ideas of what is best for their own type of operation.

Specialty clothing shops, which usually specialize in quality apparel for men or women or both at higher prices and margins, offer another potential outlet for Thames' product. Brooks Brothers, Bonwit Teller, Roger Kent, Lord & Taylor, and Saks Fifth Avenue are examples of specialty shops, although there are many smaller ones of strictly local reputation. Some of the specialty shops advertise in the daily press and quality magazines (e.g., *The New Yorker*). Also, some of the specialty shops, like Brooks Brothers, have a number of outlets. There are also chains of women's specialty stores that are less quality-oriented and lower-priced, such as Touraine and Lerner shops.

One of the particularly valuable features of the higher-grade specialty shops, from the customer's viewpoint, is personal customer relations that frequently develop with the sales staff in contrast to department store service, which is usually impersonal. So if the sales staff of these specialty shops can be won over to a new brand, there is an excellent opportunity for immediate sizable sales from this category of outlet.

Price cutting or discounting is common in most kinds of retailing in the United States, but is concentrated mostly in lower-quality, limited-line chains and discount stores. These stores try to expand sales volume by selling at very low prices with slim margins, depending on volume, high turnover ratios (low inventories), and low overhead to generate profits. Also, they often bypass national brands. Accordingly, they are not considered suitable outlets to be cultivated in behalf of a product like Thames', whose quality is important to many consumers, and which has the potential to win a substantial following in the consumer market. Advertising is usually done by radio, very heavy direct mail, and the daily press. Korvette, Zayre, and White Front Store are examples of the largest discount house chains in the United States.

Is Thames justified in trying to win a substantial share of the U.S. rainwear market? If so, what should be its distribution strategy?

4

PROMOTIONAL POLICY

Promotion is the most complex element in the marketing mix and the most difficult to carry out efficiently. Yet it can be highly productive when properly used, particularly for the purpose of changing buyers' attitudes and intentions. Promotion has a mix of its own—media advertising, direct mail, packaging, display, personal selling, and so on—and one of the toughest marketing decisions is how much expenditure to allocate to these various elements.

Promotion can play all sorts of roles—directly influencing ultimate consumers, enthusing distributors, opening the door for salesmen, soliciting inquiries for follow-up, and so on. Promotion can perform various parts of the total selling task—getting attention, developing interest, building acceptance, creating preference, and actually making the sale—or all of them at once, because it affects individuals who are at different stages in the process of coming to a purchasing decision. Finally, promotion has different time dimensions: it can lead to immediate buying action, or it can build a brand image that will pay off, like an investment, over time.

One practical way to plan promotion is first to analyze the total marketing effort and decide what it must accomplish to move the product successfully; then determine what parts of that effort can be most efficiently performed by the various kinds of promotion. Efficiency will depend on the coverage and cost of available communication means—salesmen, advertising media (e.g., magazines, radio, TV, newspapers), or displays—for reaching the potential customers for that particular product. It will also depend on the receptiveness of buyers to promotional messages, in turn based on the degree of their need or interest, the importance of the product to them, the difficulty of judging quality, and so on.

The purpose of promotion is to expand demand. It can be used both to build people's willingness and desire to buy a product, say an automobile, and to buy a particular brand or make, say a Ford or Chevrolet. Today, the most prevalent form of competition is among different brands, though the cumulative impact of many sellers promoting their own brands still has the effect of increasing total demand. And since so many brands are not greatly dissimilar, competition takes the form of promotion designed to make the small advantage of a given brand have more meaning in buyers' minds. There are many different kinds of buyers, with different interests and values, so there is plenty of scope for different appeals.

Marketers often succeed in building a body of customers who are loyal in the sense that they continue to buy the same brand most of the time, but there is always active competition for the pool of buyers who are not fully committed—who are not yet loyal to a brand or who are about to desert a brand because of dissatisfaction. Everybody fights to secure an increasing share of the market.

How much time and money can be put into the promotional task depends on how much margin per unit and how much volume the marketer has, or can expect to get. So the effect must be estimated in order to decide on the size of the budget, recognizing that advertising and selling are intended to cause the market to buy more than it otherwise would. The crucial question is always whether the advertising will bring in more net dollars than it costs, either now or in the future.

BETTER SOAP COMPANY

(Alfredo Alcindor, the advertising manager of the Better Soap Company, which had recently been organized to manufacture and sell soap in Puerto Rico, was discussing advertising strategy with Roberto Rivera, the marketing research director, and Pablo Perello, Ph.D., a consulting psychologist.)

ADVERTISING MANAGER.   Before we decide how much to spend on advertising our detergent washing powder, I think we ought to formulate a little strategy.

MARKETING RESEARCH DIRECTOR.   Well, we do know something about how women feel toward washing powders. I've seen a study made in the United States which indicates that housewives have very little motivation behind their decisions to purchase one or another of the various soap and detergent brands. This lack of motivation is ascribed to an almost complete lack of favorable attitudes toward washing and cleaning upon which to base motivational appeals, and to the failure of the soap companies to develop advertising copy which would at least contain elements or situations appealing to the more general emotional values of women.

ADVERTISING MANAGER.   That doesn't help us very much, Roberto, even if we knew that women in this country felt the same. What about it, Dr. Perello?

PSYCHOLOGIST.   Oh, I suspect that women everywhere are the same in that they get less satisfaction out of doing the laundry than they do from many other of their housekeeping activities, such as cooking for example. When a woman prepares a meal she can see her family enjoying it, but washing clothes isn't very exciting or rewarding.

ADVERTISING MANAGER. You mean, then, that motivations don't apply to soap?

PSYCHOLOGIST. Oh no, women must have *some* feelings, other than superficial attitudes on cleaning, whitening, brightening, and so forth, toward the various soap brands. After weighing the rational product claims, women tend to buy the brand that "suits themselves" or, to put it another way, fits their own personalities. While attitudes toward soaps and detergents may not be strong enough to be considered "motivations," in the sense of basic human drives, they nevertheless exist, and taken together they constitute the "product image" of a brand.

ADVERTISING MANAGER. So what? How do we try to take business away from Kit, which happens to be the largest selling brand here? As a matter of fact, it accounts for over half of total sales of mild detergents. No other brand has even 20 percent of the market.

MARKETING RESEARCH DIRECTOR. I think I can throw some light on that. We did a survey that shows Kit buyers have different kinds of personalities from buyers of other brands taken as a whole. For example, when we gave housewives a list of twenty adjectives and asked them to choose the ten that they thought best described themselves, all of them tended to choose adjectives like friendly, dependable, practical, healthy, and hardworking, rather than pretty, lovable, appealing.

PSYCHOLOGIST. That's their self-image. It doesn't mean they don't like to think of themselves as appealing, pretty, and so on, but just that they put more premium on other virtues than the feminine, frilly ones.

MARKETING RESEARCH DIRECTOR. You know, Dr. Perello, the funny thing is that when we went on and asked them to name the adjectives that best described what their husbands wanted them to be, they chose almost the opposite qualities. Then they did choose the feminine ones.

ADVERTISING MANAGER. What a bunch of frustrated females!

PSYCHOLOGIST. Not necessarily, Sr. Alcindor. Maybe they're just realists.

MARKETING RESEARCH DIRECTOR. Well, that's where the Kit users come in the strongest. Compared with non-Kit users, they tend to rate themselves lower on the feminine adjectives like pretty, appealing, and at the same time they rate their husbands' desires even higher.

ADVERTISING MANAGER. How can that help us, Roberto?

MARKETING RESEARCH DIRECTOR. Well, we just have to do our advertising so that our product image fits that self-image.

PSYCHOLOGIST. Or maybe you should do the reverse. I'm a psychologist, not a marketing man, but maybe the non-Kit users, although representing a smaller potential market, are more susceptible to new advertising appeals and thus represent a better possible payoff.

What advertising strategy should Better Soap follow in terms of the kind of housewives to appeal to and the kind of appeals to use? How does your decision affect packaging, brand name, and advertising?

CANTWELL PACKING COMPANY

Cantwell Packing Company's vice-president in charge of sales, Mr. Harold McGowan, attended a meeting about the proposed fall–winter advertising budget with the company's advertising agency, Hamilton & Calston.

Cantwell packed tomato ketchup, tomato juice cocktail, sliced pickled beets, red cabbage, canned tomatoes, and succotash—all for distribution throughout New England. Its selling prices were about 10 percent less than those of nationally advertised brands; thus its shelf prices in the supermarket also were usually a few cents lower.

Cantwell had retained Hamilton & Calston for a number of years. In the past year, as in the four preceding years, Cantwell's sales totaled slightly over $3 million, with a before-tax profit of about $195,000. The year's advertising budget was $120,000—evenly divided between the spring–summer and fall–winter campaigns.

Agency's Campaign Plan

At the meeting, the agency presented the following plan for the six-month fall–winter campaign.

AIMS

Whenever we submit a plan for advertising and sales promotion, we feel that our client has every right to ask: "What will this advertising do for me?" "What will I get back for the money I spend?"

This plan has three aims: to gain new consumers, to sell more Cantwell products to present consumers, and to move *all* Cantwell products. The first is the big objective; the other two are corollaries.

SALES POTENTIALS

The first question we should face when thinking about adding Cantwell customers in New England, or adding sales by whatever means, is the size of the market. Is there room in this market for more Cantwell sales? Is the market saturated? Is competition so strong that no further progress can be made?

A panel survey among housewives on food products shows, for example, that New England contains 5.8 percent of the U.S. population and accounts for 5.4 percent of ketchup sales. In short, it is just slightly on the minus side of being a completely normal market for this product.

If we apply 5.4 percent to the annual national sales of ketchup, we find that New England probably purchased 1,677,000 cases (24 bottles per case). Your sales constitute but a small part of this total. No brand of ketchup is so strongly entrenched in this territory that it makes a successful bid for new business by Cantwell in any way impossible.

The picture is much the same for canned tomatoes and tomato juice. The figures for succotash show a total estimated New England consumption of only 18,400 cases. No figures as to potential seem to be available on pickled beets or red cabbage.

The local representative of a national packer has told us that he believed there was good opportunity for sales increase in the New England market for canned tomatoes, and that his company's sales were slowly increasing.

He was not optimistic about increasing sales for pickled beets and red cabbage. He had recently made a survey on red cabbage, and reported that distribution in New England for red cabbage of all brands was poor, sales volume weak, and demand almost nonexistent. In view of this, we do not believe that your advertising should devote more than mere mention or listing of red cabbage as a Cantwell product.

As to national growth, the demand for ketchup and chili sauce has evidently more than doubled during the past ten years, and there is no reason to believe that this trend will not continue. Demand for tomato juice has increased 90 percent during the same period. On the other hand, demand for canned tomatoes and for canned beets has shown but slight increase.

Our conclusion is that there is more than enough market in New England for the types of products you offer to warrant an effort to sell more Cantwell items, and that no competitor is strong enough in this territory to stymie your effort.

HOW MUCH IS A NEW CONSUMER WORTH?

Possibly you have never had occasion to consider sales from just this angle, "How much is a new consumer worth?" Actually, of course, we mean a new family of consumers, for whom the wife and mother is the purchasing agent.

Newspapers and magazines figure that it is worth an investment of $10 to $20 to get a new subscriber.

Published statistics indicate that the average New England family spends $1,530 per year in food stores. It is obvious, then, that the value of a new customer of a food store runs into many dollars.

Let us endeavor to pin this down a bit further. If we assume that a food store chain gets no more than a fourth of the $1,530 a family spends annually for food, that amounts to $382. If their gross profit is 20 percent, the figure of gross profit per customer comes to $76. It seems to us that a new customer would easily be worth this gross profit.

Another way to look at it is to consider the cost of trading stamps, which some chain stores use, amounting to up to two cents per dollar of sales. The obvious first purpose of the trading stamp offer is to get more of the consumer's food dollar. If a store is now getting $382 per year of the customer's food expenditure, it is obvious that it is shooting for the other three-quarters, or $1,148. In short, it is investing $7.64 to get additional gross of $1,148. *This expenditure is in addition to all advertising and all other sales promotion.* It gives a little inkling as to what a customer is worth.

Let us now refer to another food store chain. Unit sales per week (average for one store) on ketchup amount to 542 bottles, on which the gross store profit is $43.36. Similar figures on tomato juice are 424 cans with a gross store profit of $42.40. On canned tomatoes the similar figures are 562 cans per week at a gross profit to the store of $44.96. No breakdown is given for canned beets or red cabbage. The figures for succotash are 12 cans per week at a gross store profit of 98¢. On these four items alone the store has a weekly gross profit of $131, or more than $6,500 annually.

We realize that this may not be the picture of the average store. It does, however, show what products such as yours contribute to the profit of a well-conducted supermarket.

We shall now attempt to arrive at some idea of what a new customer is worth to Cantwell. Undoubtedly you could do a better job in making such an estimate than we can, because you may draw upon your figures of cost and profit as well as deeper knowledge of your own business.

We earlier derived an estimate of 1,677,000 cases of ketchup as the normal New England demand. In this area there are 3,891,500 households. Thus, the average annual consumption per household of ketchup is 0.431 cases or approximately 10 bottles; or, at 40¢ per bottle, the expenditure is $4. We can only make an assumption on the similar figures for your other items, but, all told, we roughly estimate that of items such as you provide, the total annual expenditure per year is $12. Of this figure perhaps $3 represents your gross profit.

The question then is: How much is it worth to you to gain an added $3 of gross profit? Judging from what other lines of business pay and are willing to pay for a new consumer household, we believe the gaining of a new customer who buys and continues to buy Cantwell products is well worth two years' gross profit, or $6.

Our proposed campaign for New England, as you will see shortly, costs $65,000-$70,000. If our sole aim were to obtain new customers, this would mean that the advertising and sales promotion, plus the added effort of your brokers, must net approximately 11,250 new Cantwell households to make your advertising and sales promotion investment pay off, not immediately, but let us say within two or three years. We believe it is perfectly possible to reach this goal of obtaining 11,250 new customers.

As previously stated, this is a rough way of estimating a goal and of evaluating it. We think, however, that the evaluation of this is low rather than high.

The corollary aim of selling more Cantwell products to present household customers and the aim of broadening the public consciousness and acceptance of Cantwell, may simply be put down as plus values, although they are actually much more than that.

You have told us that because of a short crop of tomatoes, the size of your pack on Cantwell ketchup will be limited. Your feeling is that you can sell all of this pack without resort to advertising or sales promotion.

We believe that it would be a grave mistake not to advertise Cantwell ketchup. It is the best-known item in your line. It is the one product with which the public associates the name Cantwell.

One of the objects of your advertising is to build public acceptance of Cantwell, and your ketchup is the vehicle for such advertising. To call a halt in the advertising of your best known product means losing ground. You have years of investment in the advertising of this product. You surely do not wish to jeopardize this investment. Therefore, you should continue to advertise ketchup as a matter of insurance for the future.

There is a second reason why we want to include Cantwell ketchup in all advertising, even though the stress of the advertising will be put on canned tomatoes or pickled beets: the advertising vitally needs the quick Cantwell identification by reader or listener, which only your ketchup provides. Accordingly, we recommend that the ad budget for the fall–winter campaign be increased to $70,000.

Proposal for Consumer Deals or Premiums

The agency went on to propose that the money be spent in a campaign involving deals or premiums. Reproduced below are the sections of the agency's report which set forth this proposition.

PROPOSAL

The next point is: How can we attract a new user or get a present user to buy canned tomatoes, pickled beets, or other Cantwell items? We know that it cannot be done to the extent desired with plain, straightaway advertising of the Cantwell line. We must provide some sort of a "come-on." There are three types of come-ons that would fit: a prize contest, a money-back offer, and a premium offer.

The first come-on possibility is a contest with a Cadillac, or a trip to Paris, perhaps, as a prize. To put over such a contest requires a great deal of consumer advertising. Such a message can be printed on or enclosed in a box or bag so that every package becomes an incentive to buy more. This procedure is more difficult with canned goods, in which case newspaper or television advertising would have to carry practically the whole load. The advertising cost would be far more than we can recommend.

The second come-on is a money-back offer of some sort. We wish to start the campaign with a "be our guest" offer. If the housewife will buy a bottle of famous Cantwell Tomato Ketchup and a can of Cantwell Sliced Tomatoes, or a jar of Cantwell Pickled Beets, she may send in the labels, together with her name and address, and receive promptly a shiny quarter.

From the Cantwell standpoint, there are good and bad points about such an offer. Let's take the bad points first. An offer of this nature works best when introducing a new product, especially if the new product is really novel or glamorous. It works less well for staples such as canned goods. Such an offer fits best where two products can be banded together or where, at least, they are on the same counters or shelves. We can't band Cantwell Ketchup and Sliced Tomatoes together, and the shelves where they are displayed may be several aisles apart.

On the bright side is the fact that offers of this kind on food products are extremely popular today, as you may see by viewing the food advertising in almost any newspaper. The further fact is that this offer *will* sell some Cantwell merchandise which would not otherwise be sold. It *will* bring some new customers.

Finally, it provides us with something new—the bang that we want to start a new program with advertising and sales promotion.

Actually, we are positive that you will have to refund relatively few quarters. Many women, we hope, will buy two Cantwell items, fully intending to ask for the 25-cent refund. But experience shows that only a very small percentage carry out this initial intention. Some forget to save the labels. Others save the labels but never get around to sending them in.

Generally, no more than 3 to 5 percent of the women who buy take advantage of such offers. Assuming we run the 25-cent redemption offer for thirty days, the estimated cost figure will be based on one-twelfth of your annual ketchup sale in the New England territory. You sold approximately 1,400,000 bottles last year, so an average monthly sale is 117,000 bottles. If we take 5 percent as the expected redemption rate this represents 5,850 bottles, or, at 25¢ a bottle plus 15¢ postage and handling, the estimated cost of refund to you is less than $2,500.

By no means should the success or failure of the plan, if adopted, be judged by the small number of labels that we expect would be actually sent to you.

RECOMMENDATION

The final come-on would be some sort of premium. This involves finding a premium that, in your case, has strong appeal to housewives and can be offered on a self-liquidating basis, at a price well below the price the housewife would have to pay for the premium if she had to buy it in the store. This will surely help to sell your product, without costing you a cent.

We have reviewed many possible premiums and recommend for consideration the use of two kitchen knives made by a large, famous manufacturer and distributor of kitchenware. The knives are seven in number, from which we have chosen two—a 9½-inch ham-and-bread slicer and an 8-inch French Chef knife. Each represents a $3.75 retail value that can be offered at $1 each. These knives are new and have never been previously offered as premiums.

We believe they offer unusual value to the housewife, and it is part of our advertising task to convey the extraordinary value to her. The kitchenware maker will handle all details. As mail requests arrive, you simply bundle them together and forward to his nearest distributing office.

The kitchenware manufacturer requires no payment from you and no guarantee of the number of knives that will be required. He will report to you weekly or monthly, as you desire, on the number of requests received and filled.

We believe that if this alternative is adopted, the kitchenware manufacturer should be supplied with some sort of folder or stuffer on Cantwell products that may also serve as a "thank you" note and can be enclosed with each knife or pair of knives sent out.

A second premium possibility, but one that would have to be used late in the campaign because of its seasonal appeal, consists of ten regular packets of popular flower seeds to liquidate as a premium for 50¢. These seeds would cost $3 across the counter in any garden supply or hardware store. This premium is made available by one of the largest seed houses in the country, whose seeds are known everywhere for their high quality. The company will handle all details, as in the case with the knives. The seed house imposes two conditions: you cannot have this offer if some other concern competing with your line has already contracted with it; and it must be satisfied that you are going to do a bona fide job of advertising on this premium and that its name will be mentioned in such advertising. By all means, we would want to mention the seed house's name in this advertising, because the name is an asset.

We suggest that if the knife or seed premium appeals to you, we be authorized to confirm the arrangement with the company immediately, to prevent the possibility of its being sold to one of your competitors. We wish to warn you against judging the success or failure of the campaign by the number of premiums sold. Popularity of the premium is of secondary importance and is not the criterion on which to judge the success of the campaign.

The cost of newspaper advertising to support any of these promotional programs would be $55,000 to $60,000. Store display and other expenses would be an additional $10,000.

Decision

Mr. McGovern promised to make a decision on the size of the budget and the campaign plan within a week. He also had available to guide him the results of a study of brand loyalty. (See the Appendix below.)

Should Cantwell plan to increase its level of advertising expenditures for the fall–winter campaign? For the long run? What can Cantwell do to increase its market share? What part of its product line should it promote? Which of the alternative campaign plans is preferable? Why? What bearing do the loyalty phenomena described in the Appendix have on Cantwell's problem?

Appendix: Brand Loyalty [1]

The selection of products for the study was based primarily on maximum housewife influence in brand determination and reasonably wide usage. The products chosen were: toilet soap, scouring cleanser, regular coffee (not instant), canned peas, margarine, frozen orange juice, and headache tablets.

A three-year period was chosen in order to be entirely sure of having enough time to reveal complete patterns of buying behavior with respect to loyalty or disloyalty.

The data indicate quite conclusively that a significant amount of brand loyalty does exist *within individual product groups*. (This is not to be confused with brand loyalty *across* product groups—i.e., loyalty proneness on the part of the consumer generally.)

Exhibit 1 lists the brand loyalty to individual products of each of the 66 different families who purchased seven products in above-threshold quantities. This gives a detailed picture which is useful for what it does not show, as well as for what it does show. Within these figures are plenty of instances of high brand loyalty, which show up better when the loyalty percentages are ranked separately for each product (as in Exhibit 2). But, only by looking at such an overall picture as this one, demonstrating the absence of any uniform patterns among families as to their degrees of loyalty to the different products, can we see how definitely brand loyalty is tied to individual products.

Exhibit 2 dramatizes the presence of brand loyalty among the same 66 families more forcefully by presenting the data in deciles—that is, the average loyalty to each product of the most loyal 10 percent, the second

[1] Adapted from Ross Cunningham, "Brand Loyalty—What, Where, How Much?," *Harvard Business Review*, Jan.-Feb. 1956.

EXHIBIT 1   66 Seven-Product Families Indicate that They Have
Varying Degrees of Single-Brand Loyalty to Different
Products (Percent of total-product purchases
represented by the most favored brand)

Family Number	Toilet Soap	Scouring Cleanser	Regular Coffee	Canned Peas	Margarine	Frozen Orange Juice	Headache Tablets
1	58.7	88.2	73.8	43.7	44.9	47.2	54.2
2	40.5	58.8	56.2	12.8	37.2	26.7	40.2
3	68.0	47.9	64.8	34.3	53.6	63.2	100.0
4	72.8	52.7	50.7	48.9	77.3	50.0	100.0
5	74.5	79.5	82.8	44.3	33.1	50.6	34.2
6	30.3	45.9	50.0	57.6	73.3	97.5	60.0
7	49.5	92.1	64.2	44.7	36.0	98.0	75.7
8	42.4	50.0	74.3	73.5	53.8	59.2	100.0
9	24.2	45.4	88.9	39.7	93.2	35.7	72.9
10	24.3	57.1	70.2	84.4	48.6	67.9	49.4
11	42.1	73.4	91.0	42.4	98.9	85.4	98.1
12	61.7	33.3	45.5	24.9	35.7	23.1	43.0
13	37.5	57.1	56.5	27.6	57.1	44.5	42.1
14	58.4	57.6	78.2	93.2	72.9	36.6	68.1
15	55.0	100.0	37.0	25.8	44.4	53.1	65.8
16	37.6	51.0	30.6	34.7	72.0	46.6	65.6
17	76.1	92.5	98.7	24.9	35.3	76.4	69.1
18	26.7	45.7	52.1	31.2	48.9	59.4	84.3
19	90.4	36.5	61.4	38.0	75.0	19.1	47.4
20	38.3	55.8	62.0	59.2	57.1	50.5	70.8
21	17.2	39.5	88.0	45.2	40.0	35.3	64.1
22	45.9	74.7	63.0	27.1	67.6	87.9	23.8
23	38.9	40.9	55.7	34.3	41.0	46.3	90.9
24	69.7	51.8	76.1	43.6	98.3	32.8	59.8
25	51.6	35.3	84.8	38.2	50.0	35.8	50.7
26	86.1	46.1	61.5	47.5	83.3	91.8	48.5
27	48.0	59.3	55.4	23.2	49.3	38.1	28.6
28	29.9	35.9	33.0	46.9	69.2	77.0	70.8
29	35.3	58.3	76.1	86.4	76.9	84.7	87.3
30	40.1	61.9	72.3	54.3	37.9	47.2	93.0
31	40.0	48.8	90.2	55.9	50.4	28.4	50.0
32	55.7	38.5	24.2	38.8	77.3	30.5	46.7
33	26.0	60.5	56.7	27.5	27.1	43.2	77.2
34	32.2	46.3	36.1	26.1	50.0	83.2	87.9
35	28.6	50.7	51.8	40.9	26.6	30.0	51.4
36	87.4	91.7	39.3	50.3	100.0	50.0	84.6
37	46.3	84.6	66.2	82.4	94.9	34.4	98.2
38	82.5	40.0	88.2	57.4	54.5	80.4	47.6

Family Number	Toilet Soap	Scouring Cleanser	Regular Coffee	Canned Peas	Margarine	Frozen Orange Juice	Headache Tablets
39	81.3	42.0	43.6	84.0	57.6	83.8	40.3
40	32.1	33.3	38.9	33.8	69.2	45.6	59.8
41	23.4	29.3	38.2	29.5	23.1	62.4	76.4
42	40.7	39.5	53.0	64.6	29.9	43.2	49.5
43	84.7	97.0	40.9	71.5	34.9	32.1	100.0
44	58.9	31.7	85.4	44.6	47.2	88.5	100.0
45	18.6	46.3	17.5	48.6	65.1	74.3	53.2
46	28.9	94.2	26.1	80.2	100.0	81.8	33.0
47	57.4	70.7	89.8	53.9	70.9	63.6	62.7
48	31.5	80.0	44.4	61.4	70.0	46.7	78.5
49	27.4	51.7	61.7	60.9	79.2	59.3	55.2
50	75.1	60.0	29.0	65.4	71.1	88.9	75.7
51	34.3	39.1	50.0	57.7	61.4	56.4	44.2
52	55.1	63.2	28.0	73.1	45.5	30.0	93.2
53	57.2	100.0	83.2	34.6	80.8	30.8	100.0
54	34.0	32.6	28.8	21.6	27.7	23.2	71.1
55	43.4	70.6	37.1	21.0	63.7	59.3	40.0
56	32.9	22.0	34.3	34.6	29.1	73.1	47.6
57	33.6	62.2	90.4	48.4	38.9	68.4	91.0
58	71.4	50.0	31.1	25.5	26.8	39.4	85.5
59	45.8	81.2	30.4	35.5	31.6	25.0	39.4
60	17.7	33.3	43.7	32.7	49.2	46.4	73.5
61	19.3	33.3	24.3	51.9	40.3	41.2	98.0
62	30.6	50.0	31.2	80.1	75.0	75.0	76.6
63	33.6	70.4	29.4	41.2	42.9	28.9	87.1
64	27.9	40.0	51.5	21.4	87.1	57.9	77.7
65	21.0	46.2	33.9	35.3	22.5	52.8	34.6
66	69.4	64.0	77.5	24.8	90.9	38.6	98.0

most loyal 10 percent, and so on. Naturally, there are differences in brand loyalty ranges between product classes, but these differences are not striking. Loyalties are highest for headache tablets, margarine, and scouring cleanser, and lowest for canned peas and toilet soap. Note that the deciles for the various products will not contain the same families in each case.

Are special price offers powerful incentives to switch brands? To answer this, the purchases made on manufacturers' special price inducements were deducted and favorite-brand percentages calculated on the remainder of the purchases. Exhibit 3 shows resulting decile averages in terms of single-brand loyalty for the same 66-family group as in Exhibit 2.

EXHIBIT 2   66 Seven-Product Families Show Significant Single-Brand Loyalty within Product Groups (Percentile averages for each decile for each product)

Decile	Toilet Soap	Scouring Cleanser	Regular Coffee	Canned Peas	Margarine	Frozen Orange Juice	Headache Tablets
1	84.1	95.4	91.0	84.4	96.6	91.1	99.7
2	72.2	81.4	83.7	68.2	80.8	81.8	95.2
3	60.0	67.8	74.3	57.6	73.6	71.2	86.8
4	52.5	59.8	63.7	50.3	68.7	60.5	77.0
5	43.8	54.9	57.6	45.3	57.9	53.0	72.0
6	39.3	50.1	51.5	41.1	50.4	47.4	64.4
7	34.5	46.3	43.9	35.8	46.1	43.3	54.9
8	31.1	41.3	36.9	32.6	39.2	36.7	48.8
9	27.1	36.9	31.4	26.4	33.8	31.5	43.4
10	20.2	30.8	25.4	21.4	26.1	24.9	33.4

* To be read: Among the most brand-loyal 10 percent of toilet soap purchasers, 84.1 percent were loyal to a single brand. Also, among the least brand-loyal 10 percent of toilet soap purchasers, 20.2 percent were loyal to a single brand.

EXHIBIT 3   Single-Brand Loyalty Figures for 66 Seven-Product Families Are Largely the Same After Special-Offer Purchases Are Deducted (Percentile averages for each decile for each product)

Decile	Toilet Soap	Scouring Cleanser	Regular Coffee	Canned Peas	Margarine	Frozen Orange Juice	Headache Tablets
1	86.5	100.0	91.9	84.5	98.5	91.1	99.7
2	76.1	97.8	84.2	68.4	87.1	81.3	95.2
3	65.6	85.4	76.8	58.5	76.3	71.4	86.8
4	55.0	76.9	65.6	51.5	70.0	60.4	77.0
5	47.3	69.1	57.9	47.1	61.0	52.9	72.0
6	42.5	60.1	52.1	42.3	54.0	47.4	64.4
7	38.0	51.5	44.3	36.3	49.3	42.3	54.9
8	34.1	47.9	37.3	32.7	42.8	36.7	48.8
9	30.0	43.8	31.6	26.8	36.0	31.5	43.4
10	23.5	29.1	25.7	21.5	27.4	25.0	33.4

TAWLAND CORPORATION

A two-year Tawland research and development project resulted in the "Trackmobile," a small gasoline motor-driven vehicle with two sets of tires. One was a set of rubber tires enabling it to travel on pavements; the other, at right angles, was a set of standard railroad wheels so that it could travel on railroad tracks. The rubber-tired wheels could be hydraulically lifted, making it possible for the vehicle to cross a set of tracks, settle down upon them, and continue travel on the tracks.

In the opinion of Tawland executives, the Trackmobile would replace many switching locomotives in use in factory yards. Although it was claimed that the vehicle could pull up to 200 tons, in actual tests the Trackmobile had moved up to 550 tons of loaded freight cars. Traction to move such loads was obtained by means of a hydraulic jack which slightly lifted the first attached freight car, thereby shifting the load to the wheels of the Trackmobile. It was powered by a 60-hp jeep engine, which was sufficient to equal the performance of a 20-ton switch locomotive. Patents had been applied for, but had not yet been granted.

Several factors indicated to executives that a lucrative market existed. The Trackmobile, which in many cases served the same purpose as a switching engine, and was much more versatile, had a much lower capital cost—one-seventh that of a diesel locomotive. Another appeal was its weight, which was only 6,000 pounds, as contrasted to a locomotive, which weighed 100,000 pounds. The Trackmobile was light enough to be transported by plane.

The executives of Tawland Corporation were particularly interested in the aggressive promotion of the Trackmobile because it appeared to them that such an item should be less subject to cyclical fluctuations in demand than the company's other products.

Because executives decided that they did not want to distribute this product directly to the final user, it was evident that some type of distributor was needed. It was finally decided that materials-handling specialists would be the most suitable. These specialists were firms which sold relatively few products, specializing in such items as fork-lift trucks, small tractors, and similar products.

Originally, it had been suggested that the best way of introducing the Trackmobile would be to build a special trailer for it and sell it throughout the country to distributors. However, the vice-president in charge of the wholesale division believed this type of introduction would not be sufficient. He felt it took showmanship to sell distributors and believed that the introductory program must be carefully planned and timed, and that its focus should be a show which was to include a striking demonstration.

Accordingly, a large show was held in Grand Central Station in Chicago. To this show, 300 members of the press, 100 leading industrialists, and 15 to 20 bankers had been invited. It had been arranged to use the station during a time when no trains were scheduled for arrival or departure. Facilities for cocktails, a loudspeaker system, guides, and other features believed necessary for a successful show were included. The Baltimore & Ohio Railroad had made available to the company loaded and unloaded freight cars, coal cars, and switch locomotives. Guests were first invited by mail. If they did not reply, a telegram was sent. If they still had not answered, they were called by telephone. This assured the company that attendance would be good. In order to make sure that a distributor organization would exist to back up the show, executives of Tawland had secretly shown the Trackmobile to 25 distributors and had given them franchises.

The official presentation of the Trackmobile was later described by the vice-president as a "phenomenal" success. The company and product were featured in *Time, Fortune, Business Week,* and several other leading magazines; there were stories in leading newspapers and in many trade journals. The show, which cost $8,000, yielded an advertising return considered to be worth many times this figure. Two months later, the company was still receiving inquiries at the rate of twelve per day, although no advertising expenditures had been made. Although not one Trackmobile had as yet been produced, the company had $900,000 worth of orders on its books.

Tawland executives had come to the conclusion that the distributors should sell the product on the basis of demonstrations in the customers' plants, because experience had indicated that four out of five demonstrations resulted in a sale. In order to assure the proper utilization of the Trackmobiles, the conditions of sale to a user included one clause permitting the distributor to spend up to three days in a customer's plant to instruct the latter's personnel, and another clause stating that the distributor alone was to be allowed to furnish technical service.

The price of a Trackmobile was $15,900 delivered. Distributors paid $12,750 f.o.b. plant. It was carefully pointed out to the distributors, however, that their margin included a $250 provision for the cost of demonstration, $225 freight, $300 cost of instruction, and $125 for three months' service, making the distributor's full cost $13,650.

Was this a well-conceived promotional program? Can Tawland look forward to a good volume of sales? What is involved in building demand for a product like the Trackmobile?

WHITING CORPORATION

The principal product line of the wholesale division of the Whiting Corporation was electric chain hoists, small electrically operated mechanical hoists which had numerous applications throughout industry. Until recently, executives of Whiting Corporation had lacked confidence in the company's ability to distribute the product, because the Whiting name was relatively unknown in the chain hoist business. Executives were inclined to conclude that they could not get the leading mill supply houses to handle the product.

The hoists, which were quoted at an average price of $230 a unit, were generally sold to the final user by the mill supply house salesman who called upon the customer together with Whiting representatives. These customers would sometimes be entertained, and extensive negotiations would often follow.

The new vice-president of the wholesale division became convinced that this type of distribution was both ineffective and unprofitable, because selling expenses exceeded $100 per hoist while the company's gross margin on the product was only $60.

One of the first steps undertaken by the vice-president of the wholesale division was to rewrite the catalogue describing the electric chain hoist in order that it have more appeal to the ultimate buyer and the distributor. The new catalogue emphasized the usefulness of electric chain hoists (see Exhibit 1), whereas the previous catalogue had concerned itself primarily with explaining the technical features of the Whiting product. After the new catalogue was completed, the wholesale division embarked on a program developed by the vice-president, which he called the "cream of the crop" program.

The initial step in the plan was to establish a strong distributor organization. Executives determined the number and type of distributors that were desired in each area. Each salesman was then instructed to call upon the best distributors in his territory in an effort to get them to handle the hoists. In order to assure the selection of good distributors who would aggressively sell the product, the requirement was set that each distributor must maintain at least five electric hoists in stock and have at least three salesmen in his employ.

An adjunct to the "cream of the crop" program was a new discount schedule. The standard trade discount given by manufacturers to distributors was 25 percent and 5 percent. However, in launching the "cream of the crop" plan, additional discounts for volume were to be given. If a distributor, during the first six months of the fiscal year, bought eight hoists, he obtained a retroactive discount of 3 percent. For ten hoists he obtained 4 percent, fifteen hoists 5 percent, twenty-two hoists 7 percent, and thirty hoists 10 percent. These discounts were to be given at the end of each six months' period.

Once the manager of the distributing organization had agreed to cooperate in the "cream of the crop" plan, a sales meeting was arranged for the distributor's salesmen, and the Whiting salesman presented the plan to the sales force. The company outfitted each Whiting salesman with a presentation manual, to be used as a visual aid before the audience of salesmen. These manuals cost $1,000 to prepare.

The distributors' salesmen were supplied smaller presentation manuals to use in selling hoists to the final user. To insure that the distributors' salesmen would use the books, the supply was limited and invoices at $10 per book were sent. The invoices were not to be paid, but served as a reminder of the book's value.

EXHIBIT 1 New Catalogue Description of Electric Hoist

Some Lifting Methods
ARE THE PEAK OF _IN-EFFICIENCY!_

THESE METHODS
CAUSE YOUR COSTS TO RISE

The hand-hoist . . .
users are never
accused of speeding

The block and tackle . . .
belongs to the dark ages

The "hernia method" . . .
slow, costly and dangerous

Why not
lift the faster,
safer, less costly
way with a...

WHITING
ELECTRIC HOIST

29 Models — Capacities from 500 to 4,000 lbs.

WHITING CORPORATION, Harvey, Illinois
Manufacturer of Cranes, Hoists and other
Industrial Equipment for over 60 years.

Each page in the book described one sales feature of Whiting hoists to the distributor salesmen. The vice-president believed that a distributor salesman using the manual as an aid would be forced to give a slower and more complete and understandable presentation. A supply of small giveaway catalogues describing the hoists was furnished to each distributor.

During the presentation to the distributor's sales force, the Whiting salesmen stressed the value of selling a Whiting product, pointing out the size and reputation of the company and the wide range of products it manufactured. The presentation then showed why hoists were needed; why distributors should sell hoists; and, in detail, the superiority of Whiting hoists. Because this presentation paralleled the copy in the small giveaway catalogue, it was hoped that the distributors' salesmen, when explaining the company's catalogue to a prospect, would give a similar detailed presentation. After the Whiting salesman had explained the electric chain hoist, he proceeded to present the "cream of the crop" plan.

The basis of the plan was a belief that 20 percent of the customers accounted for 80 percent of the business for each distributor. The "cream of the crop" plan was designed to make the distributors' salesmen concentrate their efforts upon this 20 percent. The Whiting plan included active support of such efforts with a direct-mail advertising campaign. (See Exhibit 2.)

To determine which firms were the "cream of the crop," each distributor salesman first listed the firms that performed lifting operations. Next, he listed 30 accounts (of the estimated 150 accounts he handled) on a special form (Exhibit 3), including the names of individuals responsible for buying hoists. Whiting's advertising agency then sent three mailings to each firm listed, using the distributors' stationery and their salesmen's signatures.

The first mailing was a short, personalized letter with an enclosure. The second mailing was sent two weeks later, followed by the third mailing in two weeks. Each of these two mailings consisted of a short letter and an enclosure. The Whiting Corporation expected to receive about 10,000 names, and it was estimated that the cost of the campaign would be 20¢ per name per mailing. A list of the prospects, the dates of the mailing, plus a copy of the mailing, were sent to each distributor salesman, who was expected to call upon the accounts that received the mailings.

To gauge the campaign's effectiveness, Whiting required that the distributor sales manager and his salesmen list results for each account, on another form. This form covered four possibilities: the account was sold; the salesman was asked to call back; additional promotion would be required; or the account should be dropped from the list. Whiting's salesmen, executives, and advertising agency reviewed the completed forms.

An advantage of this plan, according to the vice-president, was that it was possible for the advertising agency to tabulate the list of 10,000 names in order to determine the positions of individuals who were generally responsible for the purchase of a hoist. This information was then

EXHIBIT 2   Direct Mail Promotion for "Cream of the Crop" Plan

give your
sales a LIFT with the

WHITING HOIST
"CREAM OF THE CROP" plan

Here's the first step to more sales of Whiting Electric Hoists! Each prospect name you list inside will receive a series of 3 specially personalized mailings . . . on **your** letterhead . . . signed by **you** . . . featuring the money-saving advantages of Whiting Electric Hoists.

PLEASE REMEMBER . . . LIST ONLY YOUR VERY BEST PROSPECTS!

1. Fill out completely all personal names, company names, addresses, etc.
2. For large firms, list the names of such individuals as president, works manager, production manager and purchasing agent or whoever is responsible or influential in the purchase of Whiting Electric Hoists. For small shops, list both the owner or manager and the chief mechanic.
3. For **each personal** name you list, please give us **three** of your company's letterheads and envelopes plus **15 extra** for possible spoilage.

THESE MAILINGS WILL REALLY SOFTEN YOUR PROSPECTS . . .
THEY WILL BE READY FOR YOUR CALL!
FILL OUT YOUR LIST NOW!

WHITING CORPORATION
HARVEY, ILLINOIS

EXHIBIT 3   Special Form for Distributor Salesmen

WHITING

ELECTRIC

HOIST

"CREAM OF THE CROP"

PLAN

DISTRIBUTOR SALES MANAGER'S COPY
This is your copy of the prospects selected for the Whiting Hoist "Cream-of-the-Crop" plan by the salesman whose name is shown at right. He has also been sent a copy of this which carried the following suggestions:

1. Keep this list with you constantly and use it in planning your calls to make certain that each prospect is followed up as soon as practical.
2. Note the mailing schedule and tie-in your calls with it.
3. Use code letters to keep record of calls and sales.
4. Advise your Sales Manager regarding results of your calls after follow-up of 3rd mailing.

WE SUGGEST THAT YOU CHECK EACH SALESMAN'S LIST REGULARLY. THIS WILL HELP ASSURE THE SUCCESS OF THE PLAN!

List No. .... consisting of

.... names

from ....
(names and initials of Distributor Salesman)

....
(name of Distributor Company)

MAILING SCHEDULE

Letter and Enclosure No. 1 ....

Letter and Enclosure No. 2 ....

Letter and Enclosure No. 3 ....

CODE KEYS: {
(PLACE BENEATH NUMBERS)

SOLD—"X"	CALL BACK—"Y" PLUS DATE
NEEDS MORE PROMOTION—"Z"	REMOVE FROM LIST "O"

ALL NAMES BELOW ARE FOR .... UNLESS OTHERWISE SPECIFIED
                                          City   State

1.	2.
3.	4.
5.	6.

to be used in selecting the media of the company's national advertising campaign.

Was this a well-conceived promotional program? Is it likely to be successful? Where and how does the buying urge get put into motion in a situation like this one? Does Whiting have the right kind of distribution setup?

INTERNATIONAL LATEX CORPORATION

International Latex Corporation was an important manufacturer of waterproof infants' pants, rubber kitchen gloves, bathing caps, girdles, and brassieres, sold directly to retail outlets under the brand name "Playtex." The company's record had been one of steady growth in sales, earnings, and breadth of product line. Sales had increased from less than $4 million in 1946 to more than $32 million in 1955.

Latex habitually spent a large percentage of its sales upon consumer advertising in the leading magazines and Sunday supplements, as well as maintaining a substantial cooperative advertising program. In 1955, the advertising budget was $7 million as compared to sales of about $32 million. Little use had been made of TV.

In early 1956, the executives of Latex were considering negotiating a contract for ten one-minute TV spot advertisements per day every day for five years in a minimum of the top 100 markets in the United States. Such a campaign would be the largest spot television campaign in TV history, and the TV time would be valued at $22 million annually.[1] Because of the size of the financial commitment, and the uniqueness of TV advertising for its particular product line, Latex directed its research department to test the effect of TV advertising on Playtex brassiere and girdle sales.

Playtex girdles had been an established product for many years, while Playtex brassieres had been introduced only recently.

Sales Results Test

The marketing research department in conjunction with its advertising agency, Foote, Cone and Belding, decided to test the campaign by measuring sales of stores in a TV test market against sales of stores in control cities which had no Playtex TV advertising.

The company decided to use metropolitan New York as the test area. Latex had already decided to make New York its first market if it went ahead on TV, so the test was looked upon somewhat as a head start for its first campaign. Also, success in New York would be of much more value from a promotional viewpoint than success in a lesser, easier market.

Hartford, Rochester, and Philadelphia were selected as control cities. Geographically, they surrounded New York, yet they were close enough to minimize regional variations and were large enough to have department stores and specialty shops comparable to those in New York.

---

[1] Presumably, it would be possible for Latex to cancel its advertising contracts at any time during the course of the campaign, and thus to save 70 to 80 percent of the expenditures proposed for the following eight months, and 95 to 98 percent of the expenditures thereafter.

Three one-minute TV spots per day were run in New York, Monday through Friday, for four weeks starting Monday, April 2. Two of the spots were on WABC-TV. The first of these was scheduled between 3 P.M. and 5 P.M. on the "Afternoon Film Festival," and the second between 7 P.M. and 10 P.M. The third spot was on WCBS-TV during the "Late Show" which ran from 11:15 P.M. until about 1 A.M. Equal time was devoted to the advertising of girdles and brassieres. However, in an attempt to obtain greater initial impact, all the spots during the first week were on girdles, while those of the second week were on brassieres. During the third and fourth weeks, the products were alternated on a spot-by-spot basis. A representative spot is shown in Exhibit 1.

It was realized that factory shipments were a poor and often misleading indication of store sales. Consequently, the research department decided to base its store sales figures on inventory figures adjusted for purchases. These sales figures were to be obtained by the regular Playtex salesmen who normally called on the accounts. Following a long-established company policy, Playtex salesmen had created a working relationship with almost all their accounts that permitted them to take inventory on their regular sales calls. Thus, the salesmen were not only experienced at taking inventory, but also familiar with the location of all the Playtex stock. To stimulate accurate reporting, it was decided to give each salesman an extra $25 as compensation for his effort in taking the inventory.

It was felt that the salesmen would do accurate work, and would not bias the results, if they completely understood the survey. The district sales managers of each of the four areas, as well as the eastern regional sales manager, met in New York with the research director and the vice-president of sales. The objectives, importance, and details of the tests were thoroughly explained. The meeting also covered the uses of the point-of-sale material and the salesmen's extra compensation. The district managers were made responsible for instructing the salesmen involved and supervising their activities.

Salesmen took inventory in their test accounts two weeks prior to the start of TV. They again checked inventory just before the TV, adding in any merchandise received during the period, and then calculated the sales for the two-week period. The resulting figure was broken down into the average sales in units per day for each test account. These figures for each test account in the three control cities were added together, and the total was given the base index of 100. Similar calculations were made for the test accounts in the New York market, and a sales index of 100 was established. The salesmen checked the inventory and calculated sales in the stores two weeks after the start of TV, two weeks later as the TV ended, and two weeks after the end of TV. Thus, they arrived at sales figures for three periods which were translated into index figures, as shown in Exhibit 2.

Interpretation of the girdle sales figures is complicated. The last two control area sales figures are somewhat biased by the fact that a new Playtex girdle at $5.95 was introduced in the control city of Philadelphia

EXHIBIT 1   Television Commercial

INTERNATIONAL LATEX CORPORATION
TELEVISION COMMERCIAL
THREE HUNDRED AND FIFTY FIFTH AVENUE • NEW YORK 1, N. Y. • LONGACRE 3-5000

Product : Bra
Length : one minute
Ident. : Tennis
Code No. : B-2-56-1

Friend: Wow! Set point

Marvelous form, Carol. What's your secret?

Girl: One you'd never suspect. Look.

For top form I play in Playtex . . .

My Playtex Living Bra is heavenly comfort for action all day long.

This exclusive all-elastic design never slides, rides or shifts.

My Playtex low-cut back stays low — never rides up and these exclusive elastic bias side panels adjust to every movement.

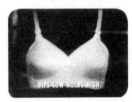

Elastic criss-cross front dips low — holds you high.

All elastic top never cuts or binds. No broken straps . . .

Glorious too for casual clothes . . .

Or loveliest dresses . . .

Try on a Playtex Living Bra at your store. You'll love it. Only $3.95. Wear Playtex Living Bras once — you'll never wear any others.

EXHIBIT 2   Sales Test Indices

	A Two weeks before TV	B First two weeks	C Second two weeks	D Two weeks after TV
Girdles				
Philadelphia Rochester Hartford	100	101	121*	117*
New York (TV)	100	139	127	176*
Brassieres				
Philadelphia Rochester Hartford	100	87	88	62
New York (TV)	100	130	116	128

* New $5.95 Playtex girdle introduced in error.

by error. The new girdle was also introduced in New York near the end of the final selling period. Because of Latex's record of highly successful introduction of new products, their accounts actively promoted the new products in an attempt to get an increasing share of the plus business.

Hooper Survey

Latex decided to do some further surveying as a check on the indications of the store sales test. Specifically, the company wanted to know the influence of its TV advertising on brand awareness, purchase consideration, and actual purchases of Playtex girdles and brassieres.

C. E. Hooper Inc. was engaged to make a series of telephone surveys of women. It was decided to do three surveys. The first was a random sample of 1,000 of the listed telephones in the New York metropolitan area; this survey was made two days before the start of the TV advertising. Second, a survey identical to the first one was made with a fresh sample of 1,000 at the end of the TV advertising. Third, from the first list of 1,000, 500 were picked at random and also surveyed two days after TV ended. Additional names were provided in case some did not answer.

The surveys were conducted by Hooper's experienced female telephone interviewers. Calls were made during both day and evening. The two questionnaires used are shown in the appendices. The first questionnaire was used on both of the groups of 1,000 respondents; the second on the 500 sample.

The results of the Hooper surveys are shown in Exhibit 3.

EXHIBIT 3   Results of Hooper Surveys

	First Sample (1,000) Before TV	Second* Sample (1,000) After TV	Third** Sample (500) Before TV	Third Sample (500) After TV
Girdles				
Brand awareness	17.1%	20.9%	17.4%	18.2%
Purchase consideration	7.4	11.0	7.8	7.4
Actual purchase (within four weeks)	1.4	4.0	1.2	1.2
Brassieres				
Brand awareness	7.4	7.4	8.6	11.4
Purchase consideration	3.5	4.0	3.6	4.2
Actual purchase	2.4	2.4	2.2	2.4

* New sample.
** Drawn from first sample.

Appendix A: First Questionnaire

This is the General Research Bureau calling. May I speak to
_____? We're making a survey on women's clothing. Will you answer
some questions for me?

1 a. Can you give me the names of several brands of girdles?
   b. Can you name any others?
2.   The next time you plan to buy a girdle, what brands would
     you consider buying?
3 a. Have you bought any girdles in the past four weeks? [*If "no,"
     skip to 4. If "yes," ask:*]
   b. What brand or brands did you buy?
4 a. Can you give me the names of several brands of brassieres?
   b. Can you name any others?
5.   The next time you plan to buy a brassiere, what brands would
     you consider buying?
6 a. Have you bought any brassieres in the past four weeks? [*If
     "no," end interview. If "yes," ask:*]
   b. What brand or brands did you buy?

Thank you very much.

Appendix B: Second Questionnaire

May I speak to _____? This is the General Research Bureau
calling again. You very kindly answered some questions on women's

clothing for me about a month ago. May I ask you those questions again? [The same questions asked on the previous survey were then repeated.]

Should the International Latex Corporation go ahead with its plans for the spot television campaign for Playtex girdles and brassieres?

SODABURST (A)

The Birds Eye Division of General Foods was readying a new home ice cream soda, Sodaburst, for test marketing in Jacksonville, Florida. In the course of developing marketing and advertising strategies for the product's introduction, Sodaburst's product manager and the advertising agency account group were considering what message strategy and appeals should be employed.

For purposes of initial test marketing Sodaburst was to be sold in two-, three-, and four-soda sizes, at retail prices of about 20¢ per soda. Retail carton size and price, as well as case size, were to be evaluated as part of the test marketing operation.

In trying to develop a clear and specific message strategy, the group had available extensive market research information, including background data on ice cream soda consumption, results of Sodaburst's product testing, housewives' opinions on the product's appropriateness for various occasions, its nutritional value, and so forth.

Product and market research information follow.

Background

Sodaburst is an instant ice cream soda, consisting of a single unit made of ice cream, syrup, and frozen carbonated water fused together and packaged in a "miniature" cylindrical ice cream container. The ice cream soda is prepared by slipping the single unit (ice cream, syrup, and frozen carbonated water) from its cylindrical container into a large glass and adding tap water. Upon contact with the tap water, the frozen carbonated water starts to release and mix with the syrup. In one minute, the soda is ready to serve.

At the time of the test marketing, the product was available in two flavors—chocolate (vanilla ice cream with chocolate syrup) and strawberry (vanilla ice cream with strawberry syrup). The product was to be sold from ice cream cabinets in the retail outlet, and had to be kept in the freezer section of the home refrigerator until ready for use.

Research indicated that about 70 percent of housewives and other adults and 80 percent of teens/children drink ice cream sodas. Among adult ice cream soda drinkers, about two-thirds consume at least one per week in summer. Teens/children exceed this usage frequency, with about 85 percent reportedly drinking at least one per week in summer. In winter, usage levels drop, as indicated in Exhibit 1.

EXHIBIT 1   Average Weekly Number of Ice Cream Sodas
Consumed Seasonally by Family

	Total	Housewives	Other Adults	Teens/Children 8–18
Summer	2.63	2.05	1.97	3.56
Winter	.94	.87	.65	1.21

Research conducted in the course of Sodaburst's early product testing revealed that on a year-round basis housewives reported their own consumption of ice cream sodas at three per month, other family adults at three per month, children 5 to 11 at three per month, and teens 12 to 17 at five per month. Field checks at soda fountains in cities throughout the country confirmed the fact that ice cream sodas enjoyed a broad base of consumption not only among children/teenagers but among adults as well.

Consumer Reaction

Several product formulations and product/package combinations were rated by consumers in a series of product use tests conducted the previous year. Exhibit 2 summarizes the ratings of the winning product formulation and product/package combination by housewives, other

EXHIBIT 2   Scale Rating of Sodaburst

	Housewives	Other Adults	Children Under 12	Children 12–17
Winning product formulation	1.21	.90	1.98	1.60
Winning product/ package combination	1.44	1.14	1.99	2.12

adults, children under 12, and children 12 to 17. (These ratings may be compared with housewives' ratings, on the same scale, of established Jell-O flavors. These latter ratings ranged from .7 to 1.3.)

Further research, in the form of an extensive home-use test, was conducted in over 400 homes, representing a cross-section of families in various income, age, and educational strata, in two cities. These tests consisted of one week's use of Sodaburst, at the conclusion of which users were questioned on possible uses and purchases of the product. Among these housewives, intent to buy was: High—64 percent, Moderate—31 percent, Low—5 percent.

These tests revealed no evidence that appeal of the product would be limited to any particular geographical area or socioeconomic group. There was some tendency toward greater acceptance of the product in lower income/education households. (However, the fact that new product acceptance is historically higher among middle- and upper-income groups would be expected to smooth out this tendency.) Respondents were asked, "If this product was sold in your supermarket, what would you expect to pay for a package of four sodas, the same size as the ones you tried?" The average expected price per soda was about 17¢; however, Exhibit 3 shows the wide range in expected price per soda.

EXHIBIT 3 Perceived Cost per Soda

Price	Percent
11¢ or less	10
12–16¢	45
17–21¢	30
22¢ or more	15

Product Appeal and Appropriateness

Those participating in the home-use test were also queried on their views of the product's appeal to adults, teenagers, and young children. Exhibit 4 reports their responses, broken down separately for those housewives with and without children.

Early exploratory research had indicated that housewives did not see the product as a substitute for fountain ice cream sodas, particularly for themselves, because it could not furnish the highly valued "going-out" experience associated with consuming fountain sodas. Rather, they saw the product as a family snack, competing with the whole spectrum of at-home snacks. Thus, the housewives who participated in the home-use

EXHIBIT 4   Housewives' Perceived Appeal of Product Among Adults, Teenagers, & Young Children

	Total	Housewives with Children	Housewives without Children
Base: Total housewives in each group	431	273	158
	%	%	%
Housewives stating product would appeal to:			
Adults			
A great deal	29	22	42
Somewhat	55	59	48
Not at all	16	19	10
	100	100	100
Teenagers			
A great deal	73	68	81
Somewhat	23	27	17
Not at all	3	4	1
Not stated	1	1	1
	100	100	100
Young Children			
A great deal	75	71	81
Somewhat	20	21	18
Not at all	5	8	1
	100	100	100

tests were asked about the product's appropriateness for various occasions. These results appear as Exhibit 5.

In earlier group interviews, after experience with the product, housewives had clearly indicated that because of its relative cost, Sodaburst would not be bought simply to satisfy teenagers/children because "kids can be satisfied with less." (Alternative snacks were seen as both "direct substitutes," such as homemade floats and sodas—10¢ to 13¢—as well as less expensive milk and cookies, soft drinks, ice cream novelties—e.g., Dixie Cups—etc.) Many housewives explicitly stated that their interest in the product was influenced by the opportunity they saw for it in promoting "family sociability" in snack-eating situations.

EXHIBIT 5   Housewives' Opinions Regarding the Product's
Appropriateness for Various Occasions

	Occasion			
	Afternoon Snacks	Dessert at Lunch	Dessert at Dinner	Evening Snacks
Very appropriate	54%	23%	19%	68%
Fairly appropriate	34	35	25	24
Not appropriate	12	42	55	7
Not stated	–	–	1	1
	100%	100%	100%	100%

	Occasion		
	Children's Parties	Teens' Parties	Adult Guests
Very appropriate	81%	71%	22%
Fairly appropriate	11	20	30
Not appropriate	7	8	47
Not stated	1	1	1
	100%	100%	100%

Specific Product Appeals

Because many instant products instill a "flavor distrust" among consumers, the flavor and taste of Sodaburst were areas of particular interest and inquiry in the home-use test research. The novelty and "magic" of the product were expected to raise doubts in some consumers' minds about its ability to provide a highly satisfying ice cream soda. Such "flavor reservations" had been expressed by about 25 percent of the housewives during Sodaburst's early product testing.

In response to questions about what specific things they liked about Sodaburst, housewives after the home-use test cited four major areas— flavor/taste, convenience, ease of preparation, and package/storage. Responses to this question, further broken down by "intent to buy," appear in Exhibit 6.

Exploratory research had also revealed that ice cream sodas, in contrast to many other snack foods, are regarded as wholesome. Thus, housewives in the home-use test were asked their opinions of the product's nutritional value. Approximately 68 percent thought the product was very or fairly nutritious, as shown in Exhibit 7. These results are also broken down by "intent to buy."

EXHIBIT 6   Specific "Likes" of Product

	Total	Intent To Buy		
		High	Moderate	Low
	%	%	%	%
All flavor/taste mentions	67	78	66	54
Tastes like a real ice cream soda	21	32	22	7
Good ice cream taste	17	17	15	19
Good flavor, taste (general)	12	8	15	11
Good chocolate taste	11	12	12	8
Refreshing, cool	4	4	4	2
All other flavor/taste mentions	12	15	8	11
All convenience mentions	61	70	67	43
All ease of preparation comments	57	58	68	43
All packaging/storage mentions	44	46	49	34

EXHIBIT 7   Nutritional Value and Intent to Buy

	Total	Intent to Buy		
		High	Moderate	Low
Perceiving product as very or fairly nutritious	68%	80%	70%	51%

Competition

Several other manufacturers were in various stages of introduction of products considered potentially competitive with Sodaburst. Included were two products from Borden Foods Company, one from Pet Milk Company, and one from National Sugar Refining Company. Information on these products is given below.

Borden's Milk Shake—"The first ice cream-thick milk shake from a can." A refrigerated product, it is made with ice cream mix and whole milk. The use theme is: "Just shake! open! pour!" The shake comes in 10¼-ounce cans retailing at two for 39¢. Each can is dated and according to Borden's has a shelf life of five months under proper refrigeration.

Borden's Moola Koola—A ready-to-drink milk-based canned product, requiring no refrigeration. Promotion theme: "new soft drink that comes from a cow." Emphasis is on fun and flavor. Moola Koola retails for 29¢ for a 9½-ounce can. A 32-ounce family size is also offered. (Both Borden drinks are vitamin-enriched and come in chocolate, strawberry, and vanilla flavors.)

Pet Milk's Big Shot—A milk additive in an aerosol container designed to look like a soda jerk. The chocolate fudge-flavored syrup is offered as the "first self-mixing milk additive that needs no refrigeration."

National Sugar Refining's Jack Frosted—A creamy chocolate milk-base additive that can make rich milk shakes and frosteds at the touch of a button. The product, in a 21-ounce aerosol can, is squirted into a glass and changes the ingredients to a shake.

What message strategy would you adopt for Sodaburst based on the consumer and market information in the case? To whom should the product be addressed? For what usage purpose(s)?

SODABURST (B)

The product manager and advertising agency account group for Sodaburst were considering what message strategy and appeals should be employed in behalf of the product. Sodaburst was the Birds Eye Division of General Foods' new home ice cream soda. (For background, see Case A.)

After extensive discussion, the following message strategy statement was approved:

> Advertising copy will be directed to an all-family audience, with particular emphasis on housewives in homes with children 5 to 17.
>
> Copy will be designed to appeal to consumers in all geographic areas and among all socioeconomic groups, except that no special effort will be made to assure appeal to members of lowest-income-quartile households.
>
> The principal objective of the advertising will be to announce that all the familiar taste enjoyment of an ice cream soda is now quickly and conveniently available at home with Sodaburst.
>
> A secondary objective will be to convince housewives of the product's quality/wholesomeness that makes it suitable for all-family consumption.
>
> The copy will dramatize the interest and excitement inherent in the totally new product concept Sodaburst represents.

The basic selling proposition submitted by the agency and agreed to by the division was: "a real ice cream soda that makes itself at home in one minute cold." In support of this basic selling proposition, the agency submitted several television commercials and print advertisements. (See Exhibits 1 through 6.) In examining these proposed advertisements, the

(Text continues on p. 184.)

EXHIBIT 1   Storyboard for Television Commercial: Commercial #1

NOTE: (QUICK CUTS)
       FRAMES # 1–6

OPEN ON ECU OF GLASS LOOKING
UP AT ROLL.

JINGLE
PLOP

TAP SWINGS OVER. CAMERA
STARTS TO PULL UP.

WATER GURGLES IN.

GURGLE

ECU OF MILK BOTTLE
TOP.

POP

MILK POURS INTO SODA.

BLIP

ECU SPOON STIRS SODA.

FIZZ

EXHIBIT 1   (cont.)

PULL BACK TO SHOT OF
COMPLETED SODA. STRAW
JABS IN.

ANNCR: (VO)
That's all there is to making
Sodaburst.

DRAW SODA TO CAMERA.

Sodaburst is a new kind of
treat from Birdseye...

ECU SODA AS STRAW POKES
ICE CREAM.

a real ice cream soda

PULL DOWN TO SHOW FROSTY
SIDE.

that makes itself at home ... in
one minute cold.

CU FREEZER DOOR OPENING.

Here's where

SEE SODABURST PACK.

you keep it.

EXHIBIT 1 (cont.)

GIRL TAKES SODABURST
AND STRAWS OUT OF
LARGE PKG.

And here's how you make it:

CU HANDS PUSHING SODABURST
ROLL OUT OF SLEEVE.

Just one Sodaburst roll

QUICK CUTS TO CU. ROLL
DROPPING INTO GLASS.

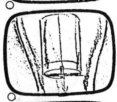

in a big glass.

WATER IN.

Water.

MILK IN.

A couple of blips of milk

STIR, THEN. . .

Stir.

EXHIBIT 1   (cont.)

DISCOVER SODAS ON TRAY
TURNING TOWARD FAMILY IN
REAR.

And let her go.
In a minute you've got a real
ice cream soda.

WOMAN TAKES SPOONFUL OF
ICE CREAM.

Big healthy scoop of vanailla
ice-cream.

MAN ENJOYING SODA.

Frothy crown.

GIRL ENJOYING SODA.

Gobs of flavor, and lots of
fun.

FAMILY GROUP.

Who likes Sodaburst? Who
doesn't!

CUT TO ECU OF SODA BEING
DRUNK. AS SODA DISAPPEARS.
SUPER: WIPES ON. "MAKES
ITSELF AT HOME IN ONE
MINUTE COLD."

It's a real ice cream soda
that makes itself at home. . .
in one minute cold.

EXHIBIT 1   (cont.)

PULL BACK TO SEE BOY.
SHEEPISH LOOK ON FACE AS
HE MAKES LOUD GURGLE AT
BOTTOM. HE SUCKS UP SUPER.

Strawberry or chocolate. . .

PUTS EMPTY GLASS DOWN NEXT
TO TWO BOXES, ONE
CHOCOLATE, ONE STRAWBERRY.

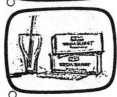

both in the ice cream freezer
at your store.

BIRD FLIES IN PULLING SUPER:
"YOU KNOW THEY'RE GOOD. THE
LITTLE BIRDSEYE TELLS YOU."

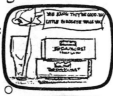

And you know they're good.

The little Birdseye tells you

MUSIC: BUTTON

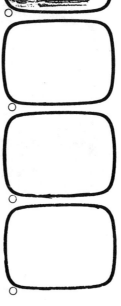

EXHIBIT 2   Storyboard for Television Commercial: Commercial #2

OPEN ON ECU SMALL BOY'S HANDS
REMOVING PAPER FROM END OF
A STRAW.

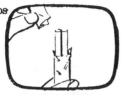

MUSIC: GAY, BOUNCY TYPE

CUT TO ECU PROFILE SHOT OF BOY,
BLOWING PAPER OFF END OF STRAW.

PAN WITH PAPER AS IT LANDS
ACROSS TABLE AT BASE OF A
FULL GLASS OF SODABURST.

ANNCR: (VO)

Fun. . .is a Sodaburst -

CAMERA MOVES UP SODABURST TO
SMALL GIRL'S FACE. HOVERING
OVER IT LAUGHING. SHE HAS AN
ICE CREAM MUSTACHE.

The real ice cream soda
that makes itself at home. . . ..

CUT TO MCU 11 YEAR BOY
DRINKING SODA.

in one minute cold.

MOVE IN TO ECU HIS FACE.
HE MAKES SLURPING NOISE AND
HIS EYES QUICKLY TURN LEFT
TO SEE IF HIS FATHER HAS
CAUGHT HIM.

They'll love it. . .
(SLURPING NOISE)

EXHIBIT 2   (cont.)

QUICK CUT TO ECU FATHER'S FACE, HE IS JUST ABOUT TO TAKE BITE OF ICE CREAM. HIS EYES TURN RIGHT AND GIVE BOY A "WHY ARE YOU DOING THAT" LOOK.

SLURPING STOPS AS FATHER EYES BOY

QUICK CUT BACK TO ECU BOY'S FACE, EYES DOWN, SMILING, BUT SLIGHTLY EMBARRASSED THAT HE WAS CAUGHT SLURPING.

CUT TO LONG SHOT MOTHER AT END OF TABLE ABOUT TO OPEN BOX OF SODABURST.

So will you. . .

CUT TO ECU HANDS OPENING BOX.

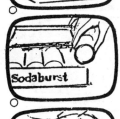

because it's never been so easy to give your family such a special treat!

ECU HAND REMOVES ONE SODABURST.

All you have to do is

ECU HAND PUSHES SODABURST OUT OF CONTAINER AND DROPS IT OUT OF FRAME.

plop Sodaburst

EXHIBIT 2 (cont.)

CU SODABURST IN GLASS.

into a big glass

CUT TO CU WATER POURING INTO GLASS.

add water

STAY ON GLASS AS SODABURST STARTS TO MAKE ITSELF.

and wait a minute for the frozen cube of bubbles to turn Sodaburst

DISSOLVE TO SODA ALREADY MADE.

into a real ice cream soda!

CUT TO CU MILK POURING INTO GLASS.

Now. . .a little milk

CU SPOON STIRRING.

a little
stir

EXHIBIT 2 (cont.)

SPOON DIGS INTO ICE CREAM.

and dig right in

ECU ICE CREAM ON SPOON.

to a mound of rich, creamy
vanilla ice cream

CUT TO ECU MOTHER DRINKING
SODA.

in a fresh fruit strawberry
or a deep chocolate soda.

CUT TO BIRDS EYE LOGO ON
SODABURST PKG.

Birds Eye has put 4 of them
in a pkg.

PULL BACK TO SEE NAME
SODABURST, TOO.

and dropped them

CONTINUE PULLING BACK SO YOU
SEE ENTIRE SODABURST PKG.

in your grocer's ice cream
freezer

EXHIBIT 2 (cont.)

PULL BACK MORE TO SHOW MOTHER'S ALMOST EMPTY GLASS NEXT TO PKG. SUPER: "MAKES ITSELF AT HOME IN ONE MINUTE COLD", YOU DO NOT SEE MOTHER'S FACE, BUT STRAW MOVES SLIGHTLY AND SODA LEVEL LOWERS SO THERE IS NONE LEFT.

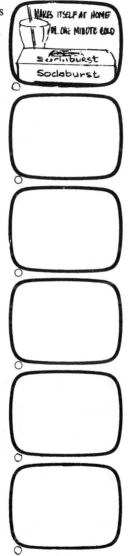

Pick up Sodaburst. . .and treat your family to a real ice cream soda that makes itself at home, (SLURP SOUND) in one minute cold.

EXHIBIT 3   Storyboard for Television Commercial: Commercial #3

OPEN ON BLANK SCREEN.

(YOUNG MOTHER VO):
All right. . .who wants a real
ice cream soda?

TWO HANDS (LITTLE BOY AND
LITTLE GIRL) SHOOT UP INTO
FRAME WAVING
ENTHUSIASTICALLY.

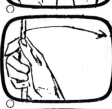

O.K. . .

CUT TO CHILD OPENING
DOOR AND. . .

get the Sodabursts
(SOUND)

TAKING PRODUCT OUT OF
FREEZING COMPARTMENT.

out of the freezer
(DOOR SLAM)

OTHER CHILD OPENS
CUPBOARD AND. . .

and the

TAKES OUT GLASSES.

big glasses out of the
cupboard

EXHIBIT 3   (cont.)

ALL CHILDREN'S HANDS AS
THEY TAKE TOP OFF SODA CUP

now. . .

PUT SODA IN GLASS.

(SOUND)

ECU MOTHER'S FACE SHE
IS HELPING THEM WITH HER
MOUTH.

Thaaaat's right. . .

now. . . .

THEY POUR CUP OF WATER
INTO GLASSES

a cup of water and wait

a minute

ECU TABLE TOP PROFILE BOTTOM
OF SODA GLASS AS IT BEGINS
TO BUBBLE. .ON CUE SUPER
"MAKES ITSELF AT HOME IN
1 MINUTE COLD" CAMERA
MOVES AROUND TO

ANNCR: (VO) Yep. . . .that's all there
is to making Sodaburst the real
ice cream soda that makes
itself at home in one minute cold.

TABLE TOP SHOT, SODA
IN FOREGROUND WITH CHILDREN
BEHIND WAITING WISTFULLY.
DISSOLVE TO. . .

Just put 'em in a glass. . .add

water. . .and sit tight while

the little frozen cube turns

Sodaburst into

EXHIBIT 3   (cont.)

ECU TOP SHOT OF GLASS
MOVE AROUND GLASS TO SEE. . .

The finest, frothiest ice
cream soda you've ever made.

SPOON COMES IN TO STIR.
PULLS UP ICE CREAM.

Healthy helping of real ice cream. . .
luscious syrup

PULL BACK SLOWLY TO APPROACH
FULL SHOT OF GLASS.

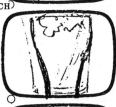

and plenty of real soda
fountain fizz. . . .

QUICK CUT TO CU CHILD
TAPPING STRAWS ON TABLE TO
REMOVE PAPER.

all yours at home. . .

FULL SHOT OF FULLY MADE
SODA. CHILD PUTS STRAWS IN
AND PULLS OFF SCREEN.

in one minute cold! Call this
a miracle?

CHILDREN DRINKING
SODA.

Birdseye calls it Sodaburst.

EXHIBIT 3 (cont.)

PAN TO MOTHER WITH SODA
ALMOST READY TO DRINK,
SHE STIRS AND SIPS.

chocolate or strawberry. . .in
your grocers freezer.

SHE LOOKS UP.

WOMAN SPEAKS:

And you know they're
good. . .

ZOOM IN LOGO TIGHT AND

(WOMAN VO:)
The little Birds Eye.

BACK TO FULL SHOT
OF PKG.

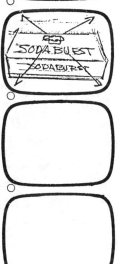

tells you.

EXHIBIT 4A   Layout of Print Advertisement: Ad#1, Left-hand Page

You are looking at
a real ice cream soda
about to happen

EXHIBIT 4B   Right-hand Page

see,
it happened!

No fooling!
Now you can make
real ice cream sodas
at home.
Just pop one
Sodaburst
into a big
glass

and add
plain tap water.
That's all.

In one minute
you've got a good
old-fashioned ice
cream soda,
brimming with rich
vanilla ice cream,
luscious syrup
and plenty
of real
soda
fountain
fizz.
Chocolate or
Strawberry
Both flavors
in the ice cream
cabinet at your
store.
And you know they're
good. The little
Birds Eye tells you.

Sodaburst! The real ice cream soda
that makes itself at home in 1 minute cold!

EXHIBIT 5 Layout of Print Advertisement: Ad #2

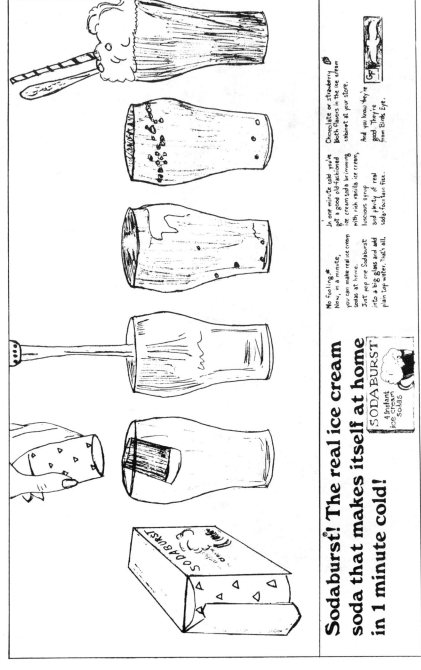

Sodaburst!® The real ice cream soda that makes itself at home in 1 minute cold!

SODABURST
4 instant ice cream sodas

No fooling.*
Now, in a minute, you can make real ice cream sodas at home. Just pop one Sodaburst into a big glass and add plain tap water. That's all.

In one minute cold you've got a good old-fashioned ice cream soda brimming with rich vanilla ice cream, luscious syrup and plenty of real soda-fountain fizz.

Chocolate or strawberry. Both flavors in the ice cream cabinet at your store.

And you know they're good. They're from Birds Eye.

EXHIBIT 6   Layout of Print Advertisement: Ad #3

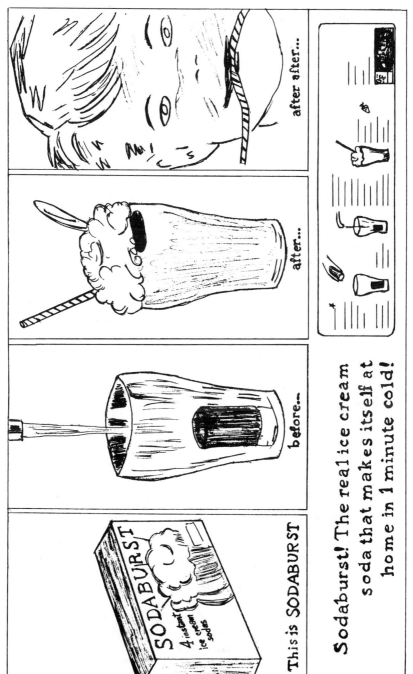

* Note: Body copy similar to other print ads.

Sodaburst product manager and his staff wondered which ones best implemented the agreed-upon message statement.

Which of the proposed TV commercials best implements the message strategy selected by the product manager? Why? Which is the best print execution? Why?

NORTHWESTERN MUTUAL LIFE INSURANCE COMPANY

In the summer of 1971, Mr. Richard S. Haggman, Superintendent of Advertising for Northwestern Mutual Life Insurance Company, was undertaking an extensive review of the company's advertising efforts. This review was precipitated by several factors. First, although Northwestern was among the largest life insurance companies in the United States, a 1970 Gallup study had indicated that, with the general public, it ranked thirty-fourth in awareness among fifty-five life insurance companies studied. Second, a recent survey of Northwestern's own agents had revealed that over half of those responding believed the current national campaign to be only "fair" or "poor" in terms of effectiveness. Third, reactions to the company's recent magazine advertisements had not approached the levels of earlier years—in terms of either Starch readership ratings or reprint orders from agents, both traditional criteria at NML.

Company and Industry Background

Northwestern was chartered by the state of Wisconsin in 1857 as a mutual insurance company—that is, one organized to write insurance for its owners rather than to make a profit for its owners like a stock company. The company, like many of its mutual counterparts, concentrated initially on life insurance only. Recently it had begun to offer disability income insurance. By contrast, companies like Travelers, Aetna, Allstate, State Farm, and INA had been offering all lines of insurance—including many kinds of property and liability insurance.

Northwestern had not branched out in this manner, but issued only life, annuity, and disability income policies. The company wrote no health insurance; neither did it write group insurance. Instead, each policy was sold on an individual basis, whether to a family member or to a business. In spite of this strategy, Northwestern was among the largest life insurance companies in the United States, and was the largest company specializing in individual life insurance. Exhibit 1 shows Northwestern's overall position—seventh largest—among the top ten companies in terms of assets. As can be seen in Exhibit 1, the mutual companies were a dominant

EXHIBIT 1 Largest Life Insurance Companies Ranked by Assets
(All figures—$000)

Company	Assets	Life Insurance in Force	Increase in Life Ins. in Force	Premium & Annuity Income	Net Investment Income	Total Income	Net Gain from Operations [1]
Prudential	29,134,352	156,775,266	10,538,653	3,798,270	1,413,780	5,212,050	54,662
Metropolitan	27,865,762	167,283,940	9,779,886	3,722,232	1,399,527	5,121,759	26,893
Equitable	14,371,372	76,909,206	6,156,466	1,750,071	699,495	2,449,566	715
New York Life	10,741,138	50,317,456	4,284,214	1,217,545	508,144	1,725,689	47
John Hancock	10,048,444	60,896,318	4,230,574	1,240,801	466,359	1,707,160	18,414
Aetna [2]	7,214,675	59,883,313	4,351,567	1,832,346	344,775	2,177,121	56,856
Northwestern	6,124,984	19,477,040	1,291,925	558,216	317,166	875,382	14,245
Conn. General [2]	5,065,289	36,064,588	3,965,447	980,873	246,688	1,227,561	12,746
Travelers [2]	4,709,713	58,386,609	5,614,791	1,497,601	206,376	1,703,977	35,143
Mass. Mutual	4,287,684	19,614,214	1,358,225	543,256	221,109	764,365	10,401
Totals—Top 50	171,862,259	1,031,450,846	76,690,750	25,055,117	8,375,965	33,431,082	591,953

[1] After dividends to policyholders and federal income tax.
[2] Stock company.

Source: *Fortune,* May 1971, pp. 194–95.

185

factor in the life insurance business, controlling about two-thirds of the assets of the industry. Both mutuals and stock companies paid dividends to owners of participating policies. However, because stock companies issued fewer of these policies and because they also paid dividends to shareholders, the ratio of policyholder dividends paid to premiums received was considerably lower for stock companies than for mutuals. This situation gave most mutuals a cost advantage over the stock companies and helped maintain the former's dominance in the field.

By having high standards of risk acceptance, by keeping operating expenses to a minimum, and by earning a better than average return on its investments, Northwestern had for some years been paying dividends equal to approximately one-third of premiums received. This was well above the average. As a consequence, Northwestern regularly ranked number one in low net cost among major life insurance companies.

Marketing at Northwestern

The company's overriding marketing objective, as delineated in the company's 1970 Strategic Plan and reaffirmed in the 1971 Plan, was "to continue to be the leading American company providing family and business security by specializing in life insurance and related services for the individual." In order to maintain this position company officials believed they had to:

1. Penetrate the expanding family market more strongly
2. Delineate and develop specific submarkets, such as college and business/professional categories
3. Create a greater awareness of Northwestern by groups other than its own policyholders—e.g., government, the academic world, the general public

It was hoped that the achievement of these goals would lead to increases in new business in terms of volume (face amount), premiums, and lives—Northwestern's standard performance measures. Of these three, the company put its primary emphasis on new premiums, and the Strategic Plan called for more than doubling 1970 new premiums (of approximately $45 million) by 1978. Most of this growth would have to come from existing insurance plans, because the company did not anticipate a major change in its product line.

Northwestern's product line had evolved over the years, of course. The basic policies—whole life, limited-payment life, endowment, and term—had been introduced within the first twenty years of the company's existence. Major changes came around 1910, when the company adapted these policies to business use, and during the 1930s, when the company began to insure pension plans. Other changes had taken the forms of making existing plans adaptable to a greater variety of uses and of expanding the number of settlement options available.

There had been two significant additions to Northwestern's portfolio in recent years. Extra Ordinary Life, introduced in 1968, was a combination term/permanent plan with a minimum face value of $20,000. Its popularity was attested to by the fact that recent statistics showed it to represent nearly a third of first-year premiums and showed the greatest percentage increase over 1970 of any plan. A disability-income policy was introduced in 1969. Sales of this policy were growing steadily, but its premiums were still an insignificant portion of Northwestern's income. Exhibit 2 illustrates the company's product line as of 1970.

EXHIBIT 2   1970 New Business by Plan of Insurance

	Volume (in millions)
Ordinary Business	
Life (whole and limited payment)	$788
Extra ordinary life	718
Endowment (retirement income)	40
Term and combination	404
Annuities	
Retirement	45
Variable	20
Conversions [1]	125
	$2,140

[1] Term policies which are converted to permanent insurance.

Note: The proportion of new business made up of various plans differs for volume (face amount) and for premiums. Endowments and annuities represent a greater percentage of premium dollar than they do volume; for term policies the situation is reversed.

Most of the over 125,000 individuals to whom new NML insurance was sold each year were between 18 and 34 years old, with 25 the single age at which the largest number of policies were bought. Relative to all American insureds, Northwestern customers had a higher annual income, were more highly educated, and were more likely to be professionals or entrepreneurs. Exhibit 3 shows a comparison of Northwestern and industry business on several demographic dimensions. The company also issued many policies to women. In 1970, women accounted for nearly one-quarter of the lives covered by new life insurance (not annuity) business. These

EXHIBIT 3   Northwestern and Insurance Industry Customer Profiles:
Age, Occupation, Income

New Policies Issued by Age

	Northwestern		Industry	
	1960	1970	1960	1970
Under 15 years	17%	18%	15%	13%
15–24	19	22	24	32
25–34	29	32	31	28
35–44	23	17	20	15
45 and over	12	11	10	12

Adult Male Policies Issued by Occupation

	Northwestern		Industry	
	1965	1970	1965	1970
Professionals	29%	28%	15%	13%
Managers and proprietors	23	25	23	21
Clerical and sales	20	14	14	14
Craftsmen	13	16	26	26
Students	14	16	10	13
Other	1	1	12	13

Adult Male Policies Issued by Income

	Northwestern		Industry		
	1965	1970	1965	1970	
Less than $10,000	61%	38%	74%	62%	Less than $10,000
$10,000–14,999	21	30	21	32	$10,000–24,999
$15,000–29,999	15	25	5	6	$25,000 and over
$30,000 and over	3	7			

policies, however, represented only 11 percent of the face amount of this business. The average man bought life insurance valued at $22,500; for a woman the comparable figure was $8,500.

Nearly 18 percent of the new policies issued in 1970 were classified as juvenile insurance—i.e., they covered individuals 13 years old or younger. As was true for insurance on the lives of women, juvenile policies had a low average face value—approximately $6,500.

Separate from the family protection and juvenile markets, Northwestern emphasized the sale of both ordinary and annuity policies to businesses. These policies were used to underwrite such things as pension and trust funds, keyman coverage, and business purchase agreements. A breakdown of Northwestern business by market served is found in Exhibit 4.

EXHIBIT 4   1970 New Business by Type of Market

By Type of Market	Volume (in millions)
Regular [1]	$1,765
Juvenile	120
Employee benefit plans [2]	
Corporate pension and profit sharing	70
H.R. 10[3]	11
Tax-deferred annuity	48

[1] Includes ordinary insurance for both family protection and business markets, with the former representing some 80 to 85% of the total.

[2] Comprise both annuities and ordinary insurance in approximately equal proportions.

[3] Also called Keogh Plans, after the sponsor of the bill enabling self-employed persons to set up pension plans for themselves and their employees.

Northwestern insurance was sold only through authorized agents, including nearly 2,800 full-time personnel, 700 part-time agents, and 350 college agents. There were no brokers.[1] This sales force was specially trained by Northwestern to be of maximum service to the high-quality market which typified the company's prospects. By industry standards the Northwestern agency force was well above average—more than one in five members of the Million Dollar Round Table, one-third Chartered Life Underwriters. The lapse rate for all NML policies in force was 2.3 percent compared with 5.9 percent for the industry as a whole. Northwestern's policyholders not only renewed their insurance with the company; they also bought additional insurance. In 1970, 50 percent of the new volume came from sales to persons already covered by Northwestern policies.

Despite the high quality of the sales force, the company did have an agent turnover problem, albeit to a lesser degree than the industry as a whole. In addition, Northwestern believed that more agents were needed

[1] Agents for other insurance companies were not permitted to sell Northwestern policies, although Northwestern agents could sell policies from other companies if Northwestern did not provide the type of coverage involved.

to meet future sales goals. Thus the company was constantly recruiting new agents and seeking to cut the proportion of those who failed.

Company Advertising

Traditionally, the company's advertising had sought to develop a quality image, trying to presell the name and values of NML. More specific information on past target audiences, creative themes, media, and budget follow.

Target Audience. Northwestern directed its advertising primarily to policyholders and prospective policyholders. Prospects were defined largely in terms of having the same demographics as present policyholders. Further, the advertising directed at these overlapping groups was expected to have a significant impact on agents and, to a lesser extent, on the general public.

As noted in the description of a typical purchaser, the company considered its prime prospects to be well-educated, upper-income men. The sales agents addressed the bulk of their efforts to this group. In terms of occupation, the company defined the men who bought the largest amounts of insurance as having jobs that would classify them as being in the upper or upper-middle social classes (e.g., business executives, physicians, small-business owners, attorneys, etc.). Initially, the age group at which the advertising aimed was the 35 to 44 bracket, but in 1962 this had been expanded to include men who were 25 to 45. By 1971, however, the most important prospects were considered to be those who were 20 to 34, because more of them were likely to be acquiring life insurance in the near future. In terms of education, some 70 percent of the company's policyholders were believed to be college-educated, compared with about 20 percent of the general population.[2] Secondary targets for Northwestern advertising were college students—those to be insured themselves and those who might represent potential agents.

Creative Themes. For some twenty years (1948 to 1968), Northwestern ran what it viewed as a distinctive campaign intended to develop a quality image through the appearance of successful business and professional leaders. These men were asked to make broad conceptual statements about life insurance, such as its value as an investment, the need for a carefully developed program, and the like. Although all were Northwestern policyowners, the leaders were not asked to endorse Northwestern insurance as such. Thus the commercial sell, which stressed Northwestern's low cost and high quality, was separated from the conceptual statement.

To add further distinction to this "Words of Experience" series, the renowned portrait photographer Yousuf Karsh of Ottawa was used for the entire campaign. As a consequence, the advertisements came to be known

---

[2] Among new policyholders, the college-educated estimate was 80%.

as the Karsh campaign. This campaign was considered very merchandisable by the agents, who purchased reprints in large numbers year after year to use as mailers or handouts. An example of a Karsh ad appears as Exhibit 5.

EXHIBIT 5   Advertisement from Karsh Campaign

Northwestern Mutual Life policyowner for 38 years. Mr. Oelman today has eleven policies with NML.

KARSH, OTTAWA

ROBERT S. OELMAN, Chairman and Chief Executive Officer, The National Cash Register Company, Dayton, Ohio

"Don't ignore the asset value life insurance offers you."

"Everyone recognizes the protection value of life insurance. It's so dramatic, in fact, that many people don't give attention to another big advantage—the dollar reserves life insurance creates. ☐ To my mind, its ever-growing cash values are a vital family asset. They're basic to security planning . . . a solid base for financial well-being. A ready source of help for emergencies, education, retirement—you name it." ☐ Your money

NML

does more for you at Northwestern Mutual Life — NML. Cash values grow fast. The dividend rate has gone up steadily: 13 times in 16 years. ☐ NML operating expenses are low. They run about one-third less, as a percentage of premiums, than the average of the 14 other largest life insurance companies. Ask the NML agent for the full story. It can pay you. Northwestern Mutual Life—Milwaukee.

Beginning in 1962, when Northwestern expanded its concept of prime prospects to include younger men, a special testimonial series was developed. These ads, which ran concurrently with the Karsh campaign, followed the same format as that series, but were less imposing. They featured younger professionals who were "on the go." An ad from this series appears as Exhibit 6

EXHIBIT 6   Advertisement from Young Men Testimonial Series

Jack Turpin has won state and national tennis championships over the last 24 years.

JACK A. TURPIN, 36. President of Hall · Mark Electronics Corporation, Dallas, Texas

"NML insurance helps stabilize our business future."

"Besides protecting my family, Northwestern Mutual life insurance is also part of my business life.

"We use it to help hold our key men. And through an NML insured stock redemption plan, we have significantly added to the asset value of both the corporation and the key men.

"Northwestern Mutual's dividends, compared to those of other life insurance companies, are remarkably high."

Your money buys more at NML

One reason is low operating expense at Northwestern Mutual. As a percentage of premiums, a recognized statistical service reports, this runs about one-third less than the average of the 14 other largest life insurance firms.

Why not call your Northwestern Mutual agent? He specializes in life insurance tailored to personal needs and delivered at low net cost.

Be sure to ask him about our dividend scale. It has been increased 12 times in the last 15 years!

NORTHWESTERN MUTUAL LIFE - MILWAUKEE NML

By 1969 there was some feeling within the company that the Karsh campaign's emphasis on older business figures as authorities was no longer so relevant to the target market. In addition, reprint sales to agents had declined markedly during the previous three years. At the suggestion of Northwestern executives, the Chicago office of J. Walter Thompson, the company's advertising agency, developed a new campaign, called the "individuals" series. The idea behind the theme was Northwestern's em-

EXHIBIT 7   Advertisement from 1969–1970 Campaign

He likes to talk about
his new job,
or about camping
with his kids,
or about the way
he does 25 push-ups
every morning.
For him, retirement is
half a lifetime away.
He doesn't dwell on it.
But someday, he wants
a small house by the sea.
Maybe even a boat.
This is his dream.
His very own.
For he is an individual.
We grew as large as we are
by recognizing
that fact.

NORTHWESTERN MUTUAL LIFE · MILWAUKEE   NML
World's largest company specializing in individual life insurance.

phasis on the individual. The creative execution in the 1969–1970 season consisted of close-ups of faces with very little body copy. (See Exhibit 7.) A different execution of the same theme followed in 1970–1971. (See Exhibit 8.)

Separate from its image/identity advertising, Northwestern ran special recruiting advertisements. In 1971, a number of these ads offered a career

EXHIBIT 8   Advertisement from 1970–1971 Campaign

booklet and phonograph record; others duplicated the regular Northwestern ads with a recruiting message appended at the bottom. On the whole, most life insurance advertising focused on either the need for life insurance or the selling achievements of the particular company's agents. Nonetheless, the creative themes used by Northwestern's competitors in 1971 varied considerably. They included Penn Mutual's gallery of agents in its Quality Club, Connecticut Mutual's stories about "Blue Chip" investments and policyholders, as well as the New England Life campaign utilizing cartoons to depict the impending accidental sudden death of distinguished-looking people in unusual settings.

Media. Northwestern traditionally emphasized magazines in its media plan. The Karsh campaign and the subsequent "individuals" ads appeared in *Time, Newsweek,* and *U.S. News & World Report. Sports Illustrated* was used for the younger-men testimonials from 1962 to 1968 and remained on the schedule to supplement the news weeklies in subsequent years. The 1971 planned media schedule appears as Exhibit 9. These same magazines were used heavily by competitors.

EXHIBIT 9   Planned Media Schedule, 1971

Publication	Cost per 4-color Bleed Page	Frequency	Total Cost	
Time	$40,906	7	$286,342	
Newsweek	25,772	6	154,632	
U.S. News & World Report	18,363	6	110,178	
Sports Illustrated	24,035	7	168,245	
Subtotal				$719,347
Trade			$ 19,383	
Recruiting			7,135	
Production			32,000	
Subtotal				58,518
Grand total				$777,865

The principal arguments in favor of the use of these magazines included:

1. Selectivity (efficiency of ad spending directed to Northwestern's traditional demographic targets)
2. Continuity (sustaining the message given the total budget)
3. Susceptibility to a story (permitting a longer message)

4. Basically serious mood
5. Merchandisability

Recruiting ads were carried in the college edition of *Time* and in the *Journal of College Placement*.

Budget. The company spent just under $800,000 for advertising in 1970; a similar amount had been budgeted for 1971, as can be seen in Exhibit 9. This figure, though double the amount spent in 1962, represented only .14 percent of the previous year's premium income. In fact, advertising as a percentage of either total premium dollars or annualized new-premium income had remained relatively constant over the previous decade.

Although Northwestern had maintained this internal advertising spending standard over time, its level of spending had not approached the external standard set by competition. In fact, only one of the companies considered by Northwestern to be its principal competitors had allocated a lower percentage of its previous year's premium income to advertising in 1970. That company, Metropolitan, had premium income high enough so that even its lower percentage for advertising supported an advertising budget of over $4 million. New York Life also spent in excess of $4 million for advertising, and Prudential topped the list with a budget of $6.3 million. If NML had allocated its advertising budget at the average rate of the other top mutual companies, its 1971 budget would have been just over $1 million. Exhibit 10 gives information on estimated 1970 advertising expenditures of major insurance companies.

The size of the budget was under question within the company for two reasons. First, the relatively low level of spending was considered to preclude the use of television, a medium used increasingly by competition. For example, according to *Advertising Age*,[3] Prudential, Metropolitan, New York Life, and John Hancock each spent more than $1 million in TV in 1970. Equitable and Mutual of New York (MONY) were expected to join this group of million-dollar TV spenders in 1971. Other major network TV buyers were Allstate and Travelers, although their budgets covered advertising for many lines of insurance. Most insurance TV advertising was concentrated on weekend sports; however, Prudential and Metropolitan, with more than $3 million each in TV, also spent heavily in entertainment programs.

Second, the impact produced by the present budget was thought to be insufficient to identify and link the campaign theme with the company. For example, about a year after Northwestern introduced its "individuals" theme, Equitable began to use a similar theme in its television commercials. Research indicated that the theme was by mid-1971 more associated with Equitable than with Northwestern. Furthermore, Prudential had borrowed the format of Northwestern's 1969–1970 campaign for its 1971 print advertising.

[3] *Advertising Age*, April 12, 1971, pp. 1, 59.

EXHIBIT 10   Estimated Competitive Advertising Expenditures

Company	Estimated 1970 Ad Budget [1] (Thousands)	1969 Premium Income (Millions)	Advertising as % of 1969 Premiums [2]
National Life	$ 350	$ 145	.24
Mutual Benefit	432	284	.15
Connecticut	650	264	.25
Massachusetts Mutual	950	475	.20
New England Life	1,100	396	.28
Mutual of New York	1,500	393	.38
John Hancock	2,226	1,141	.19
Equitable	3,409	1,809	.19
New York Life	4,200	1,130	.37
Metropolitan	4,263	3,532	.12
Prudential	6,300	3,822	.16
Total	25,380	13,391	.19

[1] Print, radio, television, and production outlays.

[2] Note that all figures are less than 1%.

Sources: Industry and advertising agency estimates.

Advertising Research Findings

Survey of Agents. As part of the major review of company advertising, Mr. Haggman conducted a mail survey of agents' attitudes toward advertising. A representative sample of some 5 percent of Northwestern's full-time agents participated in the study. These agents expressed opinions on Northwestern's current advertising and recommended ways in which it could be improved.

When asked what they saw Northwestern's advertising doing for them, 15 percent of the respondents said that it builds a quality image or prestige for agents and/or the company. Another 14 percent believed that it puts the Northwestern name in front of the public. On the other hand, more than 50 percent of the participants claimed that Northwestern advertising did "not much," "very little," or "nothing" for them.

Agents were also asked what, ideally, Northwestern advertising *should* do for them. Four categories of responses stood out. Some 20 percent of those participating thought the advertising should build the company's prestige and image by stressing the quality of the product and the agent. A similar number believed that advertising should get the Northwestern name before more people. Nearly 12 percent of the respondents wanted the advertising to emphasize the company's low net costs. An equally popular request (12 percent) was for local advertising, with the cost cooperatively shared by NML. Other suggestions ranged from "explain the products in more detail" (6 percent) to "same as now" (2 percent). In terms of an overall assessment of Northwestern's present advertising, agents were asked: "Considering what you think advertising *might do* for you, how would you rate the effectiveness of Northwestern's current national campaign?" Only 20 percent of the respondents rated the advertising as being excellent or very good, 25 percent as good, and 53 percent as either fair or poor.

Agents were also asked what specific changes they would make in Northwestern's message, media usage, or budget size. Under message, the recommendations in Exhibit 11 appeared most frequently:

EXHIBIT 11   Agents' Suggested Advertising Messages

Suggestion	Percentage Mentioning
Current message is OK	27
There's a difference: high cash values, dividends; low net cost; quality contracts	20
Quality image: we're best, let's talk about it	16
More emphasis on agent, professional image	12

In considering Northwestern's media usage, fully one-half of the respondents suggested a switch to national television. Some 21 percent of the participating agents said the company should spend more for advertising, although a few hastened to add that this increase should not be at the expense of low net cost. Another suggestion, mentioned by 18 percent of the agents, was for more local (co-op) advertising.

Syndicated Research. Mr. Haggman regularly received Starch data showing the extent to which Northwestern's magazine ads were seen and read. These data were used to compare Northwestern's ads with its own previous advertising as well as with competitive advertising. A three-year summary report appears in Exhibit 12.

More general information on consumer awareness and attitudes came from the Gallup Insurance Index, a national survey conducted in 1969 and again in 1970. This research had been developed primarily to measure changes in awareness of, and attitudes toward, major life insurance companies. These findings could be projected nationally to all men over 21 years of age. From Northwestern's point of view, the study provided a measure of the public's awareness of Northwestern and recall of its advertising.

With the general public, Northwestern ranked thirty-fourth in awareness among the fifty-five life insurance companies studied. About 10

EXHIBIT 12   Starch Readership Report

	Noted [1]	Seen Associated [2]	Read Most [3]
1967–1968			
NML (Karsh)	20	15	3
All others in category	30	21	9
1969			
NML (Individuals)	29	19	7
All others in category	27	22	5
1970			
NML (Individuals)	29	22	11
All others without			
New England Mutual	27	23	4
All others with			
New England Mutual	33	28	10

[1] The percentage of issue readers who remember, when interviewed, that they previously saw the advertisement in the issue under study.

[2] The percentage of issue readers who saw or read any part of the advertisement which clearly indicated the product or name of the advertiser.

[3] The percentage of issue readers who read 50% or more of the written material of the advertisement.

percent of the survey respondents, in both years, said they definitely had heard of Northwestern. Awareness was higher among men with incomes of $15,000 and over, professionals and businessmen, and college-educated men. Awareness of Northwestern was also higher among readers of *Time, U.S. News & World Report,* and *Sports Illustrated* (13 percent) than among nonreaders of these magazines (9 percent).

As might be expected, readers of these periodicals (5 percent) had higher recall of company advertising than nonreaders. Those who recalled the ads said that they conveyed an image of Northwestern as a large company which has gained a good reputation because it is interested in the individual and his specific needs. These people believed, further, that the ads stressed the personal qualities of Northwestern's agents.

Although Northwestern was not particularly well known, company executives believed that its policyholders had very strong positive feelings toward the company and its agents, stronger than those held by policyholders of other companies toward the latter.

Research conducted for the company by J. Walter Thompson provided some details on such favorable attitudes. For example, nearly three-quarters of the Northwestern policyholders responding to the most recent survey had expressed a "high regard" for Northwestern. Among respondents having an opinion about agent services, about 75 percent thought Northwestern's were "best." Of those who had an opinion about costs, some two-thirds mentioned Northwestern as having the lowest cost. Approximately 83 percent of the policyholders in this study had life insurance with more than one company. These particular respondents expressed an even higher regard for Northwestern than did those who owned Northwestern policies exclusively.

Among the reasons some company executives offered for the low level of awareness by nonpolicyholders was the fact that the company referred to itself by several names. Northwestern Mutual Life, NML, and the Northwestern had been used in addition to the official name, Northwestern Mutual Life Insurance Company.

Monitoring Attitudes of the Public. Separate from the research findings specific to Northwestern, Mr. Haggman received industry-wide reports from the Institute of Life Insurance. During 1967 and 1968, the research firm of Daniel Yankelovich, Inc., developed for the Institute a systematic method for tracking relevant public attitudes. The instrument used was called MAP, "monitoring the attitudes of the public." A benchmark survey was completed in 1968, and some of the same issues were measured again in 1969 and/or 1970. A selected few issues were added in the latter studies. Survey respondents included men and women, 18 years of age or older.

The attitudes explored fell into five categories:

1. The public's attitudes toward life insurance as a service
2. Attitudes toward the agent/buying situation
3. Attitudes toward the life insurance business
4. Feedback on current issues confronting the industry
5. Underlying values

Selected findings from the research appear as an appendix to this case.

One purpose of the MAP studies was to help the Institute of Life Insurance shape and evaluate its own broad industry communications programs. An additional purpose was noted in a letter from the Institute president which accompanied the initial report:

> It is hoped that this research will also be useful to the member companies of the Institute, not only in the assessment of current performance but also for long-range planning and such immediate concerns as marketing strategies or advertising directions. . . . Although this research program was not designed to answer specific questions in the latter areas, the implications of the findings do bear upon such issues.

In 1970, the Institute surveyed member firms to learn how MAP findings were being used. About 14 percent of those responding said that MAP was useful in developing advertising programs, and 8 percent said that it helped communications with the public. Thus, Mr. Haggman believed the MAP results should be considered in reviewing Northwestern's advertising program.

Major Issues

In reviewing the company's advertising situation, Mr. Haggman was concerned over general issues as well as specific details of advertising campaign planning. For example, he wondered whether a clear enough picture existed of advertising's role at Northwestern, what that role should be, and the implications in terms of specific objectives for the company's advertising. Beyond these general issues, and in light of judgments made about them, he also wanted to examine the specific dimensions of NML's advertising program, such as its target audience, basic themes, media strategy, and methods of evaluation. Moreover he questioned whether Northwestern's level of advertising spending was appropriate.

Reflecting generally on the consumer context confronting all life insurance advertising, Mr. Haggman noted: "Life insurance is low among things that really interest people . . . it doesn't have the appeal of a vacation in the Greek islands. After all, for the big payoff in life insurance, you have to die and somebody else gets the money. There's not much glamor in that."

What is advertising's role at NML? What should it be? What recommendations do you have regarding the company's advertising strategy—level of spending, target audiences, media strategy, themes, and methods of evaluation?

Appendix: Selected Findings, Yankelovich MAP Studies

There was substantial acceptance among the public of the need for life insurance. Over 60 percent [1] of the respondents believed that life insurance is as necessary as food, clothing, and shelter. An even larger number (79 percent) thought that life insurance was the best way to protect one's family against premature death. Furthermore, nearly seven out of ten persons agreed that wives should be insured.

But there was little agreement as to how much insurance a man needed. The 1970 study indicated that some 49 percent of the respondents

[1] Unless otherwise noted, data are from the original 1968 survey.

believed that a man earning $15,000 a year needed insurance equal to or greater than twice his income in order to be adequately covered. A figure that was less than twice the income was considered sufficient by 35 percent of the respondents, while all others (16 percent) were not certain of the amount. The survey also requested information on the amount of insurance coverage desirable for an average married man, 35 years old, with two children. Responses ranged from less than $10,000 to more than $50,000. With respect to women, fewer than 30 percent of those interviewed stated that women should carry as much insurance as men.

The MAP surveys also asked respondents the basis upon which they answered these questions. In 1970, the majority (53 percent) said that the real consideration is "how much the breadwinner can afford." Some 39 percent, however, based their decision on how much the family would need to be self-supporting.

Most respondents continued to believe that individuals should take care of their own insurance needs rather than relying upon the government or employers. Nonetheless, the percentage believing this declined markedly, from 73 percent in 1968 to 59 percent in 1970.

As for the kind of company from which to buy insurance, responses varied, as shown in Exhibit 13.

EXHIBIT 13   Public Preferences in Life Insurance Companies

Preferred Type of Company for Buying Life Insurance (1968):	%
"One that sells life insurance only"	32
"One that sells all kinds of insurance"	37
"One that sells all kinds of insurance plus other financial plans such as mutual funds"	29
No answer	2

Six out of ten respondents admitted that they were either "not too well informed" or "not at all informed" about life insurance. Not surprisingly, some 40 percent of them agreed that they felt uneasy when buying life insurance because they weren't sure that they were buying the right kind of policy.

This lack of self-confidence was related, in part, to suspicions about insurance agents. Three-quarters of the respondents believed that the commission system affects the recommendations that an agent makes. Furthermore, 44 percent agreed that agents "take advantage of your concern" and try "to make you feel guilty if you don't buy." One consequence of this high-pressure image of agents was that over two-thirds of the respondents said that they resent being contacted by life insurance agents.

5

MARKETING
PLANNING
AND STRATEGY

Planning and strategy focus on the overall company problem: how to match the company's resources to opportunities in the market, for long-run profitability.

Any marketing plan designed to sell the company's products or services must consider the size and nature of the product's particular advantage to users and the number and kind of people likely to be interested in that advantage. But it must also take into account the penetrability of the market. Penetrability is determined by:

1. Degree of Satisfaction with Existing Products or Services. Satisfaction in turn depends both on the intensity of need that people feel and on the degree to which existing products fill that need.

2. Communicability of the Appeals of the Proposed Product. Communicability depends on the nature of the product (how technically complex or otherwise difficult it is to explain); on the availability of suitable media to reach the particular market; on the ability of the available media to carry the message convincingly (including the authority of the particular media and the credibility of the company's own sales force); and on the readiness of people to open their minds to the message. That last factor depends, in turn, on the intensity of need as described in 1 above, and on the company image as in 3 below.

3. Company Image (or Composite Reputation). Image depends not only on the position that the company has already achieved in the various markets with its existing products and promotion but also on the skills and attitudes of the company management that caused the image to exist in the first place. The actions of management will enhance, reinforce, or detract from the image as time goes on.

4. Management Skills and Attitudes. These characteristics tend usually to reflect previous experience, because events have a way of perpetuating the existing strengths and weaknesses of management; the results of action or inaction are taken as confirmation of the original decisions, which of course caused those particular results to happen. But company strengths that are appropriate for one kind of product are not necessarily appropriate for another kind. However, it is possible for organizations to change as the result of experience; this is one reason why deliberate long-range planning has to take place, in order to develop the existing skills and attitudes and make everyone conscious of the need to grow if the company's goals are to be achieved.

5. *All of the Above Factors Are Affected by Competition.* If competitors' products, messages, images, or management strengths are better, then the penetrability of the market will be that much more difficult, more time-consuming, and more expensive.

The company must build its marketing plan on the strengths it has for penetrating a given market. Its actual strategy may be to make the most of such strengths for particular segments of the market, or for the whole mass market, but in any event its entry into the market with a new product or a new marketing program will be determined by which of its strengths are greatest in relation to the opportunities.

Timing is important. The market penetration planned for may be a future stage, but the problem is when and where to get started most economically and efficiently, so that progress can be made toward the ultimate goal. Unless the ultimate goal is envisaged from the beginning, the company may not stretch itself to the necessary effort.

One of the most important tools is pricing. Progress has to be made against competition. The price must be set high enough to maximize dollar returns, but low enough to attract buyers and to forestall other companies from trying to move in; high enough to afford flexibility (always greater downward than it is upward in pricing), but low enough to motivate salesmen and distributors.

Management must take a long-range look at the company's business and then—considering where the company wants to be five or ten years in the future, and what the company's particular strengths and weaknesses are in the market—determine the marketing efforts that are needed to reach that goal.

There always are various ways of reaching that goal, but the essence is a consistent plan, all the elements of which are self-reinforcing. And the elements do, in total, add up to the marketing mix covered in the preceding sections. A poor objective, if consistently carried through in detail, may actually be stronger than a good objective without a plan. Best of all is both a good objective *and* a good plan.

APEX CHEMICAL COMPANY

(The executive committee of Apex Chemical Company—a medium-size chemical manufacturer with annual sales of $60,000,000—is trying to

determine which of two new compounds the company should market. The two products were expected to have the same gross margin percentage. The following conversation takes place among the vice-president for research, Ralph Rogovin; the vice-president for marketing, Miles Mumford; and the president, Paul Prendigast.)

VP-RESEARCH. Compound A-115, a new electrolysis agent, is the one; there just isn't any doubt about it. Why, for precipitating a synergistic reaction in silver electrolysis, it has a distinct advantage over anything now on the market.

PRESIDENT. That makes sense, Ralph. Apex has always tried to avoid "me too" products and if this one is that much better . . . what do you think, Miles?

VP-MARKETING. Well, I favor the idea of Compound B-227, the plastic oxidizer. We have some reputation in that field; we're already known for our plastic oxidizers.

VP-RESEARCH. Yes, Miles, but this one isn't really better than the ones we already have. It belongs to the beta-prednigone group, and they just aren't as good as the stigones are. We *do* have the best stigone in the field.

PRESIDENT. Just the same, Ralph, the beta-prednigones are cutting into our stigone sales. The board of directors has been giving me a going over on that one.

VP-MARKETING. Yes, Ralph, maybe they're not as good scientists as we are—or think we are—but the buyers in the market seem to insist on buying beta-prednigones. How do you explain that? The betas have 60 percent of the market now.

VP-RESEARCH. That's your job, not mine, Miles. If we can't sell the best product—and I can prove it *is* the best, as you've seen from my data and computations—then there's something wrong with Apex's marketing effort.

PRESIDENT. What do you say to that, Miles? What *is* the explanation?

VP-MARKETING. Well, it's a very tricky field—the process in which these compounds are used is always touch-and-go; everyone is always trying something new.

VP-RESEARCH. All the more reason to put our effort behind Compound A-115, in the electrolysis field. Here we know that we have a real technical breakthrough. I agree with Paul that that's our strength.

PRESIDENT. What about that, Miles? Why not stay out of the dogfight represented by Compound B-227, if the plastic oxidizer market is as tricky as you say?

VP-MARKETING. I don't feel just right about it, Paul. I understand that the electrolysis market is pretty satisfied with the present products. We did a survey and 95 percent said they were satisfied with the Hamfield Company's product.

PRESIDENT.   It's a big market, too, isn't it, Miles?

VP-MARKETING.   Yes, about $10 million a year total.

PRESIDENT.   And only one strongly entrenched company—Hamfield?

VP-MARKETING.   Yes, I must admit it's not like the plastic oxidizer situation—where there are three strong competitors, and about a half-dozen who are selling off-brands. On the other hand, oxidizers are a $40 million market—four times as big.

PRESIDENT.   That's true, Ralph. Furthermore, our oxidizer sales represent 25 percent of our total sales.

VP-RESEARCH.   But we've been losing ground the past year. Our oxidizer sales dropped 10 percent, didn't they, Ralph? While the total oxidizer market was growing, didn't you say?

VP-MARKETING.   Well, the electrolysis field is certainly more stable. Total sales are holding level, and, as I said before, Hamfield's share is pretty constant, too.

PRESIDENT.   What about the technical requirements in the electrolysis field? With a really improved product we ought to be able . . .

VP-MARKETING.   Well, to tell you the truth, I don't know very much about the kind of people who use it, and how they . . . You see, it's really a different industry.

PRESIDENT.   What about it, Ralph?

VP-RESEARCH.   It's almost a different branch of chemistry, too. But I have plenty of confidence in our laboratory men. I can't see any reason why we should run into trouble. . . . It really does have a plus three point superiority on a scale of 100—here, the chart shows it crystal clear, Miles.

VP-MARKETING.   But aren't we spreading ourselves pretty thin—instead of concentrating where our greatest know-how . . . You've always said, Paul, that . . .

PRESIDENT.   Yes, I know, but maybe we ought to diversify, too. You know, all our eggs in one basket . . .

VP-MARKETING.   But if it's a good basket. . . .

VP-RESEARCH.   Nonsense, Miles, it's the kind of eggs you've got in the basket that counts—and Compound A-115, the electrolysis agent, is scientifically the better one.

VP-MARKETING.   Yes, but what about taking the eggs to the market? . . . Maybe people don't want to buy that particular egg from us, but they would buy Compound B-227—the plastic oxidizer.

PRESIDENT.   Eggs, eggs, eggs—I'm saying to both of you, let's just be sure we don't lay any!

If you had to choose one of these two products, which would it be? What criteria (and what ranking on each criterion) would you use in making this decision? Could you, on the basis of this brief glimpse of Apex, give it any guidelines for product strategy that would help it to do more effective developmental or pure research?

GRANDHOLM COMPANY

The Grandholm Company, a manufacturer of elevators and chairlifts for private homes, small hospitals, and apartment houses, was a well-established firm that had been in business for forty years. Sales had been slowly but steadily increasing over the period of its existence. Originally, the company's principal market was in the elaborate homes of rich industrialists; then, when that market began to decline, the company found new business in private homes where there were invalids who could not otherwise get from one floor to another. Of late, the company had found that the only way it could continue to grow was through expanding into the sale of semi-automatic elevators for commercial rest homes and small apartment houses. Its prices were higher than those of the larger elevator manufacturers, but it could do a more specialized job of adaptation to the customer's needs than its competitors apparently cared to do.

The company had developed a new model, based on a revolutionary new engineering principle, which it felt should be able to command a much larger market. The advantages of the new model were in quality of operation—easy, effortless starts and stops—and in economy of maintenance, rather than in initial cost. In fact, prices of the new model for a small apartment house would be about 20 percent higher than the previous model; for a large building, prices would be about 10 percent above those of large, nationally known competitors.

The management of the company was anxious to expand its selling activities, and felt it should hire a sales promotion manager. (Up to this point the general manager had been directly overseeing the sales promotion activities of three men.) The president narrowed the field of applicants to two men, either one of whom he thought would be satisfactory. To help him in making his selection, he obtained from each of the two candidates an account of the "one promotional effort you are proudest of." To make their accounts as objective as possible, he had his assistant rewrite them as factual reports rather than personal success stories. They are the promotions described in the Tawland and Whiting cases.[1]

Put yourself in the place of the president. Assuming that the two men were otherwise so even in their qualifications that you could not choose between them, which one would you select on the basis of the accounts of the "promotional" efforts that they submitted? More specifically: Which one would you choose, if you had to make the decision without any further delay? Why do

[1] See Chapter 4, pages 146 and 148.

you prefer this man to the other? How sure would you be of your choice? Do you think there is any difference between the relative potentialities of these two men when you look at their long-run potential rather than their chances of immediate success?

SILVERDALE DRUG COMPANY

(Scene: Silverdale Drug Company. Office of Preston ("Pete") Peterson, president. Meeting with him to discuss company policies and plans are Sheldon ("Shell") Summers, sales manager; and Thomas ("Tom") Tarkington, treasurer.)

PETERSON. I've been reading a lot of stuff about return on investment, but the idea doesn't seem to apply, in its usual form, to our particular business. Being wholesalers, our real assets are not the normal balance sheet items of buildings, equipment, inventory, bank balances. Rather *our* real assets are our customers. We've invested countless man-hours and a lot of dollars in developing them into loyal customers; and it's from those investments, in the form of continuing business, that we receive our returns—not just in the year we expend the time and money, but for many years into the future. Isn't that just as valid as the way manufacturers figure they receive returns on their investments in plant and equipment?

TARKINGTON. So what?

PETERSON. Why can't we, for purposes of making decisions about expenditures designed to increase our sales and/or profitability, look at our customers that way? As if they represented a certain capital value that can be made even more valuable by further or new kinds of expenditures? And if the increase in value is going to be greater than the cost, then that's something we ought to go ahead with.

SUMMERS. How would you do it, Pete?

PETERSON. I'm not sure. Any ideas, Tom?

TARKINGTON. Well, we could calculate their value in terms of their contribution to overhead and profit. That's the way ROI is mostly used with other kinds of investments.

SUMMERS. What would that make them worth?

TARKINGTON. Let's see. Annual sales are running at $5 million per year. Gross margin—that is, sales minus cost of goods—comes to about 15 percent; and 15 percent of $5 million is $750,000. Now, take off the costs of selling, delivery, a little for postage and telephone and even bad debts—the variable costs associated directly with servicing our customers—which add up to about $350,000. (Consider everything else overhead and profit.) This leaves us with $750,000 minus $350,000, or $400,000—the *annual contribution* that our customers make to our overhead and profit, or the *return on investment* represented by our customers. That brings us to the tricky question: How do you translate that into an investment value?

PETERSON. Suppose we use 10 percent. That is, consider that in our kind of business, we expect an investment to pay for itself in ten years; or, to put it another way, the standard for judging an investment is whether or not it will return an average of 10 percent per year. Besides, it doesn't really matter what figure we use so long as we are going to be considering alternative uses of our money. So long as the candidates for expenditure all have the same basis, we can compare them against each other.

TARKINGTON. Using 10 percent, our customers would be equivalent in value to ten times $400,000, or $4 million. But don't tell the Internal Revenue boys! Our last annual report lists our assets at $1,500,000.

PETERSON. Don't worry. There's no reason we can't have a different set of figures designed especially for making management decisions.

SUMMERS. With roughly 400 customers, that makes each one worth about $10,000. Whew! When you realize that, it becomes pretty important to do everything we can to protect our "investments," as you call them, Pete —to see to it that we don't do anything to impair their value.

PETERSON. Even more important, to see to it that they increase in value.

TARKINGTON. If you're going to do that kind of figuring, you'd better remember that they're not all of equal value. Don't forget that 65 to 75 percent of our customers account for 25 to 35 percent of our business.

SUMMERS. Well, let's not get too fancy. The next thing, you'll be telling us that we must consider depreciation—I suppose that would be the rate at which we lose customers per year through death, sellout, defection to another supplier, and so on.

TARKINGTON. It so happens I have the figures—about 5 percent per year. But that's probably offset by the normal growth of an average customer; otherwise our volume wouldn't remain very stable. So okay, if you really want me to be fancy, what about taking into account the "present value of money" and applying cash-discounted flow techniques?

SUMMERS. What in the name of? . . .

TARKINGTON. Okay, okay. It only means that money spent today has a different value—or a different cost—than money spent tomorrow. But forget it. I agree with Pete. That much refinement is meaningless. The important thing is to have a common basis of comparison for alternative uses of money *today*—or any day that you're involved in making such a decision.

PETERSON. That's enough—more than enough. Let's look at some of what you fellows are proposing to do with the developmental money we do have at our disposal. I figure that we have up to $35,000 available for investment into a long-range project to improve our sales and/or profitability.

SUMMERS. Well, you know, Pete, I want to add a new salesman, and that would cost about $10,000 per year if it ran the same as for our present salesmen. So the $35,000 we have would cover us for three to four years.

PETERSON. How many customers would that add by the end of that time, do you think?

SUMMERS. Maybe forty. Yes, I think it would be forty—that's our present average per man.

TARKINGTON. What about improving the *effectiveness* of our present salesmen, instead? How much would a really good sales-training program cost? Certainly, nowhere near as much. And how much would that add to their productivity?

SUMMERS. Not more than 2 percent—if we're lucky, 3 percent. And the cost would be just about the same as adding a new salesman. By the time we got through, it would be pretty close to $10,000.

TARKINGTON. But, Shell, that would be a one-time cost, wouldn't it? We'd spend it just once, the first year, and then we'd reap the benefit every year thereafter.

SUMMERS. Sure, but one salesman represents a 10 percent increase in number of customers, and only costs three or four times as much, figuring, as I said, that he could line up forty customers by the end of three or four years. Furthermore, if you're talking about salesmen's effectiveness, I'd rather take the money available and offer bonuses for the best sales records each year. The prospect of $3,000 or $4,000 to be divided among the top performers at the end of the year would be enough of a carrot to boost total sales 4 or 5 percent, I'd be willing to bet.

PETERSON. I'm more interested in improving the effectiveness of our customers, rather than our salesmen. Jim Vigary, who heads up Vigary and Company over in Hopkinton—I talked with him at the Wholesale Druggists Convention I went to last September—has mounted what he says is a very effective program to help his retail drug customers to be better merchants and merchandisers. He figures his payoff comes in two ways: (1) from an increase of sales through better customer performance; and (2) from becoming a preferred wholesaler source and increasing his share of the market. Costs him about $20,000 per year, but he can afford it; he's about twice as big as we are. And he estimates that in two to three years he will be reaching the point where sales of his average retailer are up by 15 percent. Suppose we just spend half as much—say, by using a consultant part-time instead of hiring a full-time merchandising specialist the way Vigary is doing it?

Well, let's do a little thinking—and figuring—and see where we come out in terms of contribution to overhead and profit over the next ten years. In other words, with $30,000 or $40,000 to invest in our customers, which way will we get the best ROI?

In what project or projects should Silverdale "invest" $35,000 in order to achieve the best "returns" over the next ten years?

TIDEWATER MILLS, INC.

Tidewater Mills, Inc., a large Virginia textile manufacturer, had annual sales totaling $120 million. The company sold direct to 300 major department stores, whereas the remainder of its 3,000 retail outlets were served through wholesalers.

The Tidewater management contemplated putting an experimental dish towel on the market. Laboratory tests indicated that the new "miracle" fabric was superior for high absorbency (50 percent greater) and lint-free characteristics. A committee studying the situation found the market potential large despite the use of automatic dishwashers. The pressing questions now were those of size, price, and retail distribution.

Towel Size

The executive committee of the company had already decided that no looms should be purchased specifically for the production of dish towels and that looms already owned by the company would have to be used. Because the company owned no narrow looms (18"–20" wide) on which dish towels were conventionally woven, this decision meant that the towels would have to be woven on looms which were 36" wide.

Because the towels had to be woven on 36" looms, it was necessary to make 36" the length of the towel. In deciding the width, the director of marketing research had assembled the following information for the use of the committee.

Several shopping trips were made by members of the marketing research department, primarily to New York stores. They found that the size of dish towels typically ranged from 17" × 32" to 18" × 36", with most of the sales volume in the 17" × 32" category. A summary of facts regarding dish towels found on the market is given in Exhibit 1.

An interview with the buyer of a large New York store resulted in the following information on size and price.

1. *Size.* The buyer said that 17" × 32" was the most common size; 20" × 30" standard for imported linen dish towels; 30" is a short towel; 36" is a long towel; width varies from 16" to 18". He believed that a length as long as 36" may be a disadvantage for hanging towels on small kitchen towel racks. However, the buyer did not consider size to be a critical factor. The overall average popular size is 17" × 32"; 18" × 36" tends to be the more expensive towel, 17" × 34" or 17" × 31¾" the less expensive towel.

EXHIBIT 1   Information on Dish Towels

Material	Size	Quality	Price
Terrycloth	29" × 15¾"	Good	$1.45
Cotton	31" × 17"	Good	.98
Cotton	32" × 16½"	Poor	.89
Cotton and small % linen	35" × 18"	Excellent	1.75
Cotton	31" × 17"	Fair	1.00
Terrycloth	28¾" × 16½"	Fair	1.10
25% linen, 75% cotton	31¾" × 17"	Good	.99
Irish linen	31½" × 16¾"	Excellent	2.25
Cotton and small % linen	32" × 17"	Fair	1.50
Cotton and small % linen	32" × 17"	Fair	1.25
Terrycloth	32" × 17"	Excellent	1.75
Linen and cotton	32" × 17"	Fair	1.25
Terrycloth	20" × 15"	Very poor	.69

2. *Price.* In this store, prices range from 98¢ to $1.95, depending on quality and size. About 80 percent of the dish towel volume in this store is at or under $1.25.

Tidewater's test laboratory reported that, even after considerable effort to lessen its tendency to shrink, the proposed toweling showed a shrink of 14.7 percent in width and 7.7 percent in length after the equivalent of six months' use and that after twelve months the total shrink was 17.4 percent in width and 8.1 percent in length. These figures contrasted with a shrink averaging around 12 percent in length and 6 percent in width after six months for competitors' dish towels already on the market. The width shrinkage was higher than the length shrinkage on the Tidewater product rather than the reverse, as was the case with competitive toweling. The reason was that Tidewater was using wide looms—36"—and, in making the width of the cloth the length of the towel, the warp had to run in the direction of the width of the towel rather than the length.[1]

The marketing research department had conducted tests to determine the size of kitchen towel most acceptable to customers. Housewives in the metropolitan Washington area were used as subjects. The housewives to be questioned were selected from a list that Tidewater had developed over the years for use in similar surveys and from new additions suggested by those already on the list. No employees or members of em-

---

[1] Alternatives, such as cutting the fabric after it left the loom, were ruled out as impractical or too costly because of the additional processing (e.g., hemming).

ployees' families were included. The memorandum from the marketing research department is summarized in the Appendix.

Price

Cost estimates by the manufacturing department indicated that quantity production of the "miracle" cloth would cost Tidewater 34¢ for a foot of the 36"-wide fabric. This estimate was for the immediate future. The department anticipated that manufacturing efficiencies, growing out of experience with the fabric, would tend to bring the direct cost down somewhat. On the other hand, it seemed likely that wage rates would increase. The future course of raw materials was extremely difficult to predict with any assurance of accuracy.

The results of the shopping trips had indicated that prices such as $1, $1.25, $1.50, and $1.75 were usual for dish towels. The $1 price was eliminated from consideration because the Tidewater management thought that it could not sell its towel at that price and still make a profit. If the towels were to be 18" wide, which was one possibility, the cost of manufacture would be 1.5 × .34 or 51¢. (If department stores, rather than supermarkets, were decided on as outlets, the wholesalers would have to charge 60¢ to get their usual 15 percent margin, and the department stores would have to charge $1 to get their usual 40 percent margin. This would accomplish distribution at a retail price of $1, but leave no margin for Tidewater.[1])

The company had a target margin of 20 percent for goods of this type in order to cover selling costs and allow for a profit. If Tidewater planned on a 20 percent margin, its selling price would be 64¢, and the wholesaler's price would be 75¢, and the retail price would be $1.25.

Recently the marketing research department had sponsored tests of alternative prices. The $1.25 price was tested against the $1.50 price by offering the 20" × 36" towel in comparable stores in comparable cities but with the difference in price. A company demonstrator was used on the first day of sale in each store, but there was no advertising. See Exhibit 2 for the results of this test.

The $1.75 price was then tested in large Midwestern department stores. Demonstrators were again used, and one store placed advertisments in two local papers. The results of the $1.75 price test are presented in Exhibit 3.

---

[1] Tidewater experience was that when it sold direct to major department stores, the additional costs incurred were just about equivalent to the wholesalers' margin.

EXHIBIT 2   Test Sales—$1.25 Stores vs. $1.50 Stores

	Test City Population	Type of Store	First-Day Sales (doz)	First 60 Days—Average Sales per Week	
				Per Store (doz)	Per Store Group (doz)
$1.25		*Large-size Stores*			
April	800,000	Average—promotional	16½	19	
February	800,000	High-class linen store	24	25	
February	800,000	Large, better type	4	17	
January	248,000	Large—promotional middle class	17½	25	
April	248,000	Large—promotional working class	10	17½	21
$1.50					
June	335,000	Large—better type	–	3⅓	
June	225,000	Mediocre—promotional type	7	3	
May	168,000	Better-type store	8½	6	4
$1.25		*Medium-size Stores*			
May	107,000	Average—promotional	10	7½	7½
$1.50					
June	130,000	Good—average	8	3	
June	102,000	High grade	3½	2	
June	93,000	Low end—promotional	8	5½	
June	84,000	Mediocre	2	3	3½
$1.25		*Small-size Stores*			
May	42,000	Promotional—good	20	25	
April	65,000	Promotional—good	20	25	
February	25,000	High-grade quality store	–	25	25
$1.50					
June	51,000	Good—average	2¼	3⅓	
May	17,000	Good—dry goods		1½	2½

EXHIBIT 3   Test Sales at $1.75

Type store	Date	Weather	Traffic	Promotion	Sales Units	Doz.
Large—middle class	Wed., 7/29	Hot, humid	Slow	Demo., no ad	58	4⅝
Large—high class	Tues., 7/28	Fair, hot	Good	Demo., no ad	92	7⅔
Large—better-type	Mon., 7/27	Fair, warm	Fairly Good	Demo., no ad	69	5¾
Large—high-class	Fri., 7/31	Fair, hot	Slow	Demo., 2 ads	80	6⅔
					299	25

Average number dozen towels sold per store: 6¼.

Channels

The director of market research prepared for the committee a summary of a survey by a women's magazine's research department. This survey had asked consumers: "In what type of store do you generally buy kitchen towels?" The responses were as shown in Exhibit 4.

EXHIBIT 4   Where Consumers Buy Kitchen Towels

Department stores—upstairs	39%
Department stores—basement	18
Discount chains & supermarkets	17
Variety stores	12
Linen shop	4
Other	7

There was some evidence that variety stores, discount chains, and supermarkets were advancing quickly in the dish towel field. Several manufacturers of lower-quality dish towels were pushing distribution through these outlets with smaller, lower-quality, closely margined goods designed to sell in 69¢ and 79¢ ranges. Supermarkets got a 25 percent markup on nonfood items, and it was not necessary to go through a wholesaler when selling to them.

If you had no further information and had to make decisions, what size, price, and type of outlet would you choose? Draw up a marketing program for the towel. Do you think your program would be successful? How many towels must be sold, at the price and size you recommend, for Tidewater to break even? (For breakeven calculation, assume that there are fixed promotional and other expenses of $200,000.)

Appendix: Marketing Research Report Summary

MEMORANDUM

Subject. Tidewater Dish Towel Survey.

Purpose. To find out the minimum width of dish towel acceptable to housewives; also their opinions regarding a good average width.

Method. Six selected samples of different widths were shown to 29 housewives of varying ages; 15 were current Tidewater testers, and 14 were new.

For the most part, different widths (12″, 13″, 13½″, 14½″, 15″, and 16″) were shown at random, starting with the median width of 14½″. Questions were also asked about ideal size and present usage.

Results. 1. Minimum shrunk width—About 36 percent of the housewives found 12″ to 13½″ the minimum they would tolerate.

2. Good acceptable width—21/29 or 72 percent found widths ranging from 14½″ to 16″ as being quite acceptable. Overall median width equals 16″.

3. Ideal width—15/29 or 52 percent preferred 15″ to 17″; while 14/29 or 48 percent preferred 18″ to 20″.

4. Type towels using now—Out of 29, 3 were found to be using linen, 10 terrycloth, and 16 cotton or combinations of cotton and rayon.

DIXIE INSTRUMENTS, INC.

In August 1956, the management of Dixie Instruments, Inc., was evaluating its hi-fi tape recorder, a product that it had been developing, in an effort to decide whether to produce the item and, if so, how to market it.

Located in Houston, Texas, Dixie Instruments had been founded in 1950 by Dr. Paulsen, a leading scientist in the field of nuclear instrumentation. Of the company's busines, 80 percent was government contract work, with the remaining sales being made to industrial and university research laboratories. The company's annual sales, which had fluctuated between $100,000 and $500,000, were currently about $200,000. During 1956 the number of employees had dropped from 100 to 60.

The hi-fi tape recorder was the outgrowth of independent experiments conducted by Mr. Cameron before he was employed by Dixie as a technician. The heart of the development was a five-position switch mechanism in the microphone barrel (dictate–record, playback, fast forward, rewind, and short back-up) that would convert a standard tape recorder for use in office dictation. For office use, these machines had the advantage of permitting erasing and rerecording without the necessity of marking a tab for the stenographer's correction. Tape recorders of increasing sensitivity were used for recording speech, for average music, and for hi-fi music. The conversion of a standard recorder did not alter the machine's sound quality.

During the past four years Mr. Cameron had bought inexpensive home tape recorders, converted them with the switch mechanism, and had successfully sold 50 in the Houston area. These units were presumably purchased primarily for office dictating use.

In July 1955, Mr. Cameron had approached Dr. Paulsen and proposed that Dixie Instruments take over the development of a hi-fi version of his dictating tape recorder in return for a royalty arrangement.

Before accepting this offer, Dr. Paulsen had his administrative assistant, Mr. Hastings, do some research into the tape recorder field. From an officer of a large national electronic firm he obtained an estimate that national sales of tape recorders were running at an annual rate in excess of 100,000. An industry publication, *Electrical Merchandising*, cited these figures on the industry's *unit* sales, as shown in Exhibit 1.

EXHIBIT 1   Tape Recorder Sales, 1953–1956

1953	275,000
1954	470,000
1955	550,000
1956 (estimated)	632,000

This same publication stated that in 1955, 20 percent of the sales were made in the under-$100 price range, 70 percent in the $100–$300 range, and 10 percent in the over-$300 range. Sales of magnetic tape were reported by this source as shown in Exhibit 2.

EXHIBIT 2   Magnetic Tape Sales, 1952–1956

1952	$ 7 million
1953	$10 "
1954	$14 "
1955	$20 "
1956 (estimated)	$30 "

Mr. Hastings found that the home recorder market had been served principally by five companies, each of which was reputed to have invested a million dollars or more in research, machinery, tooling, and market development. Prices had become very competitive. A recorder recently introduced by a large electronic manufacturer was retailing at about $140, and the quality of this machine was apparently satisfactory to most home users. There were a number of cheaper sets running as low as $40 a set retail. Other manufacturers such as Ampro, Webcor, Magnecord, and Wilcox-Gay had large sales volumes in the price range from $150 to $250 retail. For superior tonal quality, hi-fi enthusiasts could choose an Ampex, a Berlant, or one or two other makes selling between $450 and $600.

Mr. Hastings also learned that there was a considerable market for recording and reproducing machines in business offices, primarily for letter writing. This market had been served for years by Dictaphone, Ediphone, Soundscriber, Audograph, and to a limited extent by other companies. Their machines were convenient for dictation and transcription but had relatively poor sound qualities. Mr. Hastings was unable, however, to obtain any reliable estimate of the unit sales of business recording machines.

In view of the fact that Dixie Instruments' sales of nuclear instruments had dropped markedly, the company seized upon Mr. Cameron's offer as an opportunity to use temporarily idle research and production capacity.

Dr. Paulsen explained the decision by pointing out that the regular business of his company was highly technical, with wide fluctuations in demand both from year to year and seasonally within the year. For this reason, and because recent reductions in sales volume had prevented covering fixed costs, the company had been particularly anxious to find a proprietary item, the demand for which would be subject to the company's own promotional efforts.

At the time it was decided to embark on engineering development of the hi-fi tape recorder, Dr. Paulsen estimated that manufacturing costs would total $100 per instrument. It was assumed that such a machine would retail readily at $300, leaving an adequate net profit. Consultation with a high-ranking sales executive of one of the large recorder companies tended to confirm Dr. Paulsen's approximation of price and profitability. It was originally estimated that the development program would require six months and $25,000 to reach the stage of an engineering prototype.

During development, the engineers' emphasis was on high musical quality, reflecting their belief that the home recorder market was a volume market and must be satisfied. They kept at it until they had a unit that they felt would record and play back acceptably. Company personnel believed their machine was somewhat superior to their competitors' $150–$250 home machines, and markedly superior to the dictating machines then on the market. Dixie's sales manager hoped this superiority would give him a selling point—that is, versatility. The machine could be used at home or in the office and for individual dictation or for conferences. Most other dictating machines on the market required special multiple units for satisfactory performance in conference use.

However, one result of the stress laid on quality was that the estimate of manufacturing cost was increased to approximately $140. Such a cost would require a retail price of about $500, which was considered too high to compete with other office machines or with lower-price home recorders. Dixie's quality, furthermore, was not nearly good enough to compete with Ampex and Berlant in the $500 bracket.

So, after seven months and the expenditure of $30,000, a redesign and a cost reduction program was begun. The engineers were insistent on their ideas of quality. However, after discussion with the sales department, some compromises were worked out to reduce parts cost and assembly time.

Cost reductions had to be coupled with steps toward solving the remaining operating problems or "bugs" within the unit. Among these were: speed variations causing distortion of sound, failure of switches and switch actuators, and overheating of the unit from high wattage being used in a compact case.

Finally, after the expenditure of an additional $5,000, Dr. Paulsen decided on a pilot manufacturing run of twenty machines, in order to determine whether units made and assembled by the ordinary factory worker (rather than engineers) would operate. More accurate information as to labor costs was also desired. The result of this pilot run was that only one of the twenty machines would operate satisfactorily without expensive expert doctoring. The manufacturing costs of quantity production could now be more closely estimated in the neighborhood of $132 per unit, including 20 percent annual amortization of special tooling. This indicated a retail selling price of about $400 at the desired rate of profit.

At about this time (March 1956) the controller drew up what he called a "budgetary outline," setting forth the financial results of manufacturing and selling the recorder at two different sales volumes. (See Exhibit 3.)

From the marketing standpoint, there was a question whether Dixie could achieve the same volume in home recorders as did other manufacturers. These competitors sold through distributors, who were given discounts of 50 percent off list, and who in turn sold to dealers at 40 percent off list. The sales manager felt that Dixie could not afford to give more than 40 percent, on the average, to middlemen. (It was contemplated that 40 percent would be the discount on purchases of 10 units, with special additional discounts or sales aids on larger quantities, but discounts of only 33⅓ percent on purchases of three units and only 25 percent on purchases of single units.) This meant that sales would have to be made direct to retail dealers and that Dixie's selling costs per unit would be higher than its competitors'. No additional salesmen were contemplated at the outset; salaried employees would handle initial local sales.

Furthermore, the sales manager believed that a retail price higher than $350 would reduce the potential volume of Dixie's machine in the home recorder field. On the other hand, he felt a Dixie recorder sold for use as an office dictating machine—including a foot switch, headphone, and

EXHIBIT 3 Controller's Budgetary Outlines (Dollar amounts in thousands)

	CONDITION 1				CONDITION 2			
	1,500 Recorders		Electronic Instruments	Company Total	2,000 Recorders		Electronic Instruments	Company Total
	Dollars	Percentage			Dollars	Percentage		
Sales Billed *	$341*	100.0	$180	$521	$454	100.0	$180	$634
Direct labor	40		30		52		30	
Materials & parts	129		67		171		67	
Prime cost—total	$169		$ 97	266	$223		$ 97	320
Burden—direct	14			14	16			14
Burden—allocated	25		18	43	29		17	46
Manufacturing cost	208	61.0	115	323	268	59.0	114	382
Manufacturing margin	133	39.0	65	198	186	41.0	66	252
Engineering expense	19	5.6	25	44	19	4.2	25	44
Selling expense	49	14.4	5	54	70	15.4	5	75
Royalties—Armour	3	.9		3	5	1.1		5
Cash discounts	4	1.2	1	5	5	1.1	1	6
Interest on borrowed funds	8	2.3		8	9	2.0		9
General administrative expense	30	8.8	16	46	36	7.9	15	51
Franchise tax—taxes			1	1	1	.2	1	2
Subtotal of expenses	$113	33.1	$ 48	$161	$145	31.9	$ 47	$192

	1,500 Recorders		Electronic	Company		2,000 Recorders		Electronic	Company
	Dollars	Percentage	Instruments	Total		Dollars	Percentage	Instruments	Total
Dept. profit remaining	20	5.9	17	37		41	9.1	19	60
Executive bonus—guar.	4	1.2	1	5		0		0	0
Executive bonuses—%	2	.6	2	4		8	1.8	5	13
Dept. profit remaining	$ 14					$ 33			
Royalties—Cameron	3	1.1		3		8	1.8		8
Operating profit before federal taxes	11	3.0	14	25		25	5.5	14	39

* At $210 per unit plus $17 worth of accessories.

federal excise tax—if priced in the neighborhood of $400, could compete with the existing models that were sold through strong retailing branches for about $380.

There were still engineering and manufacturing problems that would have to be solved in order to make sure the machine operated satisfactorily. The consensus of company officers was that another four months and $15,000 would be required to make a satisfactory unit. The controller also pointed out that once the technical and manufacturing problems were solved, the process of introducing the product on the competitive market would postpone the time when expected results could be achieved and that, accordingly, on the basis of his best conservative estimate, there would be an operating loss of about $50,000 in the first year (above and beyond the preliminary development expense).

Should Dixie go ahead with the recorder? If so, for what market? If you "believed" in the prospects of the recorder, and interpreted the controller's analysis as an argument against going ahead, how could you counter it in pleading your case before Dr. Paulsen? Assuming that, right or wrong, the decision is made to go ahead with the recorder, draw up the outline of a marketing program suited to the company's circumstances and your own appraisal of buying behavior for this product.

RIO RAILROAD

In 1960, the Rio Railroad, which served one of the principal inland coffee-growing areas of Brazil, suffered a serious decline in freight traffic revenues. This decline was almost wholly attributable to a drop in shipments of coffee beans. Both weather and market conditions were responsible. Although the Rio line had been prosperous enough in the past, so that its rolling equipment and tracks were in good condition, the management was worried about the future and did not feel it could stand continued annual declines in freight shipments without getting into difficulties. Passenger business was not an important source of revenue relative to freight, but it, too, was falling off slightly.

Two problems in particular bothered management: (1) dependence on the fate of one industry, with its fluctuations—plus what looked as if it might be a long-term downward trend, and (2) loss of business to trucks, as new highways were continually being opened up in the Rio's territory.

In the spring of 1962, the vice-president of sales decided to reappraise carefully his marketing effort, to make sure that he was getting as much business as possible for the railroad.

Product and Market

He began by studying the "product" offered by the railroad. The Rio was a terminal line; that is, it did not connect on the far end with another railroad. Nor did it extend to the coast, but had to depend on its connections with other carriers for through shipments.

"Time in transit" for freight movements was a problem of some importance. Within its own territory the Rio gave overnight service on carload shipments. On movements to the coast the goal was for "third morning" arrival. The challenge was to make sure the connecting carriers did not excessively delay the shipment in the process of changing crews, inspecting the cars, breaking up the train at junction points, and so forth.

Lcl (less than carload) movements of freight were ordinarily slow. Most railroads had their own particular minimum weight requirements for each car. When a car was underweight, it sat on a siding until a sufficient cargo had been assembled to make the minimum weight. As a result, lcl movements for even short hauls could take from several days to several weeks. On its own line, the Rio was generally prompt in moving lcl cars; at times, however, there had been some startling exceptions, including an eleven-day delay on one movement over a distance of only forty-five miles.

The line's carload rates were competitive with truck rates, and lower for the longer hauls. However, although the company had not made an extensive study of the situation, there was some reason to believe that lcl rates were out of line with truck competition on all merchandise originating in the eastern part of Rio's territory.

The railroad offered no pick-up and delivery service. In the case of carload shipments, however, the Rio placed the empty cars on sidings for individual shippers. These shippers were given forty-eight hours for loading the car; after that time demurrage charges were applied. Receivers of carload shipments were subject to the same restrictions on unloading, for which they were responsible. The railroad would build sidings for individual shippers and receivers, provided the customers guaranteed a minimum of carload movements.

Lcl cars, called "way cars," were loaded and unloaded at the local Rio freight sheds by station employees. The loading function was assumed by the railroad because "way cars " were already part of an assembled train.

Most Rio traffic flowed eastward out of the territory. In 1960, for example, 60 percent of the traffic was outbound, 15 percent inbound, and 25 percent local. Lcl shipments, which were primarily inbound, amounted to but one percent of total tonnage. Passenger revenue likewise was insignificant, accounting for only 3 percent of cruzeiro (Brazilian dollar) revenue. Figures for 1960 and 1959 are shown in Exhibit 1.

EXHIBIT 1   Freight Traffic Statistics

	1960	1959
Average miles of road operated	398	398
Number of tons carried *	1,928,362	2,012,974
Number of tons carried one mile	267,652,666	275,754,000
Number of tons carried one mile per mile of road	672,494	692,849
Average distance hauled, each ton, miles	138.8	137.0

* In metric tons (U.S. equivalent 2,205 pounds).

The pattern of Rio traffic reflected, of course, the basic characteristics of the territory. Most towns were small and the population was widely scattered. The largest town in the territory had a population of 5,000; the total population of the ten largest was 38,000.

There were approximately 1,250 business concerns in the line's territory. Most of these concerns were small retailers, but there were also about 200 coffee growers and 35 small manufacturers.

It was not surprising that a large share of the railroad's business came from a small number of accounts. Although the company had about 600 regular customers in 1960, 19 shippers represented 61 percent of the line's forward business; 88 shippers, each shipping 100 cars or more, represented 89 percent. Seven receivers, on the other hand, took 50 percent of the inbound freight; 26, each receiving over 100 cars, took 78 percent. Seventy-seven percent of the railroad's business came from the ten largest towns.

The company did not have many records available relating to customer potentials. There were, of course, waybills for all shipments; but much of the customer information was scattered. Consequently, the vice-president of sales was eager to build up a useful file of readily available customer information.

Organization

In simplified form, the Rio Railroad was organized as shown in Exhibit 2.

The operating department was responsible for the physical running of the railroad. Engineering and maintenance functions were part of this department. Train scheduling, dispatching, equipment purchasing, and construction were centered here as well. Reporting to two divisional superintendents were thirty-two station agents, each responsible for the operation of his particular station. Seven of these agents were entitled supervisory agents and directed the activities of one or more station employees. Other agents ran a one-man show. Supervisory agents were

EXHIBIT 2   Organization of Rio Railroad

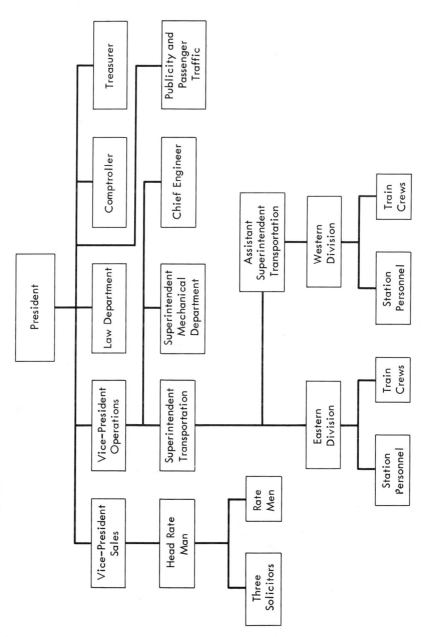

appointed jointly by the vice-president of operations and the vice-president of sales. Station agents were encouraged to join local business and fraternal groups. Most of these men were well acquainted with the businessmen in their respective towns.

With few exceptions the supervisory agents were the most capable. They were promoted from the ranks of the regular small station agents. All agents were responsible for the efficient operation of their local station, including the handling of freight; the maintenance of such records as demurrage reports, car records, freight movements, waybills, and bills of lading; the switching of cars; the operation of the freight shed; the servicing of local customers; the supervising of station employees; the scheduling of the station's work, as well as other activities.

All trains and equipment that entered the agent's station were his responsibility and were under his jurisdiction. He received and sent by telegraph (either personally or by means of his telegrapher) a stream of messages involving, ordinarily, the superintendent, train dispatchers, other agents, and the home office. The agents were generally busy men, although the burden was heaviest in the one-man stations. During the rainy season, when freight movements fell off considerably, the men did have a number of spare hours each day. They could not leave their offices, however, without permission of the superintendent and were, in a sense, "chained" by the telegraph key.

At one time the local agents had been responsible for sales solicitation. During the period of virtual railroad monopoly, the quality of such solicitation was acceptable; but most of the agents did an uninspiring job. Ordinarily they "sat' in their freight offices and waited for the business that had to come by rail anyway. Many of the men were skilled only as telegraphers and had little or no interest in customer relations. Their attitude was: "We've got the railroad. You have to use it."

The growth of truck competition forced the executives of the railroad to reappraise this sales approach. In 1958, the sales function was taken from the agents and given to the traffic department, which was in charge of rates. The name of the department was changed to sales; and the position of vice-president of sales was created and staffed by a forty-year-old man who had formerly been in the coffee business. He had three salesmen or "solicitors." One of the salesmen had the eastern half of the Rio's territory; one, the western half; and the other was a coffee specialist. Here are brief descriptions:

Mr. A was a good-natured, cigar-smoking extrovert, 45 years old. He had spent several years as a dining car supervisor before coming over to the sales department. He was a good "customers' man" and could entertain appropriately all kinds of accounts.

Mr. B had been a successful salesman for a farm equipment manufacturer until 1955, when, rather than accept a transfer to another part of the country, he became a ticket seller for the Rio. He was an avid hunter and occasionally served as guide for important customers of Rio officials. He was 30 years old.

Mr. C was the "old man" of the sales force, having been with the road thirty years. He liked to remind people of his thirty years' seniority and resented somewhat the relative progress made in the company by other men with less service. In his own words, he was "pushing 60." As an "old-timer" he knew most of the intricacies of the company, had many personal theories on running a railroad, and had made many good friends among the coffee shippers. In addition to his job as coffee specialist, Mr. C also served as "off-line" solicitor, occasionally making calls on shippers and receivers in non-Rio territories for the purpose of inducing these accounts to use the railroad's facilities.

In general, the vice-president was pleased with his solicitors. Their common weakness was a lack of any sales training. Each man operated by instinct, although the vice-president did route them as much as possible. There was no common number of calls per day, with the range in number running from two or three to fourteen or fifteen. The vice-president was worried that he had too few salesmen and felt that he should hire one, and perhaps two, new men. He based his conviction of undermanning on the fact that the railroad had never solicited a large majority of the available customers. Rather, the Rio sales efforts appeared to be concentrated on the largest, most obvious accounts. Virtually no attempts had been made to get the business of the many retailers in the area.

Many of the calls that the salesmen made were "trouble-shooting" visits in response to specific customer complaints. As a result, it was difficult to plan a salesman's visits far in advance. The salesmen worked five and one-half days a week most of the year and only five days during the rainy period. They were all paid on a yearly salary plus expense allowance basis.

To some extent, salesmen were interrupted in their rounds by visits from home office executives. Not infrequently a visiting official required a "personal chauffeur" or a hunting companion and accordingly pulled a salesman off the road. The vice-president of sales did his best to hold such interruptions to a minimum. In many cases, of course, such distractions were defended as desirable because large shippers or receivers were entertained in the process.

On their daily calls the salesmen followed no fixed pattern of behavior. By way of illustration, one of the men spent a day as follows:

Calls made: 9
Hours worked: 8½
Hours traveled: 3⅓
Lunch: 1 hour
Office time: 30 minutes
Customers seen: 6

One call of forty minutes was made on a Rio station agent. Two calls were made where a customer was not in. Two calls were made just because the salesman happened to see two customers walking on the sidewalk.

One call on a contractor resulted in that contractor's promising to ship four carloads of sand by the Rio. The contractor was willing to give the business to the railroad because the rate was no higher and the salesman "asked for the business at the right time."

Another call was made on a fertilizer dealer. The dealer turned down the salesman's offer to build a shed on the railroad trackside.

In a third call the salesman asked an automobile dealer with several agencies, "Why did you receive some cars last month by truck? After all, we bought a truck from you last spring because we thought you gave us all your business." The car dealer explained somewhat impatiently that most of his cars did come by railroad, but that for one of his agencies the trucking was more convenient.

The effectiveness of a salesman's efforts was ordinarily difficult to measure. Most of the shippers and receivers dealt in hundreds of cars, and a salesman's request for increased business might or might not result in the future use of a few additional cars. Furthermore, as one salesman said, "What can we offer the shipper?" To some extent salesmen tried to convert or retain customers by entertaining them. Several retailers in the western section referred to railroad solicitors in general as: "They walk in, offer you a cigar, chat a while and then ask, 'How many cars are you shipping by us next month?'"

Rates

While established truck rates were not too far out of line with railroad rates, many trucks hauling merchandise into the Rio's territory from the coast were willing to take a return load at a price sufficient to cover direct costs only. This "back haul" problem was of real concern. Some coffee shippers made wide use of this low-priced transportation.

There were, however, a few limitations to this form of transportation to the shipper: (a) During the bad season, truck movement on the highway was likely to be more hazardous than rail movement. (b) Many trucks were so undependable or so poorly equipped that commodities might arrive at the market late or in poor condition. (c) Some of these trucks were "fly-by-night" operations, so that the shipper had no financial recourse in case of trouble.

But, in general, truck competition was severe; and even the "regular" operators, without much or any rate advantage, provided the buyer with store-door delivery, smaller lot shipments, rapid service, and efficient freight handling that was hard to meet. Trucks, for example, delivered full truck loads at the coast a day earlier than rail. On incoming shipments, truck competition was intensified by the fact that many metropolitan shippers on the coast shied away from the trouble of transporting their merchandise to the nearest railroad station and relied instead on long-haul trucks.

The attitude of the local businessman toward the Rio Railroad was generally favorable. But the outspoken comments of one well-respected retailing merchant might be noted: "There is nothing wrong with the Rio rates. But it keeps its transportation advantages a secret to businessmen." The road received its largest share of criticism from businessmen in the western part of the territory who resented a cutback in passenger service in their area.

Relation of Sales to Operations

The railroad was faced with a difficult problem in reconciling the interests of the operating department with those of the sales department. A few of the common conflicts were:

1. Local agents were responsible for the economical handling of trains and cars and yet individual shippers and receivers often complained that such things as train schedules, demurrage charges, switching fees, humping practices, and freight house limitations were detrimental to their interests.
2. To stop a long freight train was costly because it meant idle time, delayed schedules, overtime operations, and so forth. Thus, freight car conductors were sometimes tempted to go through a small station without stopping, if the only freight for that station consisted of some lcl merchandise.
3. Local agents were responsible to the operating department and yet they constantly had to meet and negotiate with customers. Customer requests for agent time often conflicted with agent responsibilities at the local station. As one of the better agents said, "My operation would be a failure if I didn't constantly break a few rules."
4. In order to continue making profits, the railroad was forced to watch its expenses with care. Several steps had been taken by top management to hold operating costs to a minimum. In the slack months, for example, rolling stock was leased to other railroads. During these same months four to five of the smallest Rio stations were closed, all customers being advised to contact the agent in the nearest town. Over the years the trend had been for the closing and consolidation of small stations. At the same time permanent work forces at the individual stations were cut to the very minimum. Indeed, some of the supervisory agents complained that these drastic personnel reductions had reduced them to the status of clerks. These agents also complained that they had no time for anything but details.

From top management's point of view there was little conflict between the vice-presidents of sales and of operations. Both these men realized their mutual dependence and consulted each other frequently. Both realized the importance of each other's functions, and were always willing to compromise for the best interests of the road. The vice-president of sales, however, wanted to define more precisely the respective customer functions of the agents and of the salesmen. He was anxious to insure the maximum contribution to profits by both agents and salesmen.

What kind of long-range program should the vice-president of sales set up to reverse the decline in freight shipments? (Be sure to consider all demand factors, all elements of the marketing mix.) Does the president need to act?

INDEX
OF
CASES

ABOUT
THE AUTHORS

EDWARD C. BURSK is Professor (Emeritus) of Business Administration, Harvard Business School, and for over 25 years was Editor of the *Harvard Business Review*. Among his many books are *Text and Cases in Marketing: A Scientific Approach*, the four-volume *The World of Business* (co-editor), and the Bursk-Greyser companion volume to this one, *Advanced Cases in Marketing Management;* he has also written numerous articles on marketing and selling. As Educational Director of the International Marketing Institute, he has shaped the marketing training of hundreds of international executives. He served as vice-president and publications chairman of the American Marketing Association. Professor Bursk is a member of the Hall of Fame in Distribution, and earned the Parlin Award for distinguished contribution to the science of marketing. He is currently engaged in management consulting in Cambridge.

STEPHEN A. GREYSER is Professor of Business Administration, Harvard Business School; Executive Director of the Marketing Science Institute, a nonprofit research center in marketing associated with HBS; and Editorial Board Secretary, *Harvard Business Review*. Among his books are *Cases in Advertising and Communications Management, Advertising in America: The Consumer View* (co-author), and the Bursk-Greyser companion volume to this one, *Advanced Cases in Marketing Management*. He has also written extensively on marketing and advertising, and is a frequent interpreter of public policy issues involving marketing. He also is responsible for numerous HBR studies of executives' attitudes toward business and social institutions. He has served as a national director and publications board chairman of AMA, as well as president of the American Academy of Advertising. He is also a faculty principal of the consulting firm, Management Analysis Center.